ANIMAL RIGHTS LAW

Do animals have legal rights? This pioneering book tells readers everything they need to know about animal rights law.

The book starts with an overview of anti-cruelty and animal welfare laws, before focusing on progress towards granting basic rights and legal personhood to animals. It uses straightforward examples from over 30 legal systems from both the civil and common law traditions, and is based on the Animal Rights Law course which the authors teach at the University of Cambridge. To help readers understand the legal evolution, it explains the ethics, legal theory, and social issues behind animal rights and connected topics such as property, standing, dignity, and human rights.

The book's companion website (bloomsbury.pub/animal-rights-law) provides links to key references and journals, as well as briefs on the latest cases in this fast-changing area, and gives readers the tools to investigate their own legal systems with a list of jurisdiction-specific bibliographic references.

Rich in exercises and study aids, this easy-to-use introduction is a prime resource for law students as well as anyone else who wants to understand how the law is changing to protect animals.

Animal Rights Law

Raffael N Fasel
and
Sean C Butler

·HART·
OXFORD · LONDON · NEW YORK · NEW DELHI · SYDNEY

HART PUBLISHING

Bloomsbury Publishing Plc

Kemp House, Chawley Park, Cumnor Hill, Oxford, OX2 9PH, UK

1385 Broadway, New York, NY 10018, USA

29 Earlsfort Terrace, Dublin 2, Ireland

HART PUBLISHING, the Hart/Stag logo, BLOOMSBURY and the Diana logo are
trademarks of Bloomsbury Publishing Plc

First published in Great Britain 2023

A catalogue record for this book is available from the British Library.

Library of Congress Cataloging-in-Publication data

Names: Fasel, Raffael N, author. | Butler, Sean C, author.

Title: Animal rights law / Raffael N Fasel and Sean C Butler.

Description: Oxford, UK ; New York, NY : Hart Publishing, an Imprint of Bloomsbury Publishing, 2023. | Includes
bibliographical references and index. | Summary: "Do animals have legal rights? This pioneering book tells readers
everything they need to know about animal rights law. The book starts with an overview of anti-cruelty and animal welfare
laws, before focusing on progress towards granting basic rights and legal personhood to animals. It uses straightforward
examples from over 30 legal systems from both the civil and common law traditions, and is based on the Animal Rights Law
course which the authors teach at the University of Cambridge. To help readers understand the legal evolution, it explains
the ethics, legal theory, and social issues behind animal rights and connected topics such as property, standing, dignity,
and human rights. The book's companion website (bloomsbury.pub/animal-rights-law) provides links to key references and
journals, as well as briefs on the latest cases in this fast-changing area, and gives readers the tools to investigate their
own legal systems with a list of jurisdiction-specific bibliographic references. Rich in exercises and study aids, this
easy-to-use introduction is a prime resource for law students as well as anyone else who wants to
understand how the law is changing to protect animals."—Provided by publisher.

Identifiers: LCCN 2022046033 | ISBN 9781509956463 (hardback) | ISBN 9781509956104 (paperback) |
ISBN 9781509956128 (pdf) | ISBN 9781509956111 (Epub)

Subjects: LCSH: Animals—Law and legislation. | Animal welfare—Law and legislation. | Animal rights.

Classification: LCC K3620 .F37 2023 | DDC 344.04/9—dc23/eng/20221201

LC record available at https://lccn.loc.gov/2022046033

ISBN: PB: 978-1-50995-610-4
        ePDF: 978-1-50995-612-8
        ePub: 978-1-50995-611-1

Typeset by Compuscript Ltd, Shannon
Printed and bound in Great Britain by CPI Group (UK) Ltd, Croydon CR0 4YY

To find out more about our authors and books visit www.hartpublishing.co.uk. Here you will find extracts,
author information, details of forthcoming events and the option to sign up for our newsletters.

To our students

Acknowledgements

When we first started lecturing Animal Rights Law at the Cambridge Law Faculty in 2017, our work was considerably complicated by the fact that there was no textbook covering this increasingly rich and dynamic field. In the years since, animal rights law has grown in both breadth and depth, and with it the need for a book that covers the key aspects of this new field of law. This textbook hopes to fill that gap. Tracing the structure and broad content of the Cambridge course, the book is the product of numerous years of study and teaching. It would not exist without the help and stimulating ideas of many others from whom we have learned along the way and to whom we would like to express our gratitude.

Before starting the Cambridge course, we approached some of the preeminent Animal Law Lecturers in the US, all of whom generously encouraged us and helped us to get started: Jon Lovvorn, Kristen Stilt, Steve Wise, and David Wolfson.

A few years after we started teaching Animal Rights Law, we realised there was much more to be done. On 26 April 2019, we officially launched the Cambridge Centre for Animal Rights Law to conduct and support teaching and research. Soon after the Centre opened, we were contacted by Timothy Midura, President, Executive Director, and General Counsel of the Brooks Institute for Animal Rights Law & Policy. He offered to fund our Centre so as 'to put wind in your sails', to use his words. And the Centre has been sailing on ever since.

Many colleagues supported the textbook when it was but an idea. Michael Bowman, Simon Brooman, Sherry Colb, Joshua Dienstag, Teresa Gimenez Candela, Meg Good, Jed Goodfellow, Michael Hoeflich, Piper Hoffman, Amanda Kennedy, Joanna Kyriakakis, Christine Elizabeth Parker, Nancy Perry and Howard Crystal, Raj Reddy, Sophie Riley, Debbie Rook, Aaron Timoshanko, Steven White, and Steve Wise all responded with encouragement to an informal survey we circulated, and helped us establish that there is great demand for a global textbook on animal rights law.

The process of researching, writing, rewriting, and formatting the book would not have been possible without the help of our team of brilliant Research Assistants. From climbing the University Library tower to search for books, to translating laws from far-away jurisdictions, to last-minute manuscript checks – their efforts to make this book what it is now knew almost no limits, and nor do our thanks to them: Katharina Braun, Pablo Pérez Castelló, Motunrayo Esan, Michael Gold, Sam Groom, Ankita Shanker, Nico Stubler, and Zoe Tongue.

To ensure that the content of the pages that follow meets the highest academic standards possible for us, we relied on the expertise of some of the leading thinkers, writers, and teachers in animal rights law who generously commented on chapters of the book: John Adenitire, Charlotte Blattner, Macarena Montes Franceschini, Visa Kurki, Tomasz Pietrzykowski, and Joe Wills. We remain indebted to them for their help. Special thanks are owed to Joshua Jowitt who kindly read the whole manuscript and put it through its paces.

Roberta Bassi, our editor at Hart Publishing, believed in the book from when it was just a proposal. It would never have seen the light of day without her enthusiasm and continuous support. Her exemplary efficiency, professionalism, and warmth set the standard for what the publishing industry should strive.

Finally, we would like to thank Giordana Campagna and Penelope Butler, our (respective!) wives, for their patience and support throughout the process.

Cambridge, July 2022

Contents

Table of Figures

Table of Cases

Ecuador

Europe

Germany

India

Pakistan

Switzerland

UK

USA

Where available, links to these cases can be accessed on the textbook's companion website.

Table of Legislation

Domestic Law

Introduction

The legal scholar Roscoe Pound once famously noted: 'Law must be stable and yet it cannot stand still' (1923: 1). Pound's point was that law's job of securing order is in tension with the changing nature of social realities. As circumstances and people's values shift, so must the law, lest it become obsolete.

In recent decades, important changes have been underway in many societies concerning how humans perceive other animals. Thanks to a wealth of scientific studies, there is growing understanding of the sentience – the capacity to have feelings such as pain, fear, or joy – that unites humans with animals as diverse as mice, crabs, bears, and gulls. There is also increasing awareness of the many other astounding capacities of animals, ranging from the puzzle-solving minds of octopuses, to empathetic chickens, to crows constructing their own tools. Interest in animals and their needs has furthermore witnessed a boost due to the current salience of pandemics and the risk of zoonotic diseases, as well as the climate crisis that has become a reality affecting not only humans but also non-humans. As humans' understanding of animals and their relationships with them are changing, the idea has gained a foothold in some countries that animals should have similar rights protections to humans. For instance, in a survey conducted in 2015, 32 per cent of Americans agreed with the statement that 'animals deserve the exact same rights as people to be free from harm and exploitation' (Riffkin, 2015) – a 7 per cent increase from 2008.

These changes in public perception and opinion have arrived at the door of law: more and more scholars are arguing that fundamental rights or legal personhood should be granted to some animals; and animal rights lawyers are trying to translate these arguments into practice by petitioning courts and lawmakers for change. For example, in the first half of 2022 alone, several animal rights cases and proposals made international headlines. In January, the Constitutional Court of Ecuador ruled that the Ecuadorian Constitution's protection of the rights of nature also gives rights to individual animals, such as the chorongo monkey Estrellita on whose behalf a lawsuit was brought. In February, the citizens of the Swiss canton (ie state) of Basel-Stadt went to the ballot box to decide on whether to change the bill of rights of their constitution to include the rights to life and to bodily and mental integrity for non-human primates. And in June, the New York State Court of Appeals – the state's highest court – had to decide on whether Happy, an elephant kept in the Bronx Zoo, should be considered a legal person with the right to bodily integrity and moved to a sanctuary.

Legal education is trying to catch up with these developments. According to a database from the animal law organisation Global Animal Law (2021), some 200 universities around the world offer Animal Law courses. This is a significant number considering that, in 1988, Pace University in the US was the first law school in the world to start offering an Animal Law course. What is more, there is growing interest in education about questions of right-holdership, legal personhood, and legal dignity for animals. This trend is reflected in the increasing number of courses at universities around the world that are specifically focused on animal rights law. Despite this interest, however, there has so far been no textbook devoted entirely to questions of animal rights law.

The textbook you are holding in your hands or reading on a screen is the first to fill this gap and to map the emerging field of animal rights law. Following Pound's quote above, this textbook is about whether and how the law should adapt to accommodate and enable the changes we are seeing in public understanding and opinion, in litigation and law reform proposals, as well as in legal education. As its title reveals, the textbook has a threefold focus: it is about animals, rights, and law.

First, it is a book about *animals*. Animals are all around us – often involuntarily, but sometimes voluntarily. Depending on the country in which you are reading this book, animals such as cats, dogs, guinea pigs, rabbits, or even lizards and snakes, may be companions for humans. Other animals, such as chickens, fish, cows, sheep, pigs, and turkeys, are likely to be used for food or clothing. Yet others, such as goats, sheep, or reindeer, could be used for herding and sustenance. Others still, including mice, rats, guinea pigs, rabbits, birds, or monkeys, are used for experimentation. Some horses, elephants, monkeys, dolphins, and sea lions may be used for entertainment, while other horses, elephants, monkeys, dolphins, and sea lions may lead lives in the wild that are relatively unaffected by humans. Foxes, rats, squirrels, racoons, or monkeys could live near human settlements, and buffalos, coyotes, eagles, ravens, and turtles are sacred to some human communities.

But not only are human relationships with animals complex and multifaceted, humans themselves are animals, biologically speaking. Like all the above-mentioned animals, humans form part of the biological kingdom *Animalia* and therefore differ from plants, fungi, and other organisms such as bacteria. As we will see in this book, many animal rights proponents emphasise the evolutionary connections between the species *Homo sapiens* (the human species, which is a species of primate) and other animal species. And they point out animals' sentience, their vulnerability, and their interests in having their life, bodily and mental integrity, social relationships, access to food, shelter, and healthy environments protected. These connections are by some used as an argument against artificially separating 'humans' from 'animals', including in the language we use. While we will come across reasons supporting this view, this textbook follows the human-focus that is characteristic of current law and uses the terms 'humans' and 'animals' separately.

Second, the textbook focuses on *rights*. In newspaper articles and on social media, one regularly encounters claims about animals' rights. For instance, when Harambe the gorilla was shot in 2016 after having grabbed a child who climbed into his enclosure, some on social media asserted that Harambe's right to life had been violated. Harambe did not actually have such a right. But around 79 per cent of UN Member States do have laws protecting animals against cruelty (so-called 'anti-cruelty laws'), and some also have laws that protect animals' welfare in positive ways, such as by requiring people keeping animals to provide them with food and suitable living conditions (so-called 'welfare laws'). Anti-cruelty and welfare laws (which together we call 'animal protection laws') are sometimes said to confer 'rights' on animals. However, as we will see, such laws at most confer rights in a *thin* sense. Current animal 'rights' are for the most part simply the correlatives of human duties. For instance, humans in many legal systems have a duty not to impose unnecessary suffering on animals when using and killing them. This is sometimes said to correspond to a right in animals not to suffer unnecessarily when used and killed. However, in virtually all legal systems, animals currently lack rights protecting their fundamental interests in life, bodily integrity, and liberty in ways that human rights protect humans' corresponding interests. In other words, animals lack rights in a richer sense, which we call *thick rights*. As thick rights, animal rights would provide a complex set of protections for their holders' fundamental interests, they could not easily be infringed, they could be privately enforced, and they could evolve dynamically.

'Animal rights law' understood in this way can be seen as a subfield of 'animal law': a more general field that also covers animal protection laws, as well as the position of animals in areas such as family law, trust law, and criminal law. This textbook provides an overview of anti-cruelty and welfare protections for animals (which form the focus of 'animal welfare law') and discusses why such laws can be said to confer thin rights on animals. This is mainly by way of background, however. Its primary focus is on 'animal rights law', that is, on the questions raised by the rising efforts around the world to grant animals thick rights.

Finally, this is a textbook about *law*. As such, it is interested in the institutions, processes, concepts, and mechanisms surrounding the creation, maintenance, change, and enforcement of legal norms regulating animals. To be sure, these legal norms do not exist in a vacuum. They are influenced and shaped by other frameworks, practices, and norms, including from philosophy, history, religion, psychology, and ethology. The textbook draws on such interdisciplinary perspectives when charting the history of animal rights law, debating its moral foundations, exploring its relationship to religious beliefs and human psychology, as well as surveying how it can track (and sometimes fail to track) insights from ethology. Despite including perspectives from other disciplines, however, the textbook's focus is on animal rights law as a distinct legal field. This field is inspired by what is going on in neighbouring fields, but it raises characteristically legal issues that demand legal solutions.

Consider an example. When in 2016 Judge María Alejandra Mauricio of the Third Court of Guarantees in Mendoza, Argentina, was confronted with the question whether the chimpanzee Cecilia should be moved from a zoo to a sanctuary, she could not answer that question solely by relying on philosophical, biological, or religious arguments. Rather, she had to develop legal answers to distinctly legal questions such as: can Cecilia benefit from *habeas corpus* protection? Are the interests of animals protected under the right to a healthy and balanced environment, which is enshrined in Article 41 of the Argentinian Constitution? And, what the Judge herself called 'the great question': 'are the great apes – orangutans, bonobos, gorillas, and chimpanzees – non human legal persons?' (Judicial Branch of Mendoza, Third Court of Guarantees 2016, 22). In chapter seven, we will discuss how Judge Mauricio answered these questions in what became the first ruling in the world to grant *habeas corpus* protection to an animal. In many of the other chapters, we will study the concepts and instruments that legal scholars, courts, and lawyers more generally have developed to understand, implement, and progress animal rights law.

The first book to portray animal rights law, this textbook reflects the breadth and diversity of perspectives that make up this new field. Rather than focusing on one legal system or one approach to animal rights, it is a global textbook, in at least two respects. First, in its geographic ambit: unlike many animal law textbooks, it analyses animal rights law as a phenomenon spanning many parts of the world. To illustrate this, it draws on examples from a wide range of countries and legal traditions, and analyses overarching topics such as the legal theory of animal rights and the social movement aspects behind animal rights in a way that opens the field to readers from a variety of backgrounds. Second, the book is global in a substantive sense, describing not only one theory or approach to animal rights, but a plurality of approaches. Wherever possible, the textbook presents the voices of a variety of thinkers – some of whom support animal rights, while others are critical of it. This engagement with a diversity of points of view is necessary to paint the field with the depth required to give readers a well-rounded picture.

As a textbook that maps the key areas of animal rights law in just over 200 pages, this book necessarily takes the nature of an introductory text. For us to be able to limit ourselves to providing an overview of the basic issues meant that we had to pass over more advanced considerations, many country-specific issues, as well as questions that are not widely discussed. The textbook cannot therefore serve as a substitute for more detailed engagement with primary and secondary literature, as well as with the laws of all countries. However, it is ideally suited as a springboard for such further investigations. To facilitate more detailed and specific engagement with animal rights laws, the chapters in this book point to relevant references that allow readers to follow up on key issues and end with a list of 'Useful References', which have been selected with a view to both widen and deepen understanding. On the textbook's companion website, readers will find an even larger treasure trove of sources allowing them to further pursue their interests in animal rights law. The website contains: updates on important new cases and legislation; supplementary chapter-specific references; jurisdiction-specific references; and a repository of key journals.

We will use this symbol in the margin to indicate topics about which you can find more information on the online resource bloomsbury.pub/animal-rights-law:

As an educational text, this book does not give any definitive answers to contested questions, and instead aims to equip readers with the tools they need to understand the central debates, cases, and issues. Readers are assisted in thinking about and identifying their own answers to pivotal questions by 'Exercises' at the end of key sections and at the end of all the chapters. Although a background in law will help understand the chapters that follow, it is not required. A summary of the 'Central Issues' at the beginning of each chapter facilitates readers' comprehension of the discussions that follow, and the glossary at the end of the book will further assist readers in their mastery of the basic concepts, including technical legal terms.

When you arrive at the end of this textbook, you will understand the manifold ways in which people in legal systems around the world are being required to rethink laws that were long thought stable and useful, but which are increasingly challenged in the 'dawn' of animal rights law that we are currently seeing (Fasel and Butler 2020: 1). You will possess the toolkit to critically assess these developments, and you will be able to determine whether the social realities of animal rights are changing in a way that – according to Pound – law can no longer ignore.

The book's structure is as follows.

Chapter one lays the foundation for the rest of the textbook by providing an overview of the status quo of animal protection law around the world. Drawing on a wide range of legal systems, we focus on the key themes that characterise animals' legal status. In many countries, animals are considered to be ownable things, whereas in others they have a status as more than simple property. The chapter also discusses different laws protecting animals, ranging from anti-cruelty laws to more progressive welfare laws. We then consider constitutional norms which regulate animals in a handful of countries, before finally turning to international legal rules relating to animals. This overview of animal law will serve as the basis against which readers can assess the increasingly popular arguments – discussed in the rest of the textbook – that existing legal protections for animals are insufficient and animals should be granted thick rights or similar protections.

In chapter two, we address the debate between those who argue that humans can continue to own, use, and kill animals, as long as they treat them humanely in the process (so-called Welfarists) and those who argue that all use and killing of animals should end and that animals should cease to be property (so-called Abolitionists). The chapter begins by charting the view of so-called Classic Welfarists, whose theories still underlie most modern animal protection laws. We then address the Abolitionist critique that emerged as a response to Classic Welfarism and discuss some of its strengths and weaknesses. In response to Abolitionism, in turn, some developed a hybrid theory between Classic Welfarism and Abolitionism – called New Welfarism – which the chapter examines in the same way. Finally, we draw attention to how recent animal rights scholarship is trying to move beyond the dichotomy between Welfarism and Abolitionism.

Philosophy, and moral philosophy in particular, is an important source of inspiration for animal rights lawyers. Chapter three gives an introduction to the most influential philosophical approaches to animal rights. It begins by discussing four key approaches that support animal rights in the broad sense: Peter Singer's utilitarianism, Tom Regan's deontological approach, Martha Nussbaum's capabilities approach, and Sue Donaldson and Will Kymlicka's political approach. The chapter then turns to three philosophical approaches that criticise animal rights or aspects of the animal rights idea. We call these critiques the Ecofeminist Critique, the Conservationist Critique, and the Contractualist Critique.

Chapter four moves from philosophy to legal theory by providing a primer on the key legal theory questions that animal rights lawyers need to be able to answer. As we will see, some are sceptical of the idea of legal rights for animals because they think that it is little more than 'loose talk' by animal lovers. To address the sceptics' concerns, the chapter first analyses whether animals can have legal rights at all. To do so, it presents and analyses the two dominant theories about the functions of rights: the choice (or will)-based approach, and the interest-based approach. Finding that at least under the interest-based approach animals are fit to have rights, the chapter then asks whether, in fact, animals already possess some rights. Here, we distinguish between thick and thin rights conceptions – referred to above – which take contrasting views on this point. Finally, the chapter looks into the much-debated question whether, to have rights, animals would need to cease to be property and become legal persons or whether they could remain property.

In chapter five, we turn to the relationship between animal rights (understood as thick rights) and human rights. Specifically, we focus on the question whether animal rights and human rights are conflicting projects that undermine each other – as some critics claim – or whether they are cut from the same conceptual cloth and are mutually supportive in practice – as others argue. We first look at the common explanations given by those who argue that only humans should have rights. We then discuss the opposite arguments put forward by animal rights proponents who believe that animal rights and human rights are in harmony. Even if human and animal rights are mutually supportive, however, conflicts between them could still arise. For this reason, the chapter's last section analyses different legal tools – focusing on the proportionality test, the prioritisation of the interests of minorities, and the Species Membership Approach – that could help resolve such conflicts.

In the past two decades, courts around the world have been confronted with a new phenomenon: cases brought on behalf of animals arguing that they should be recognised as legal persons and/or afforded certain thick rights. Chapter six is dedicated to portraying and analysing the most important cases. It begins by discussing cases that deal with the issue of legal standing: the legal capacity to bring a case in the first place, which has proven to be a stumbling block for a lot of animal rights litigation. The chapter then turns to cases in which courts were asked to issue a writ of *habeas corpus*. Here, the chapter will return to the Cecilia case mentioned above – the first case in which an animal was recognised as a legal person with *habeas corpus* protection – as well as other prominent *habeas corpus* litigation, and will discuss the reasons why most of these cases have failed so far. Finally, the chapter examines cases that concern the extension of rights going beyond *habeas corpus*. In this section, we analyse case law dealing with animals' rights to life, to bodily and mental integrity, to liberty, and to food, as well as legal personhood.

Animal rights reform is not only sought through the courts, but also through changes to legislation. In chapter seven, we focus on domestic and international proposals to introduce thick animal rights via legislation, which we understand to include international treaties, declarations, and national constitutions, as well as statutes. Because there is currently no binding legislation on animal rights anywhere, the chapter concentrates on the key proposals that have been put forward for such legislation. We begin by canvassing the laws that have been proposed on the domestic level, before turning to proposals for treaties and declarations on the international level. Lastly, because of the absence of binding animal rights legislation, we ask what considerations those drafting future animal rights laws should take into account. In this last section as well as all other sections of the chapter, we focus on four themes that help us parse animal rights legislation: scope (which animals are covered); legal status (the proposed legal categorisation of animals); procedural rights (how animals could claim their rights in court); and substantive rights (which substantive protections animals would receive).

Chapter eight, finally, considers whether animal rights is a social justice issue in the tradition of other large movements such as abolitionism and feminism. To explore this increasingly widespread view, the chapter first explores potential links between animal rights and the human abolitionist movement, which will also allow us to cast more light on the Abolitionist approach discussed in chapter two. Focusing in particular on the feminist movement, the chapter then considers overlaps with animal rights and the proximity between these issues, as well as some important differences. In this section, we also consider the question of when emphasising similarities with other social justice issues can become problematic. To do so, we examine two heavily criticised analogies and comparisons that some in the animal rights movement have made with other social justice causes. Lastly, we discuss the lessons that animal rights proponents can learn from other movements, including the importance of direct action, consciousness-raising, the opportunities provided by social media, and the need for political compromise.

The conclusion summarises the key insights of the textbook and points to potential future developments in the field.

1

The Current Legal Status of Animals

I. Introduction

Legal systems around the world regulate the behaviour of human beings in almost all areas of life. What humans are (and are not) allowed to do with non-human animals is no exception. As in other domains of law, there is great diversity in how different legal systems treat animals, ranging from those that have few legal rules pertaining to animals, to others that have developed elaborate legal frameworks to regulate their lives. To make things even more complex, some states (especially federal states) apply different rules to animals depending on where these animals are within the country; and, since relatively recently, there has been an increasing number of national constitutional norms (ie rules) and international legal instruments concerning animals. This chapter maps the current legal status of animals around the world. In so doing it will help readers understand where laws protecting animals come from historically, what they look like, and what they achieve.

To illustrate the current state of animal law, this chapter draws on a variety of different countries, some from the common law tradition (such as India, Jamaica, the UK, or the US), others from the civil law family (such as Austria, China, Germany, or Nicaragua). Traditionally, courts play an important role as law-makers in common law countries by setting precedent. Civil law systems, by contrast, accord a more important role to systematic legislation by parliament, called 'codes'. As we will see, despite this traditional difference, legislation plays an important role in animal law even in common law systems.

By the end of this chapter, you will understand the basic framework of animal law in different legal systems, and will have the tools to explore the particular legal rules of your own legal system. On the companion website, you will find legal-system specific references based on continent, which may contain additional information about your own country.

The chapter will furthermore lay the foundation for the rest of this textbook. It will help you understand why voices have become louder in proposing that existing legal protections for animals are insufficient and that animals should be granted fundamental legal rights. As we will see, not all the legal rules that apply to animals necessarily protect them, and not all animals have the same levels of protection. Moreover, even laws that are meant to protect animals are not always effective in practice because of issues around compliance and enforcement. Nevertheless, there has been a trend toward increasing animal protection in many legal systems, and, in a few cases, even toward granting animals fundamental legal rights and legal personhood – a point we will return to in subsequent chapters.

The chapter is structured as follows. We first describe animals' legal status as simple property in some legal systems, and then discuss legal systems that grant animals a status as more than simple property. In the third section, we analyse different laws protecting animals, ranging from those that protect animals against cruelty to those that protect them from welfare infringements that go beyond cruelty. Finally, we will look at the emerging constitutional and international legal rules relating to animals.

Central Issues

1. A key feature of animals' current legal status is that legal systems around the world generally consider them ownable property (or 'things'). However, some legal systems formally distinguish between animals and inanimate property such as bikes or books, and even more countries protect animals in other ways that make them more than 'mere' property.

2. Many countries possess anti-cruelty laws that protect animals from inhumane treatment. These laws proliferated in Western legal systems in the nineteenth century as scientific understanding of animals' natures grew, but more general laws that serve to protect animals can be traced back at least as far as the third millennium BCE.

3. Numerous legal systems go beyond mere anti-cruelty laws and have more general animal welfare laws. These laws are characterised by the fact that they protect animals in positive ways and provide for criminal and administrative enforcement mechanisms.

4. Some countries also possess constitutional provisions that concern animals. These provisions range from competence norms (ie powers to make new laws), to state objectives, to more direct legal protections.

5. There are also a limited number of international laws that apply to animals. This is particularly the case in the EU and the states that are members of the Council of Europe.

6. Laws protecting animals often suffer from a lack of compliance and enforcement. The limited available data suggest that laws are enforced differently with regard to different species, and that there is a general reluctance on the part of authorities to take animal protection offences as seriously as other offences.

II. The Property Status of Animals

Arguably the most consistent defining trait of animals' current legal status is that legal systems around the world consider them property. This means that animals can be owned, bought, used, inherited, rented out, sold, and destroyed in similar ways to other objects (eg books or bikes). That animals can be owned in the first place is generally traced back to the fact that they are considered things (or objects) in law, rather than persons (or subjects).

This section will discuss the main legal implications of animals' property status and will also consider the steps that some countries have taken to change the property status of animals to strengthen protection of their interests.

A. Animals as Simple Property

According to the animal law scholar Thomas Kelch, the relationship between humans and animals 'has remained virtually untouched' in the past 4,000 years (Kelch 2012: 25). From a legal perspective, one of the factors that has remained constant is the fact that humans have been able to own animals for a very long time. For example, in Mesopotamia, human ownership over agricultural animals was legally recognised as early as the seventeenth century BCE.

Particularly important today is the fact that the law of ancient Rome categorised animals as ownable 'things'. According to the distinction made by the famous Roman jurist Gaius, law can be divided into three categories: persons, things, and actions (ie procedural devices to bring suits). With some exceptions, only human beings could be persons. However, not all human beings fell into that category. Notoriously, some humans were considered slaves and thus things. Animals, too, were in the category of things over which property rights could be established. Persons had virtually absolute control over things and could therefore use or kill animals largely without restrictions.

The Roman categorisation of animals as property has had a lasting impact on modern legal systems, especially in the Western world which has built its legal systems on Roman legal concepts. Through European colonisation or voluntary adoption of Western legal norms, the Roman categorisation of animals as things has also influenced many other legal systems. To this day, numerous legal systems follow the view that animals are things that humans can own like other objects. More specifically, animals are generally considered 'movable' property that – in contrast to 'immovable' property such as real estate – can be traded with few constraints.

Consider, for example, the legal status of animals in Cameroon. Cameroonian law categorises animals as moveable property, and this provision can be found in its

Civil Code (2005). The provision employs these features from Roman law due to the fact that the country was a former French and German colony:

Article 528 – Cameroon Civil Code (2005)

Entities are moveable by nature if they can be transported from one place to another, either because they can move themselves, like animals, or because they can change place only in virtue of an external force, like inanimate things.

In other states that consider animals as simple property, animals are sometimes not even mentioned explicitly. This is the case, for example, in China, which has voluntarily followed the model of European civil codes, specifically the German Civil Code. In China's newly adopted Civil Code from 2020, animals are simply subsumed under more general property headings, such as 'moveable properties':

Article 266 – Chinese Civil Code (2020)

Private individuals shall have ownership of their legal income, houses, daily necessities, production tools, raw materials, and other immovable and movable properties.

That animals are included in this provision can be inferred for instance from other rules in the Chinese Civil Code that make it clear that animals are subject to ownership. For example, when discussing state ownership, the Civil Code states:

Article 251 – Chinese Civil Code (2020)

All wild animal and plant resources that are state-owned by law are owned by the state.

The fact that animals' property status is not always mentioned explicitly should not hide the fact that it has profound implications throughout the legal system. This is true not only in the domain of private law, but also other domains such as criminal law and public law.

Take, for instance, tort law (considered a part of private law). Because animals are considered property, not persons, they cannot claim remedies for any harm that is inflicted on them. Instead, if an animal is harmed, only their *owner* (usually a human being) can claim remedies, and only if they (the owner) can show that they have suffered a loss. In many legal systems, animals are treated like other pieces of moveable property in such cases. For instance, if your neighbour runs over your cat Coyopa and she dies as a result, then you can claim damages from your neighbour just like you could if they ran over your football. Generally, the amount of damages you can claim is assessed based on Coyopa's market value at the time of her death. As we will see in the next subsection, some legal systems allow owners to claim damages for emotional loss in the case of injury or death of companion animals – but this is still relatively rare. The reason why damages for a cat and damages for a football are assessed similarly is that animals are legally objects, not persons. As well as meaning they cannot benefit from legal action, the fact that animals are not legal persons also means that they are not legally responsible for harms they cause. For example, the rules of tort law require the owner of an animal to compensate other persons if they are harmed by the animal. You might incur such tort liability, for example, if Coyopa entered your neighbour's house and scratched their expensive furniture. Coyopa does not incur any liability herself.

Another illustration is health law (a part of public law). Legal systems generally allow the killing of animals if they are considered to pose a danger to public health (which generally means human health). Due to animals' status as property, such killings can be carried out legally, in the same way that other objects can be destroyed in situations of emergency. In many legal systems, compensation is often payable for the owner whose animals are killed, also determined largely by market value.

Consider for example Singapore's Infectious Disease Act 1976. In case of disease the Act provides that:

Article 13(1) – Singapore Infectious Disease Act (1976)

The Director [of Medical Services of the Ministry of Health] may order the destruction of any animal and the disposal of any food or water wherever found if he considers such animal, food or water to be a source for the transmission of an infectious disease.

Laws such as this have become particularly relevant since the COVID-19 outbreak, as numerous countries have considered or carried out large-scale killings of animals suspected of being hosts to the virus. In November 2020, for instance, Denmark was reported to have ordered the killing of 17 million minks – which were farmed in the country for their fur – in an attempt to stop them from passing the (potentially mutated) virus back onto humans.

B. Animals as More than Simple Property

While animals remain property in all legal systems, in many countries they are no longer 'mere' property. Put differently, some countries have taken steps toward distinguishing animals from inanimate forms of property such as bikes or books. This has generally involved recognising that animals have inherent value (ie value in and of themselves, regardless of whether they are useful or valued by someone else). This recognition has occurred in two ways: first, the enactment of specific laws that protect animals' wellbeing in ways that bikes or books are not protected; second, and more rarely, the explicit recognition in law that animals are not simple or mere property.

Many countries have adopted the first approach and enacted animal protection laws of various forms and strengths. We will look at these laws in more detail in the next section. Our focus in this subsection is instead on the second way: acknowledging legally that animals are not simple property but possess a status that goes beyond mere thinghood. This approach has been followed by fewer countries, although their number is growing. The first country to have changed its law to recognise that animals are not identical to other kinds of property was Austria. Before the Austrian Parliament changed the Austrian Civil Code in 1988, animals were implicitly included in the category of things that serve humans and other persons:

Article 285 – Austrian Civil Code (1811)

Everything that is different from the person, and that serves a human use, is called a thing in the legal sense.

Since 1988, the Civil Code contains an additional provision making clear that animals are not mere things:

Article 285a – Austrian Civil Code (1811)

Animals are not things; they are protected by special laws. The laws that apply to things are applicable to animals only insofar as no deviating regulations exist.

Numerous countries have followed the Austrian example, including the Czech Republic, France, Germany, Poland, Slovakia, and Switzerland. In some countries, the change in animals' legal status was recorded not in the civil code but in more specific legislation. Poland, for example, amended its Animal Protection Act (1997) to reflect animals' status as beings that are more than simple property:

Article 1 – Polish Animal Protection Act (1997)

An animal, as a living being capable of suffering, is not a thing. Man owes him respect, protection, and care.

Regardless of where exactly in the law the recognition occurs, the process of undoing the thinghood of animals is referred to as *dereification* (referring to the process of undoing the thinghood (Latin *re* or *res*) of animals). Animals have been made things, so they can legally also be unmade things.

However, it is important to note that while many countries have legally recognised that animals are more than simple property, they have not turned them into legal persons either. Instead, animals in these countries now formally occupy an intermediate position between thinghood and personhood.

One of the potential issues with this intermediate position is that it does not fully remove animals from the scope of the rules that govern property. To see this, have a closer look at the above-mentioned Article 285a of the Austrian Civil Code (1811). While the first sentence of this provision ('Animals are not things, they are protected by special laws') appears to lift animals from their property status, the second sentence ('The laws that apply to things are applicable to animals only insofar as no deviating regulations exist') brings them back down. The reason for this lies in the qualification 'insofar as no deviating regulations exist', which means that animals are practically treated as property *unless* there are any specific laws that require treating them differently. The main laws to do that are animal protection laws (which we will discuss in the next section). However, other areas of law can foresee special rules, too. For instance, as we saw above, tort law may provide for rules that allow for the compensation of emotional loss in the case of a dead or injured companion animal whereas no such compensation would be given for inanimate property.

Some have suggested that the dereification of animals has been 'mainly symbolic' (eg Vink 2020: 87). The intermediate legal status, they argue, makes little practical difference for animals as they are still treated as property in many contexts. What seems to support this view is that there are numerous legal systems (such as Israel and Mexico) that have adopted the first way identified above: they have not formally recognised animals as more than mere things, but have passed animal welfare laws and other 'special laws' that only apply to animals, thereby implicitly recognising that animals are more than mere things. Many animal rights scholars in fact believe that animals' legal status as property makes it difficult or even impossible for them to ever possess fundamental rights akin to human rights. We will return to this question in chapters two and four.

Exercise 1: Animals as Simple Property or More

1. In which respects do the animals you know differ from objects around you, like your pen or laptop? Are animals closer to objects or humans in your view?
2. Try to find out how your own legal system classifies animals: Does it express what the formal status of animals is? Are animals considered simple property? Are there laws that recognise animals as more than simple property? If yes, in what way?
3. Do you think provisions such as Article 285a of the Austrian Civil Code or Article 1 of the Polish Animal Protection Act have mainly symbolic value? Is symbolic value important? Discuss these questions with a friend or fellow student.

III. Legislation Protecting Animals

As mentioned in the previous section, many countries have adopted special legal rules that apply only to animals and not to other forms of property. The most important such set of rules are the laws that protect animals' wellbeing. Depending on the legal system, these laws range from rather limited rules that only protect animals from cruelty (so-called 'anti-cruelty laws') to broader and more protective 'animal welfare laws' (which are sometimes also called 'animal protection laws', although we apply that term in a broader sense to also cover anti-cruelty laws). In 2021, out of 193 UN Member States, at least 152 countries (79 per cent) had some form of animal protection law. Of the 152 countries with animal protection laws, 73 had only anti-cruelty laws (38 per cent), and 79 had anti-cruelty and animal welfare laws (41 per cent) (see Figure 1).

Figure 1 Countries with and without animal protection laws (2021)

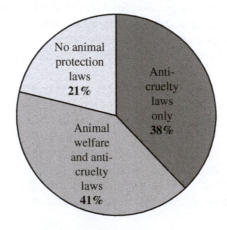

This section begins by considering the history of legal rules protecting animals. It then sheds light on anti-cruelty norms and discusses what distinguishes animal welfare laws from such norms. Finally, it analyses the species-specific provisions as well as exclusions and exceptions that both types of animal protection laws can contain.

A. The History of Animal Protection

As we saw in the previous section, laws that deal with animals as ownable things date back millennia. Laws that not only *deal with* but also serve to *protect* animals have a similarly long history. For example, around 2100 BCE the Chinese Emperor Da Yu decreed: 'For three months in summer, fishing nets must not be cast into the rivers and streams so as to ensure the thriving of fish and turtles' (Cao 2015: 18). Around 1100 BCE, the Xi Zhou Dynasty had in force an order that, at certain times of year, six types of animals could not be harmed (although it is unclear what animals were meant). In the third century BCE, the Indian Emperor Asoka had edicts carved into rocks. One of edicts provided that 'Here [apparently referring to a specific holy place] no animal shall be killed or sacrificed' (cited in Organ 1970: 78). There were further provisions against the slaughter of parrots, geese, partridges, ants, pregnant pigs, and animals under six months old.

Even though early laws such as these likely served to protect animals in practice, they were not always enacted with that purpose in mind. For example, laws regulating sacrificial animals may have been primarily enacted for spiritual purposes, not to protect animals from suffering or being killed. Even centuries on, laws that had the *effect* of protecting animals were often created with the *aim* of protecting humans. For example, when the English Parliament passed the Slaughter of Beasts Act (1488) to ban the killing of animals within the city walls of London and other towns, its primary goal was to protect humans from the pollution and smell caused by such activities, rather than to protect animals from pain and death.

This changed in recent centuries, when laws were increasingly being enacted with the aim of protecting animals – even though that aim would usually still stand alongside other, more human-centric aims. In the West, this was the case during the modern era when new laws were created that were specifically aimed at prohibiting the cruel treatment of certain types of animals. One of the first such laws was the Act against Plowing by the Tayle, and pulling the Wooll off living Sheep (1635), passed by the Irish Parliament to ban the cruel practices of attaching ploughs to horses' tails and tearing off wool from living sheep instead of shearing them. The Act made its aims explicit with regard to the former practice, noting that 'plowing by the tail' leads to the problem that '(besides the cruelty used to the beasts) the breed of horses is much impaired in this kingdome, to the great prejudice thereof'.

Other Western laws prohibiting animal cruelty include the Massachusetts Body of Liberties (1641), enacted in the former Massachusetts Bay Colony, which provided: 'No man shall exercise any Tirranny or Crueltie towards any bruite Creature which are usuallie kept for man's use'. Similar legislation followed in numerous other US states, including Maine (1821), New York (1829), Michigan (1838), and New Hampshire (1843). Many European states also adopted their first animal protection legislation during this time. For example, following the UK's Martin's Act of 1822, France (1850), Sweden (1857), and the Netherlands (1886) enacted similar anti-cruelty laws. In many cases, anti-cruelty provisions were simply added to existing laws. With time, however, it became more common to create standalone anti-cruelty acts.

This wave of animal protection legislation during the nineteenth century coincided with significant advances in human knowledge about animals' biological functions and needs. The term 'pathocentrism' (see Blattner 2019a: 282) is sometimes used to describe the shift that occurred during this period from human-centric animal 'protection' laws to laws that were entirely (or at least primarily) enacted with the aim of protecting animals from pain and suffering (*páthos* in ancient Greek).

Scientific advances maintained their role in driving progress in animal protection legislation throughout the twentieth century, as animal ethology and neuroscience were gaining acceptance as fields of study within the scientific community. In the UK, for example, increasing knowledge of animals' complex behaviours and needs served as the basis for fundamental changes in approach to, and improvements in, animal protection laws in the 1960s. Precipitated by the publication of Ruth Harrison's *Animal Machines* (1964) – a widely influential book describing intensive animal farming – the UK government set up the Brambell Committee with the mission of examining the conditions of farmed animals and proposing welfare standards to protect their interests. The Committee's 1965 Report noted the basic similarities that exist between the sensations of which humans and many other animals are capable, and emphasised the need to protect animals' physical as well as emotional health and to provide living conditions that are appropriate to their species. The Report served as the foundations for the so-called 'Five Freedoms', which were codified in their present form in 1979 by the UK Farm Animal Welfare Council. These Freedoms are:

(1) Freedom from hunger and thirst
(2) Freedom from discomfort
(3) Freedom from pain, injury or disease
(4) Freedom to express normal behaviour
(5) Freedom from fear and distress

The Brambell Report and similar reports in other countries played an important part in moving animal protection laws beyond mere protection from cruelty and into a broader and more positive understanding of animal welfare. Recommendations such as the Five Freedoms have made their way into animal welfare laws across the world. Consider the following two examples:

Article 24 – Malaysian Animal Welfare Act (2015)

(1) The owner or a licensee [of an animal] shall have the duty to–

(a) take reasonable steps to ensure that the needs of an animal are fulfilled, which includes

  (i) its need for a suitable environment;
  (ii) its need for a suitable diet;
  (iii) the need for it to be able to exhibit its normal behaviour patterns;
  (iv) the need for it to be housed with or apart from other animals; and
  (v) the need for it to be protected from pain, suffering, injury and disease; ...

Article 3 – Costa Rican Animal Welfare Act (1994)

The basic conditions for the welfare of the animals are the following:

(a) Satisfaction of hunger and thirst;
(b) Ability to develop according to their normal patterns of behaviour;

(c)   Death caused without pain and, if possible, under professional supervision;
(d)   Absence of physical discomfort and pain;
(e)   Preservation and treatment of diseases.

Today, legislative changes which aim to protect animals' welfare in ways that go beyond mere protection from cruelty are often promoted by reference to animals' 'sentience', which is the capacity to have feelings such as pain, fear, and joy. As the Brambell Report foreshadowed, comparisons between humans' sentience and that of other animals play an important role in animal protection debates, and they have become increasingly common in recent years.

However, the fact that many modern laws enacted to protect animals are based on the recognition that animals are sentient does not rule out that they can also pursue other aims. The European Union (EU) Council Regulation on the protection of animals at the time of killing (2009), for example, is evocative of earlier laws we discussed above which pursued both animal- and human-centric purposes. Consider Paragraph 4 of its preamble:

Paragraph 4 – EU Council Regulation on the protection of animals at the time of killing (2009)

Animal welfare is a [European] Community value … The protection of animals at the time of slaughter or killing is a matter of public concern that affects consumer attitudes towards agricultural products. In addition, improving the protection of animals at the time of slaughter contributes to higher meat quality and indirectly has a positive impact on occupational safety in slaughterhouses.

Exercise 2: The History of Animal Protection in Your Own Country

Prepare a timeline of animal protection laws in your own country, starting with the first laws. To assist you in this task, you may want to consult the jurisdiction-specific references provided on the textbook's website.

The following factors can help you to start forming a well-rounded picture of how and why these laws developed:

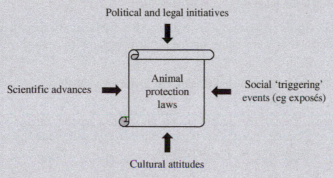

B. Anti-Cruelty Laws

As we saw above, some countries have adopted animal protection laws that aim to safeguard animals' welfare in complex ways, including by trying to ensure living conditions appropriate to their species. Before these countries had such laws, however, they mainly had laws prohibiting cruelty against animals. In fact, as we saw above, 38 per cent of countries still today only protect animals through such less far-ranging anti-cruelty laws (and 21 per cent even have no such laws).

As their name suggests, 'anti-cruelty' laws are primarily aimed at protecting animals from cruel treatment. Although there is considerable diversity in the anti-cruelty laws of different legal systems, they all have in common the recognition that practices which inflict suffering on animals are wrong and should be prevented, unless there are reasons that justify these practices.

Some anti-cruelty laws are framed in a broad way, prohibiting unspecified acts of cruelty against an unspecified range of animals. Take, for example, the following anti-cruelty provision which adopts a rather general approach to describing cruel conduct, from the US state of New Mexico:

Paragraph 30-18-1 – New Mexico Statutes (2011)

... B. Cruelty to animals consists of a person:

(1)   negligently mistreating, injuring, killing without lawful justification or tormenting an animal; or

(2)   abandoning or failing to provide necessary sustenance to an animal under that person's custody or control.

Pakistan's Prevention of Cruelty to Animals Act (1890), which is still in force today, takes a similar approach in that it leaves largely open the categories of animals that are protected. However, it is more specific in identifying banned cruel practices:

Article 3 – Pakistani Act on the Prevention of Cruelty to Animals Act (1890)

If any person–

(a)   overdrives, beats, or otherwise treats any animal so as to subject it to unnecessary pain or suffering, or

(b)   binds, keeps, carries or consigns for carriage any animal in such manner or position as to subject it to unnecessary pain or suffering ...

In 2019, the US Congress passed a federal law that was equally specific with regard to the cruel practices that were being banned, but general with regard to the animals it protects:

Paragraph 48 – Preventing Animal Cruelty and Torture Act (2019)

(a) Offenses

(1)   CRUSHING.–It shall be unlawful for any person to purposely engage in animal crushing in or affecting interstate or foreign commerce or within the special maritime and territorial jurisdiction of the United States ...

(f) Definitions ...

(1)   the term 'animal crushing' means actual conduct in which one or more living non-human mammals, birds, reptiles, or amphibians is purposely crushed, burned, drowned, suffocated, impaled, or otherwise subjected to serious bodily injury ...

This particular Act was created in response to so-called 'animal crush' videos in which people crushed, tortured, and killed small animals such as kittens or hamsters. Building on a law from 2010 which prohibited the creation and distribution of such videos, the 2019 Act also banned the underlying cruel practices. Until 2019 the US had no national anti-cruelty law, with states' laws filling the void.

Still other anti-cruelty laws are framed in narrower ways and protect specific animals, usually from species-specific forms of cruel treatment. For example, the Turkish Animal Protection Act (2004) protects companion animals from specific cruel practices:

Article 8 – Turkish Animal Protection Act (2004)

... Surgical interventions aimed at changing the external appearance of pets or other non-therapeutic treatments such as the cutting of tails and ears, the removal of vocal cords and removal of nails or teeth are prohibited ...

Although many narrow anti-cruelty norms are rather limited in their reach, they can in principle also protect animals' interests in more wide-ranging ways. Consider for example the following provision from Luxembourg, which includes in a list of prohibited cruel treatments the killing of animals for purely economic reasons – the first of its kind:

Article 12 – Luxembourg Law on the Protection of Animals (2018)

It is forbidden:

... (13) To eliminate animals for exclusively economic reasons ...

Finally, as the Luxembourg Law illustrates, anti-cruelty norms are often part of more comprehensive animal welfare laws. These norms are often couched as prohibitions of inflicting 'unnecessary' or 'unreasonable' suffering on animals. For instance, the Animal Care and Protection Act (2001) of the Australian state of Queensland provides:

Section 18 – Queensland Animal Care and Protection Act (2001)

... (2) ... a person is taken to be cruel to an animal if the person does any of the following to the animal–

(a) causes it pain that, in the circumstances, is unjustifiable, unnecessary or unreasonable
...

In laws such as these, the anti-cruelty-related provisions are supplemented with more wide-ranging animal welfare protections. It is to these protections that we turn now.

C. Animal Welfare Laws

Although anti-cruelty laws are strictly speaking also aimed at improving animals' welfare, the term 'animal welfare law' is sometimes reserved for more wide-ranging laws that go beyond protecting animals from mere cruelty. Animal welfare laws currently exist in 41 per cent of countries. These laws are generally driven by scientific insights about the behaviour and needs of animals, and the resulting demand for laws that protect their interests in more complete ways and with due regard to their species.

There is great diversity in animal welfare laws, not least due to the vast array of activities involving animals which they may govern, including chicken farming, puppy breeding, transporting livestock, managing zoos, and the handling of animals in laboratories. Nevertheless, it is possible to identify two main features that are characteristic of animal welfare laws: (1) they contain provisions promoting animals' welfare in positive ways; and (2) they provide for both criminal and administrative control mechanisms for their enforcement.

(1) The first and arguably most characteristic feature of animal welfare laws is that they are not limited to 'negatively' prohibiting certain types of cruel practices or acts against animals. Instead, they also create certain *'positive' requirements* to promote animals' wellbeing. These requirements are sometimes spelled out concretely, often following the framework of the Five Freedoms mentioned above. In other cases, they are encapsulated in more general clauses. An example of this latter approach is Paragraph 2 of the German Animal Protection Act 1972:

Paragraph 2 – German Animal Protection Act (1972)

Any person keeping, caring for or required to care for an animal,

(1)   must feed, care for, and provide shelter to the animal in a way that is appropriate to its species, behaviour, and needs; ...

Another example from the UK is the Animal Welfare Act (2006) – applicable in England and Wales – which enshrines a welfare duty in its section 9:

Section 9 – Animal Welfare Act (2006)

(1)   A person commits an offence if he does not take such steps as are reasonable in all the circumstances to ensure that the needs of an animal for which he is responsible are met to the extent required by good practice. ...

The general reference to take 'reasonable' steps is clarified somewhat in section 9(2), which defines animals' needs by alluding to the Five Freedoms.

(2) The second characteristic feature of animal welfare laws is that, by contrast to anti-cruelty laws, they are not solely enforced through criminal penalties. Rather, they provide for *both criminal and administrative enforcement mechanisms*. Depending on the legal system, criminal controls generally involve the police, public prosecutors, and courts and result in criminal convictions, whereas administrative controls generally involve state animal welfare agencies and result in measures such as prohibitions on keeping animals.

Take criminal enforcement. Depending on the severity of the violation of an animal's interests, animal welfare laws allow punishing offenders with fines (for less severe infractions) and/or imprisonment (for more severe infractions). Although there are some legal systems in which animal welfare violations are merely considered misdemeanours (ie minor offences) an increasing number of legal systems consider at least severe welfare violations to be felonies (ie severe offences). The Norwegian Animal Welfare Act (2009) serves as an illustrative example for the different levels of criminal severity:

Paragraph 37 – Norwegian Animal Welfare Act (2009)

Intentional or grossly negligent violation of the requirements in or under this Act or decision issued under this Act is punishable with fines or imprisonment for a maximum of 1 year, or both, provided the offence is not subject to more severe penal provisions. Aiding and abetting are punished in the same way. Serious violations are punishable with imprisonment for a maximum of 3 years. When determining the seriousness of the violation, the scale and effect of the violation and the level of guilt shall be taken into account.

Criminal punishments are generally regarded as playing an important role due to their punitive and deterrent functions. However, in practice, administrative measures have just as central a role, not least because they can be imposed by other state agencies and usually with fewer procedural hurdles than criminal penalties. The Nicaraguan Law for the Protection and Welfare of Domestic Animals and Domesticated Wild Animals (2011), for example, lists the following possible administrative sanctions:

Article 68 – Nicaraguan Law for the Protection and Welfare of Domestic Animals and Domesticated Wild Animals (2011)

Administrative sanctions include:

(a) Admonition;
(b) Fines;
(c) Confiscation for serious and very serious offences;
(d) Temporary or permanent closure of establishments for one year for serious offences and two years for very serious offences;
(e) Temporary or definitive prohibition of the exercise of trade in animals for one year for serious offences and two years for very serious ones;
(f) Prohibition of possessing animals for two years for serious offences and five years for very serious ones; ...

Another important administrative instrument that animal welfare acts provide for is licensing. Welfare laws often require certain premises, activities, and/or people to be licensed in order to work with animals. For example, to run an animal testing laboratory, a boarding kennel or cattery, or a slaughterhouse, a licence from a governmental agency is often required. In many cases, this can mean that the premises are inspected and approved as suitable before an initial licence is granted. Licensing thus allows animal welfare laws to exert control not just after violations have already happened (as is primarily the case with criminal penalties), but to attempt to ensure in advance that no violations occur. Take the example of the Jamaican Animals (Control of Experiments) Act (1949), which regulates animal testing:

Section 3 – Jamaican Animals (Control of Experiments) Act (1949)

(1) No person except a licensee shall perform any experiment.
(2) No licensee shall perform any experiment except in accordance with the terms of his license and subject to the restrictions imposed by this Act.

In order for licensing to be more likely to have its desired effect of ensuring compliance with animal welfare laws, however, it is also necessary that regular (and ideally unannounced) checks are carried out to make sure licence-holders remain in compliance with the terms of their licence. If the licence-holder is found not to comply, they can either be cautioned or, depending on the severity of the violations, lose the licence. Consider the same Act for illustration:

Section 10 – Jamaican Animals (Control of Experiments) Act (1949)

(3) Every licensee under this Act shall permit any person authorized in writing as aforesaid to enter and inspect, for the purpose of securing compliance with the provisions of this Act, any place specified in such licensee's licence for the performance of experiments.

Section 13 – Jamaican Animals (Control of Experiments) Act (1949)

It shall be a condition of every licence or permit under this Act that such licence or permit may be revoked at any time by the person granting it on his being satisfied that such licence or permit ought to be revoked.

D. Species-Specific Provisions

Due to the detailed level of protection of many animal welfare laws, they ordinarily contain provisions that are specific to certain species or groups of species. This is also true for some anti-cruelty laws that contain more granular requirements.

Depending on the legal system, such species-specific provisions can be found in the animal protection act itself or in implementing legislation. This is the case, for example, in Switzerland, where the Animal Protection Ordinance (2008) implements and concretises the Animal Welfare Act (2008)'s more general welfare-related duties. For instance, it contains an entire article dealing with the requirements for housing horses:

Article 59 – Swiss Animal Welfare Ordinance (2008)

(1)   Horses must not be kept tethered. Tethering for a brief period of time during feeding, provision of care, transport, overnight treks, during events or in similar situations does not fall under this requirement. Horses that are newly introduced to a stable or that are in military service may be tethered for a maximum period of three weeks. ...

(3)   Horses must have visual, auditory, and olfactory contact with one other horse. In justified cases, the cantonal authorities can issue a temporary exemption for an old horse kept individually. ...

This provision illustrates how scientific insights into the behaviour and needs of horses – social animals that like to roam freely – can shape species-specific welfare requirements. However, species-specific provisions need not always be primarily driven by scientific knowledge. Sometimes the grounds for distinguishing between different species or other groups of animals are more political. For example, in the Directive 2010/63/EU on the protection of animals used for scientific purposes, the EU specifically highlighted in the preamble that 'the use of non-human primates is of the greatest concern to the public', stating that:

Paragraph 17 – EU Directive 2010/63/EU on the protection of animals used for scientific purposes

... the use of non-human primates should be permitted only in those biomedical areas essential for the benefit of human beings, for which no other alternative replacement methods are yet available ...

Experiments on animals that generate less public concern, by contrast, have not solicited a similar legal response. For example, there is no campaign for mouse emancipation despite their being widely experimented on.

As this example suggests, animal protection laws often draw politically motivated distinctions between different species of animals and can thus lead to starkly different levels of protection for animals despite having relatively similar needs. One example that stands out are the relatively high levels of legal protection that companion animals such as cats and dogs possess when compared to farmed animals such as chickens, cows, or pigs. For example, according to the Code of Practice for the Welfare of Dogs (2017) – a non-binding instrument in England and Wales that is indicative of minimum legal standards and has evidential value in practice – there is a duty to ensure that dogs' emotional needs are met. At the same time, Paragraph 40 of Schedule 2 to the Welfare of Animals at the Time of Killing (England) Regulations (2015) allows for the 'gassing' of pigs. This is despite the fact that studies have shown that gassing inflicts considerable suffering on pigs, who are as sensitive as dogs and have other basic needs in common with them (eg Department for Environment, Food & Rural Affairs 2021: 48).

E. Limits of Animal Protection Laws: Exclusions and Exceptions

What even strong animal welfare laws have in common with simple anti-cruelty legislation is that they do not cover all animals nor all situations. Rather, they have specific limitations of their reach. These limitations fall broadly into two categories: *exclusions* of particular species or groups of species from the scope of the law or from specific provisions within the law; and *exceptions* that allow certain practices that would otherwise be illegal.

Let us start with *exclusions*. Most animal protection acts determine at the outset what their *scope* is, that is, the kinds of animals they protect. Sometimes, this occurs in one of the first provisions which define what an 'animal' is for the purposes of the law. One particularly striking example is the US federal Animal Welfare Act (1966) which excludes some important categories of animals from the scope of its protection by setting out what animals are not 'animals' for the purposes of the Act:

Paragraph 2132 – US Animal Welfare Act (1966)

(g) The term "animal" means any live or dead dog, cat, monkey (nonhuman primate mammal), guinea pig, hamster, rabbit, or such other warm-blooded animal ...; but such term excludes (1) birds, rats of the genus Rattus, and mice of the genus Mus, bred for use in research, (2) horses not used for research purposes, and (3) other farm animals, such as, but not limited to live-stock or poultry ...

As David Wolfson and Mariann Sullivan (2004) have pointed out, the exclusion of farmed animals and laboratory mice and rats from the Animal Welfare Act's scope of protection makes that Act inapplicable to over 98 per cent of all land animals used in the US.

New Zealand's Animal Welfare Act (1999) adopts a less exclusive approach:

Section 2 – New Zealand Animal Welfare Act (1999)

(1) ... animal–

(a)   means any live member of the animal kingdom that is–

    (i)   a mammal; or

(ii)   a bird; or
(iii)   a reptile; or
(iv)   an amphibian; or
(v)   a fish (bony or cartilaginous); or
(vi)   any octopus, squid, crab, lobster, or crayfish (including freshwater crayfish); or
(vii)   any other member of the animal kingdom which is declared from time to time by the Governor-General, by Order in Council, to be an animal for the purposes of this Act; ...

However, even this relatively inclusive Act does not protect all animals. For instance, its protection does not extend to molluscs or insects.

The other feature that characterises some animal protection laws is the use of *exceptions* which explicitly allow behaviour that would otherwise be unlawful. One frequent example are exceptions that are granted to certain religious communities from the general requirement of stunning animals before slaughtering them.

Take, for example, the Spanish Law on the care of animals, their exploitation, transport, experimentation, and sacrifice (2007), which exempts certain religious communities from having to comply with the requirement to stun animals before killing them:

Article 6 – Spanish Law on the care of animals, their exploitation, transport, experimentation, and sacrifice (2007)

(3) When the slaughter of the animals is carried out according to the rites of Churches, Confessions, or religious Communities registered in the Registry of Religious Entities, and the obligations regarding stunning are incompatible with the prescriptions of the respective religious rite, then the competent authorities shall not demand compliance with said obligations ...

Although still common, such exceptions have been revoked in some legal systems, including Switzerland (1893), Slovenia (2013), Denmark (2014), and in the Walloon and Flemish regions of Belgium (2019). We will return to these exceptions in chapter five.

Another important example is the use of exceptions for the production of farmed animals, common in North America. The gist of these exceptions is that they make the legal provisions that prohibit the cruel treatment of animals or that mandate specific care for animals inapplicable to farming. Consider Canada, where welfare laws both on the federal and provincial level contain numerous animal welfare norms. However, almost all of these laws exempt so-called 'generally accepted farming practices', that is, practices relating to the rearing of animals as livestock that are common to most farming operations. For example, the Animal Protection Act (2018) of Saskatchewan provides:

Section 2 – Saskatchewan Animal Protection Act (2018)

(3) Notwithstanding anything in this Act, an animal is not considered to be in distress if it is handled: ...

(b) in accordance with generally accepted practices of animal management

Provisions such as this allow farming operations to avoid incurring criminal or administrative responsibility for how they handle their animals, which has economic benefits for them. However, as animal lawyers have pointed out, these laws introduce not only a double standard that treats farmed animals differently from other animals, but they also undermine the purpose of animal welfare law to the extent that they allow the farming industry to create its own rules that derogate from animal protection (see eg Cassuto and Eckhardt 2016).

Exercise 3: Animal Protection Laws in Your Own Country and Beyond

1. How would you classify your own legal system? Does it have laws protecting animals? Are they mainly focused on prohibiting cruelty toward animals? Or do they go beyond mere prohibitions of cruelty?
2. Which (if any) of the two characteristic elements of animal welfare acts can you find in your country's laws? If none, look into the laws of a neighbouring country.
3. What kinds of animals do the animal protection laws of your country (or a neighbouring country) cover? To answer this question of scope, have a close look at the first few articles in the relevant animal protection laws. Do you think these laws include enough animals, or should they include more?
4. 'It is unfair that some legal systems have revoked the exceptions previously granted to religious communities to slaughter animals according to their own rites.' Do you agree or disagree with this statement? Why?
5. Go back to the timeline you drew of animal protection laws in your own country in Exercise 2: can you draw the future of that timeline? How will animals be protected in your country in 10, 30, and 100 years?

IV. Constitutional Law

The legal rules relating to animals that this chapter has considered so far have mostly been based on statutory legislation enacted by parliaments of different countries. However, in some legal systems, animals are regulated not only through parliamentary legislation but also in the constitution. Since constitutions are at the top of the legal hierarchy, constitutional norms are generally more difficult to change than statutes (requiring for example a supermajority in parliament and/or a referendum) and they can trump statutes that contradict them. The constitution can therefore be a desirable place for animal protection norms.

As this section shows, constitutional protection for animals is rarer and less advanced than statutory animal welfare protection. We will therefore only address the most important points here. Existing constitutional provisions on animals can roughly be divided into three types: (1) competence norms; (2) state objectives; and (3) more direct legal protections.

A. Competence Norms

The first type of constitutional provision that makes mention of animals are competence norms. These norms are not directly aimed at protecting animals. Instead, they assign the power to public bodies to create legislation to protect animals. Such norms are typical for decentralised legal systems where constitutions identify whether national or state (or other lower level) bodies have the competence to regulate animal protection matters. Consider, for example, the following provision from Bolivia, which is a decentralised state:

Article 302 – Constitution of Bolivia (2009)

(I) The following are the exclusive authority of the autonomous municipal governments, within their jurisdiction: …

(5) To preserve, conserve and contribute to the protection of the environment and natural resources, wild fauna and domestic animals.

B. State Objectives

A number of constitutions also enshrine animal protection as so-called 'state objectives', that is, goals that the state aims to achieve. In contrast to other constitutional norms like constitutional rights, state objectives are primarily aspirational and do not create any binding obligations that could be enforced in court (ie they are not justiciable). However, they are of symbolic significance because they recognise animal protection as a value in a country's apex form of law. State objectives can also practically help promote animal protection as they can be used by courts to interpret other constitutional norms as well as legislation.

A good example of a state objective can be found in the German Constitution (the 'Basic Law'), which was amended in 2002 as follows:

Article 20a – German Basic Law (1949)

… Mindful also of its responsibility toward future generations, the state shall protect the natural foundations of life and animals by legislation and, in accordance with law and justice, by executive and judicial action, all within the framework of the constitutional order.

This constitutional recognition of animal protection has allowed German courts to give weight to the interests of animals in cases where their interests conflict with other constitutional norms, including humans' constitutional rights. For example, the German Constitutional Court relied on this state objective when determining that the human right to sexual autonomy can justifiably be limited when it comes to zoophilia (Constitutional Court of Germany 2015).

Another example is the Indian Constitution (1950) which was amended in 1976 to include the following provision:

Article 51A – Constitution of India (1950)

It shall be the duty of every citizen of India– …

(g) to protect and improve the natural environment including forests, lakes, rivers and wild life, and to have compassion for living creatures

While this 'duty' is not directly enforceable in court, it has been invoked by Indian courts in their case law. For example, the Indian Supreme Court made reference to the provision when it found that *jallikattu* races (in which bulls are chased and pulled down, often harming and sometimes killing the animals) violated the Prevention of Cruelty to Animals Act (1960) (Supreme Court of India 2014). We will return to this case in chapter six.

C. Direct Legal Protections

Finally, there are constitutional norms that protect animals in more direct ways that are ordinarily enforceable. Only a few legal systems possess such constitutional provisions, and they all take somewhat different forms.

Consider for instance the Constitution of Brazil (1988), which provides that:

Article 225 – Constitution of Brazil (1988)

Everyone has the right to an ecologically balanced environment, which is a public good for the people's use and is essential for a healthy life. The Government and the community have a duty to defend and to preserve the environment for present and future generations.

§1. To assure the effectiveness of this right, it is the responsibility of the Government to: …

(VII) protect the fauna and the flora, prohibiting, as provided by law, all practices that jeopardize their ecological functions, cause extinction of species or subject animals to cruelty.

Animal protection organisations have been able to directly rely on this article and the Brazilian Supreme Court has granted their legal challenges regarding, for example, the unconstitutionality of cockfighting or the *Farra do Boi* festival which involves the chasing, attacking, and killing of oxen (Federal Supreme Court of Brazil 1997).

An even more wide-ranging protection for animals was introduced in the Swiss Constitution in 1992. As the first country in the world to do so, Switzerland granted constitutional recognition to the dignity of animals:

Article 120 – Constitution of Switzerland (1999)

(2) The Confederation shall legislate on the use of reproductive and genetic material from animals, plants and other organisms. In doing so, it shall take account of the dignity of living beings as well as the safety of human beings, animals and the environment, and shall protect the genetic diversity of animal and plant species.

In spite of this provision being embedded in the context of non-human gene technology, the protection of animals' dignity is regarded as having effect in all areas of Swiss law. While there is some debate as to the concrete legal implications of animal dignity (especially whether it is or should be as absolute as human dignity), there is consensus that it recognises animals as beings with inherent value, that is, beings that matter in themselves and ought to be protected as such. The Swiss Federal Supreme Court has, for example, invoked animals' dignity to rule unconstitutional an animal experiment involving macaques, arguing that the macaques' inherent interests outweighed the scientists' interests in conducting the experiment (Federal Supreme Court of Switzerland 2009).

V. International Law

Once we move beyond domestic law and enter the domain of international law, there are arguably even fewer norms protecting animals. Specifically, there is currently no global treaty that protects animals in the way that, for example, global human rights treaties protect humans around the world. As we will consider in chapter seven, there have been proposals for international declarations of animal rights. However, none of these proposals has been adopted so far.

What does exist are international treaties that *relate to* animals. Perhaps the most prominent one is the Convention on International Trade in Endangered Species of Wild Fauna and Flora (CITES) from 1973, to which most states are parties. CITES's primary purpose is to protect endangered animals and plants. However, in contrast to the domestic laws that we analysed in the previous sections, CITES does not generally aim at protecting *individual* animals from harm. Rather, its principal aim is to protect *species* from extinction.

There are other treaties that do not focus on the level of species and create requirements to protect individual animals. However, because their priorities lie elsewhere, these treaties generally only protect animal welfare in marginal ways. The International Convention concerning the Transit of Animals, Meat and Other Products of Animal Origin (1935), for example, in Article 5 provides among other things that:

> … With a view to meeting the various difficulties arising in the course of transit, the exporting countries shall take steps to see that the animals are properly loaded and suitably fed and that they receive all necessary attention, in order to avoid unnecessary suffering.

However, the focus of this Convention (which has only been ratified by six states) is not on protecting animal welfare but on ensuring that live animals and other animal products are transported in a sanitary way so as to not lose their market value.

Animals' interests are protected more directly at the regional (ie continental) level. While there have been efforts to this effect on different continents, Europe stands out in terms of the international animal welfare instruments it has established over the past decades. The Council of Europe (an international organisation distinct and separate from the EU) in particular has played a pioneering role in creating numerous regional international treaties to further the protection of animal welfare. These treaties cover a range of different subject matter and include the European Conventions for the Protection of Animals kept for Farming Purposes (1976), for the Protection of Animals for Slaughter (1979), for the Protection of Animals during International Transport (1968, revised in 2003), for the Protection of Pet Animals (1987), and for the Protection of Vertebrate Animals used for Experimental and Other Scientific Purposes (1986).

In addition to the Council of Europe, the EU has enacted its own animal welfare instruments which are binding on all its Member States (all of whom are also Council of Europe members). These EU instruments include diverse laws aimed at protecting animals during transport and slaughter, as well as animals kept for farming purposes, used for experiments, kept as companion animals, used for their fur, or held in zoos.

Even though these instruments are already guided by the fact that animals are capable of feeling pain and having other sensations, it was the explicit recognition of their sentience by the Treaty of Lisbon in 2008 that made headlines. Since 2008, the EU's Treaty on the Functioning of the European Union (TFEU; 1957) – one of the EU's two core treaties – has contained the following article:

Article 13 – Treaty on the Functioning of the European Union (TFEU; 1957)

In formulating and implementing the Union's agriculture, fisheries, transport, internal market, research and technological development and space policies, the Union and the Member States shall, since animals are sentient beings, pay full regard to the welfare requirements of animals, while respecting the legislative or administrative provisions and customs of the Member States relating in particular to religious rites, cultural traditions and regional heritage.

The precise implications of this provision are not clear yet. However, it seems to play a comparable role to the constitutional state objectives which we discussed in section IV, with courts such as the EU Court of Justice invoking it to interpret other EU animal welfare laws in more protective ways.

Exercise 4: Constitutional and International Law

1. In your view, why is it important that constitutions enshrine animal protection? Which constitutional norms are the most significant? Alternatively, is it sufficient to protect animals in normal legislation (ie statutes)?

2. How about international law? Have a look at the International Convention for the Protection of Animals (not in force), which the Committee for the Convention for the Protection of Animals proposed in 1988 (you can access it on the textbook's website). Thinking about domestic anti-cruelty and animal welfare laws, how would you classify the Convention itself as compared to its protocols? What do you think are some of the advantages (and disadvantages) of having international legal instruments protecting animals?

VI. Animal Protection Laws in Practice

What the law requires and what actually happens in reality are frequently not the same thing. This seems particularly true for animal law, where there is often a significant gap between the law on the books and law in action. When studying animal protection laws such as the ones we discussed in this chapter, it is therefore important to keep in mind that compliance with these laws may often be found wanting. Let us briefly consider this problem and some of its causes.

One of the first issues that we encounter is that there is not only limited data on compliance with animal protection laws, but that there are also different ways of assessing compliance. For example, one can try to measure compliance by focusing on prosecutions brought, the severity of punishment, the rates of inspections, etc – but will in any case likely only get a partial picture.

The data from countries that do track compliance (generally by focusing on numbers of prosecutions and punishments/administrative measures) points not only to considerable differences between enforcement in different regions but also a tendency not to take animal welfare offences as seriously as other offences.

Consider the example of Switzerland, a federal state which provides a relatively high level of protection to animals. Data collected on animal welfare-related offences by the non-governmental organisation *Tier im Recht* (2021) reveals stark discrepancies between how different cantons (ie states) enforce animal law: the Canton of Bern, for example, recorded a total of 267 cases in 2020 (2.56 cases per 10,000 inhabitants). The Canton of Jura, by contrast, only recorded four cases (0.54 per 10,000 inhabitants). Even more problematically, there is a significant number of unreported or undetected welfare violations. As *Tier im Recht* points out, this can be inferred from the fact that, despite the millions of animals that are kept in Switzerland, there was a total of only 1,919 cases recorded in the entire country in 2020. What is more, the cases that are recorded reveal additional problems. First, enforcement seems to be taken more seriously when companion animals (especially dogs and cats) are concerned, whereas cases involving farmed animals are rarer, despite the greater number of such animals. Second, for all violations, the penalties handed out are often insubstantial and are far below the maximum penalties that the Swiss Animal Welfare Act 2008 allows. For example, this Act allows for imprisonment of up to three years for severe violations, but the most severe sentence ever handed out (in 2017) was of imprisonment for 120 days. It was the sanction for a person who shook and beat a puppy and then abandoned the injured animal for hours so that, when found, the puppy had to be euthanised.

What are some of the causes for enforcement problems such as those illustrated by the Swiss case? Writing in the context of the US – which faces similar issues – Bruce Wagman, Sonia Waisman, and Pamela Frasch (2019) have highlighted four causes that are likely also to be applicable elsewhere. First, responsible state officials (police, prosecutors, judges, etc) rarely receive the *training* they require to investigate and prosecute animal protection cases. Second, these officials may have *personal biases* that lead them to view cases involving animals as less important. Third, *scarce resources* (personal, financial, or otherwise) can lead officials to prioritise cases that involve human victims, and to put animal cases on the back burner. Finally, officials may come under *pressure from the community* to drop a case if it involves pursuing citizens who have good standing in the community.

Such limitations on public prosecution may be offset to some extent by private prosecution, which is possible in some legal systems. For instance, in the UK the Royal Society for the Prevention of Cruelty to Animals (RSPCA) – a private charity founded in 1824 – has its own inspectors who gather evidence and a team that decides which cases to litigate using its right to instigate criminal prosecutions privately (a right that all citizens have in England and Wales). For example, in 2019 the RSPCA success-fully secured 1,432 convictions of 661 defendants. Charges brought by the RSPCA were dismissed in respect of only 44 defendants. The RSPCA's prosecution success rate (convicted defendants as a proportion of all defendants) was 93.7 per cent. Despite this success, the RSPCA in 2021 decided to transfer its prosecution work to public prosecutors. Private prosecution is, after all, not without its problems. Because private organisations tend to be less accountable and transparent than public authorities, private enforcement done poorly can be more bane than boon.

What is more, also in the UK, farmed animals are significantly underrepresented in animal welfare cases, and penalties issued are well below the maximum penalties possible under UK animal welfare law. Furthermore, the RSPCA does not have the power to appeal judicial decisions. That power seems very rare even in countries that allow for private enforcement. One notable exception was the so-called *Tieranwalt* (animal attorney) in the Swiss Canton of Zurich, which existed from 1992 to 2010. The *Tieranwalt* was a private attorney who was independent from the cantonal authorities and who was granted the rights to bring prosecutions in criminal cases and even to appeal decisions.

Alternative mechanisms to enhance compliance have been proposed in recent times. These have included, for instance, improving data gathering for enforcement by making mandatory the installation of CCTV monitoring in slaughterhouses, which was done in the UK in 2018. It remains to be seen whether such alternative approaches can make a dent in the current compliance and enforcement deficit.

VII. Conclusion

This chapter has provided an overview of the current legal status of animals around the world. As we saw, there is considerable divergence in the levels of protections that different countries afford to animals, ranging from the absence of protections, to protections against mere cruelty, to more wide-ranging animal welfare protec-tions. These are again all applied differently to different types of animals, making clear that animal welfare protection is often guided not only by insights into animals' sentience and needs, but also by political considerations about the respective place of companion, farmed, and other animals in society. What is more, as we saw, even well-balanced laws often suffer from a lack of compliance or under-enforcement.

One of the issues that has shone through our discussion is that, even in legal systems that have extensive legal protections for animals, the status of these beings is still significantly different from that of human beings – despite the fact that animals have similar needs and interests in life, bodily integrity, or freedom. Perhaps most importantly, animals can be owned by humans, whereas legal ownership of humans is unthinkable today. As we will see in chapter two, some believe that as long as animals remain property they cannot have proper legal protections for their interests. Animal welfare laws, on this view, have a natural limit to what they can achieve because they ultimately have to operate within a framework that regards animals as goods that humans can use for their own purposes. This is sometimes referred to as the 'property paradigm', and is nicely illustrated by the following provision in the Russian Civil Code:

Article 137 – Russian Civil Code (1994)

The general rules on property apply to animals insofar as the law or other legal acts do not provide otherwise. In the exercise of rights, cruelty to animals, contrary to the principles of humanity, is not allowed.

In other words, humans have legal duties to treat animals humanely (or, in some countries, even with fuller regard to their welfare needs), but these duties are ultimately embedded in a broader property framework which allows humans to exercise ownership rights over animals. Chapter four will address whether this means that animals can have no rights whatsoever under current laws, and chapter six will turn to recent cases in which a limited number of legal systems have started to afford stronger legal protections to animals, including legal personhood and thick rights.

Exercise 5: The Current Legal Status of Animals

1. Many people believe that animals' interests are insufficiently protected by law. Try to make two small lists, one about the animal protection laws in this chapter generally, and one for those in your own country (you can do this exercise in groups, by having each group focus on a different list). Consider in each:

   a) what their key deficiencies are, and
   b) what the key legal reforms might be.

2. George Orwell wrote in *Animal Farm* that 'All animals are equal but some are more equal than others.' Write an essay of 500 words in which you reflect on this quotation in light of what you have learned about the status of different kinds of animals in legal systems around the world.

3. Do you think that animals' property status means that animal welfare laws cannot develop beyond a certain level of protection? If so, what could an alternative system look like that would allow better protection of animals' interests?

4. How, in your view, could compliance with animal protection laws be improved?

Useful References

Bielska-Brodziak, A, Drapalska-Grochowicz, M and Suska, M (2020) 'Symbolic Protection of Animals' 3 *Society Register* 103.

Eisen, J and Stilt, K (2016) 'Protection and Status of Animals' in R Grote, F Lachenmann, and R Wolfrum (eds), *Max Planck Encyclopedia of Comparative Constitutional Law*, available at oxcon.ouplaw.com/view/10.1093/law-mpeccol/law-mpeccol-e71?prd=OXCON.

Elischer, M (2019) 'The Five Freedoms: A History Lesson in Animal Care and Welfare', available at www.canr.msu.edu/news/an_animal_welfare_history_lesson_on_the_five_freedoms.

Global Animal Law (2021) 'Legislation Database', available at www.globalanimallaw.org/database/index.html.

Lundmark, F et al (2014) 'Intentions and Values in Animal Welfare Legislation and Standards' 27 *Journal of Agricultural and Environmental Ethics* 991.

Vapnek, J and Chapman, M (2010) 'Legislative and Regulatory Options for Animal Welfare' (Food and Agriculture Organization of the United Nations), available at www.fao.org/3/i1907e/i1907e01.pdf.

Whitfort, A (2012) 'Evaluating China's Draft Animal Protection Law' 34 *Sydney Law Review* 347.

World Animal Protection (2020) 'Animal Protection Index', available at api.worldanimalprotection.org.

2

Welfarism vs Abolitionism, a Dichotomy?

I. Introduction

Is it possible that animal protection laws have inherent limits to what they can achieve? Could they even positively undermine attempts to achieve full protection of animals' interests? In this chapter, we will analyse the view that even properly enforced animal welfare laws are detrimental to animal wellbeing because they condone animals' property status and allow the use and killing of animals for human ends.

This view, known as Abolitionism, directly challenges the paradigm of Classic Welfarism – the view that humans are allowed to own, use, and kill animals, but must treat them humanely in the process. Classic Welfarism is the model on which animal protection laws have been based at least since the nineteenth century, but in response to the Abolitionist challenge, a new view gained traction in the 2000s. This New Welfarism adopts Classic Welfarism's requirement to treat animals humanely when owned and used for human purposes, but goes further by holding that animals should be granted rights against certain types of uses and killings.

In this chapter, we will address the central tenets of Classic Welfarism, Abolitionism, and New Welfarism, focusing in particular on the debate – heated in the early 2010s – between Abolitionists and New Welfarists. As we will see, this debate is as much about different philosophical outlooks on the appropriate treatment of animals as it is about diverging advocacy strategies. Finally, we will consider recent developments that question the continuing relevance of the welfare-abolition dichotomy for the future of animal rights law.

Central Issues

1. Animal rights scholarship and, to some degree, advocacy was consumed in the past two decades by a debate between two camps: Abolitionists on the one hand, and Classic and New Welfarists on the other.

2.   According to Classic Welfarism, animals can be owned, used, and killed because humans' interests weigh heavier than animals'. However, animals must not be caused any unnecessary suffering. This outlook has been criticised because, among other reasons, it fails to give sufficient consideration to sentient animals' interests in not suffering and in not being killed.

3.   Abolitionists argue that animals should have the right not to be property and that most, if not all, types of use and killing of animals should be banned, which they believe cannot be achieved as long as animals remain property. Abolitionism's concomitant rejection of welfare reforms has been the subject of criticism, including on the grounds that it sacrifices improvements for the sake of theoretical purity and that its goal to abolish companion animals antagonises many who would otherwise be sympathetic to animal rights.

4.   New Welfarism is a hybrid position: its adherents believe that animals should have certain rights and that these rights can be achieved through welfare reforms. This outlook has been criticised on numerous grounds, including that the means it promotes undermine its end, and that it makes people feel comfortable with animal exploitation.

5.   By developing alternative animal rights theories that are often framed in less divisive terms, much of scholarship in recent years has either implicitly or explicitly moved away from the debate between Abolitionists and Classic and New Welfarists.

II. Classic Welfarism

As we saw in chapter one, the nineteenth century witnessed a surge in animal protection legislation in many parts of the world. The philosophical framework that underpinned this surge is Classic Welfarism. According to Classic Welfarism, animals should be treated humanely because they can suffer, but they may nevertheless be owned, used, and killed because human interests are considered to be morally weightier than non-human interests. Who exactly advocated Classic Welfarism? What does it entail? And what are some of its shortcomings?

A. Bigger Cages! Classic Welfarism and the Humane Treatment of Animals

Classic Welfarism emerged in the eighteenth century as a countermovement to the Cartesian view of animals as automatons, which had been prevalent since the mid-seventeenth century. René Descartes, the French philosopher who popularised this view and after whom it is named, famously described animals as *'bête-machine'* (animal machine) that, in contrast to humans, lack reason and a soul. Descartes himself did not seem to believe that this precludes animals from feeling pain. But that did not stop many of his followers from regarding his view as licence to treat animals as insensitive objects, including by dissecting and experimenting on living animals.

Classic Welfarists challenged the Cartesian paradigm by arguing that animals are due moral consideration. Even if they do not possess rationality or a soul, proponents of this new view held, many animals are sensitive beings who can feel pain and experience happiness. Two of the first modern thinkers to develop arguments in favour of promoting animals' wellbeing by curtailing cruelty against them were the Scottish philosopher Francis Hutcheson (1694–1746) and the British clergyman Humphrey Primatt (1734–1776). Yet it took a secular rendering of their Christian theories by the English utilitarian philosopher and legal reformer Jeremy Bentham (1748–1832) for Classic Welfarism to become as influential as it did in the nineteenth century.

Although Bentham did not write any treatises on animals, he made the implications of his utilitarian philosophy (about which we say more in chapter three) for animal welfare evident in a much-cited footnote of his *An Introduction to the Principles of Morals and Legislation* (1789). In the context of discussing who is susceptible of happiness and of having law promote that happiness, Bentham argues that animals have been unjustly treated as insensitive things in law. Rejecting the view that it is the 'blackness' or 'villosity' of one's skin that should determine whether someone matters morally, he goes on to ask:

> What else is it that should trace the insuperable line? Is it the faculty of reason, or, perhaps, the faculty of discourse? But a full-grown horse or dog, is beyond comparison a more rational, as well as a more conversible [*sic*] animal, than an infant of a day, or a week, or even a month, old … the question is not, Can they *reason*? nor, Can they *talk*? but, Can they *suffer*? (Bentham 1789, 1970, 283 note b).

Bentham's view, that it is the ability to suffer – to feel pain – that makes a being matter morally, was adopted and amplified by John Stuart Mill (1806–1873), another pivotal utilitarian thinker, and it more recently became the principal tenet of Peter Singer's influential *Animal Liberation* (1975), which we discuss in chapter three.

According to the Classic Welfarist doctrine which Bentham helped shape, animals matter morally by virtue of their sentience (ie their ability to feel and to experience the world subjectively) and are owed equal consideration of their interests in not suffering. The law should therefore protect them from cruelty. Nevertheless, Classic Welfarists do not take issue with the fact that animals are property and can be used and killed for human purposes. Classic Welfarists simply insist that animals must be treated humanely in the process. If we were to put this in slogan form, we could say that Classic Welfarism advocates 'bigger cages!'. That is, it champions laws that aim to ensure that animal suffering is minimised, for example by setting minimum sizes of cages in which farrowing pigs are kept. However, Classic Welfarism does not challenge the fact that pigs are owned, used, and killed.

The reason for this is that, while Classic Welfarists such as Bentham believe that sentient animals matter morally, they believe that humans matter *more*. Bentham, for instance, claimed that humans are morally superior to animals because only humans have the ability to anticipate the future. This ability, he believed, is necessary for having an interest in not being killed. Because he believed that animals lack the ability to anticipate the future, he thought they also lack an interest in remaining alive. Bentham expressed this pithily in an anti-cruelty bill he drafted: 'Killing other animals ... is nothing: the only harm is in tormenting them while they live' (UCL, Transcribe Bentham, JB/072/214/004).

Beyond justifying human superiority, Bentham's views are also characteristic of Classic Welfarism in another way; they allow diverse human interests to outweigh animals' interest in not suffering. Casting a cloud over his above-cited footnote, Bentham wrote the following to a newspaper editor:

> I never have seen, nor ever can see, any objection to the putting of dogs and other inferior animals to pain, in the way of medical experiment, when that experiment has a determinate object, beneficial to mankind, accompanied with a fair prospect of the accomplishment of it. But I have a decided and insuperable objection to the putting of them to pain without any such view (cited in Kniess 2019, 561).

Expanding on this position in his draft anti-cruelty bill, Bentham argued that other useful purposes that justify cruelty to animals include: chastisement, food, clothing, conveyance, manufacture, preventing humans from being harmed or even just annoyed by an animal, as well as promoting useful knowledge. This list of legitimate purposes is illustrative of the broader point that, while Classic Welfarism regards sentient animals as deserving of moral and legal protection against suffering, it generally limits these protections to what Bentham calls 'wanton' cruelty: cruelty that serves no accepted human purpose (UCL, Transcribe Bentham, JB/072/214/001).

It is important to note that Classic Welfarism not only provided the intellectual foundation for the early anti-cruelty laws of the nineteenth century, it also still underpins animal protection laws today. This is true in particular for anti-cruelty laws that are limited to protecting animals from unnecessary suffering, but it also holds for more progressive animal welfare laws. Consider for example the anti-cruelty statute from the US state of New Mexico, which we encountered in chapter one:

Paragraph 30-18-1 – New Mexico Statutes (2011)

B. Cruelty to animals consists of a person:

(1) negligently mistreating, injuring, killing without lawful justification or tormenting an animal; or
(2) abandoning or failing to provide necessary sustenance to an animal under that person's custody or control.

As this statute illustrates, the law of New Mexico – as well as many other legal systems – treats animals in much the same way as Bentham proposed: it does not make owning, using, or killing them illegal. Instead, it simply protects them from suffering as long as the suffering is not required by sufficiently weighty human interests.

Despite these limitations, however, it is important to note that Classic Welfarism constituted a drastic move away from the Cartesian worldview by recognising that animals have moral status and require legal protection by virtue of their sentience. As we will see in chapter three, the idea that we owe animals equal consideration of their interests – at least as far as avoiding pain is concerned – was interpreted in more progressive ways by heirs of Classic Welfarism such as Peter Singer.

B. Critiques of Classic Welfarism

The doctrine of Classic Welfarism and the animal protection laws it inspired have become the subject of increasing criticism. The animal rights activist Henry Stephens Salt (1851–1939) was one of the first to object to the suffering inflicted on animals for food, sport, clothing, and science, and to argue for granting animals rights (Salt 1894). However, it was the legal scholar Gary Francione who has developed what is arguably the most comprehensive and sustained attack on Welfarism. Francione's arguments take aim at both Classic and New Welfarism. We focus here on the elements of his critique that primarily affect Classic Welfarism and will address his objections to New Welfarism in section IV. Understanding Francione's critique of Classic Welfarism helps us get a handle on his own position – Abolitionism – which we introduce in the next section.

At the heart of Francione's critique – which is echoed in the work of other critics such as Steven Best (2014), Sherry Colb and Michael Dorf (2016), and Corey Lee Wrenn (2016) – is his claim that the change which Classic Welfarism was supposed to bring about by giving animals' interests equal consideration has not happened. Worse, the principle of 'humane' treatment is a 'fantasy' [that makes] us feel better about exploiting animals' (Francione 2021: 6). Rather than ending animal exploitation or at least making sure that animals do not suffer when they are used, Francione argues, Classic Welfarism promotes 'happy exploitation' (2021: 59).

According to Francione and likeminded critics, the key reason for this failure is that Classic Welfarism does not challenge the basic fact that humans can own, use, and kill animals for their own ends. Instead, it only focuses on minimising suffering. In fact, these critics argue that because it does not dispute animals' status as property, Classic Welfarism cannot even achieve its limited goal of preventing unnecessary suffering. Why? The reason is that ownership creates a 'structural imbalance' (Francione 2021: 61) that puts the objects of property (ie animals) at a disadvantage vis-à-vis their owners (ie humans). Much like in the case of chattel slaves who were the property of their masters (about which we say more in chapter eight), Francione argues that ownership over animals 'necessarily result[s] in ignoring or undervaluing the interests' of these animals (2021: 34). The fact that animals can be owned thus makes it impossible to give equal consideration to their interests, including their interest not to suffer.

For Francione, one implication of animals' property status is that humans do not question the purposes for which they use animals, even when it is not necessary that they use animals for these purposes. Consider for example the use of animals as food even where other sources of nutrition are readily available. According to Francione, using and killing animals in such contexts cannot reasonably be characterised as 'necessary', yet Classic Welfarists do not oppose such practices. They simply ask how, within the accepted practice of using animals for food, suffering can be reduced to what is necessary for the practice.

Another implication is that even where Classic Welfarism requires a balancing of human interests against animal interests to determine what levels of suffering are 'necessary', human interests almost always win out. The reason for this, Francione argues, is that the balancing exercise is rigged from the start. It requires comparing the interests of humans who have property rights over animals with the interests of animals who are humans' property and lack rights of their own.

According to Francione, this means that animal protection laws will almost always protect animals only when their suffering is gratuitous and/or economically inefficient. For example, he argues that the primary reason why the Humane Slaughter Act (1958) – a federal law regulating the slaughter of animals in the US – requires the stunning of large animals such as cows, pigs, and sheep before slaughter is that this prevents the animals from flailing around, which can incur costs by injuring slaughterhouse workers and damaging carcasses.

Are these implications simply the result of poor welfare laws that could theoretically be improved? Francione thinks not. As he maintains:

> Regulation for the benefit of the property undermines the very institution of animal property. When the interests of animals, which are regarded as property, are balanced against the interests of persons who are holders of rights, and, in particular, property rights, the property must lose substantially all of the time or the property is no longer property (2021: 36).

This explains why, according to Francione, even some of the most progressive animal welfare laws that we have encountered in chapter one permit practices such as the raising and killing of animals for food which would be considered torture or worse if done to humans.

III. Abolitionism

In response to Classic Welfarism, an alternative conception emerged in the 1990s: Abolitionism. According to Abolitionism, the property status of all sentient animals and, with it, all types of use and killing of animals should be abolished. In addition, Abolitionism requires the renunciation of all animal products (so-called ethical veganism) and the education of others. Popularised by Francione's seminal book *Animals, Property, and the Law* (1995), Abolitionism has since become a vocal movement in animal rights law.

Before exploring it in more detail, we should note that Francione's account is not the only game in town. There are other animal rights models that do not follow Abolitionism, even though Francione once claimed that Abolitionism is 'the animal rights position' (Francione and Garner 2010: 4). We need therefore to distinguish the theory of Francione and his followers – which we call 'Abolitionism' with a capital A – from other animal rights conceptions. Although many of them also promote the abolition of animal exploitation, these models diverge from Francione's position for example by allowing for animals to remain property or by permitting the use of animals under certain circumstances. Call this 'abolitionism' with a small a. Our focus in this section will be on Abolitionism, which is spearheaded by Francione.

A. No Cages! The Abolitionist Case for Ending Animal Exploitation

According to Francione, nothing less than a paradigm shift is required to give animals their due. Humans should stop regarding animals as ownable things that they can use for their own ends with only few limitations. Instead, they should start viewing them as persons with intrinsic moral value. Put another way, Abolitionism demands that animals (including humans) must have a right not to be treated as property, that is, they must have 'a right to personhood' (2021: 10). This right is in the first instance a moral right, meaning that it describes how animals should be treated morally. However, once there is sufficient acceptance of it, it should also become a thick legal right (a concept we discuss in chapter four). Why do Francione and other Abolitionists focus on the right not to be property? Because they view it as the 'foundation for all other rights' (2021: 116) – one's entry ticket to the moral community. Only if one has this right, they believe, can one have any other fundamental rights.

Abolitionists argue that animals' right not to be treated as property cannot be traded off against countervailing human interests (ie it is an 'absolute right', a concept we discuss in chapter four). Hence, even if the right imposes significant cost or inconvenience on humans, it must nevertheless be respected. Abolitionists thus reject the utilitarian philosophy that underlies Classic Welfarism and which allows overriding animals' interests (eg in not suffering) when the expected gain in utility (eg scientific experiments that benefit millions of humans) is greater than the pain inflicted on the animals. Abolitionism is instead based on a deontological philosophy, according to which rights must be respected regardless of the consequences (we discuss these different philosophical approaches in chapter three).

Why do Abolitionists believe that, like humans, animals should have a right to personhood, and thus become members of the moral community? The reason, for Abolitionists, is simple: animals are sentient beings. But have not Bentham and other Classic Welfarists already recognised that animals matter morally because they can suffer? What distinguishes Abolitionism from their position?

Francione contends that although Classic Welfarists realised that sentience matters, they have not taken it to its logical conclusion. Specifically, he objects to the Welfarist view that it is justifiable to kill animals if it is done painlessly. As we saw in the previous section, Bentham and his followers adopt this view because they believe that most or all non-human animals lack the ability to anticipate and plan for the future and therefore do not have an interest in remaining alive. Building on the work of the social reformer Brigid Brophy (1929–1995), Francione contends that while such cognitive capacities may be relevant for some purposes (eg to drive cars, vote, or get a higher education), they do not tell us who has an interest in continued existence. For that, he holds, sentience is necessary and sufficient:

> Sentience is a means to an end, that of continued existence; sentience is what ensures continued survival and the continuation of conscious states. To say that a being who is sentient does not have an interest in continued existence is like saying that a being who has eyes does not have an interest in continuing to see. Seeing is what an eye *does*; perpetuating consciousness so that life continues is what subjective awareness *does* (Francione 2021: 81).

Sentience, then, has radical consequences that the Classic Welfarists misunderstood or chose to overlook: animals who are sentient not only have an interest in not suffering but also in not being used and killed. In this respect, they are no different from sentient human beings whom we would also not kill, even if some of them lack the ability to anticipate the future. This, according to Abolitionists, is what equal consideration really means: equal consideration of all sentient beings' interests in not suffering and in continuing to live.

What are the practical implications of this outlook? If we were to put it in slogan form, Abolitionism demands 'no cages!' rather than 'bigger cages!'. Concretely, by requiring that animals be given a right not to be treated as property, Abolitionism is committed to ending all forms of animal exploitation. As Francione points out, '*All* animal use – for food, clothing, entertainment, biomedical research, and so on – assumes that animals are things' (Francione 2021: 124). It must therefore be ended, rather than simply be made more humane. As he notes, we would not accept human slavery either just because it was made more humane.

Apart from ending the use and killing of animals for food, sport, and experimentation, Abolitionism also demands an end to domesticated animals themselves – including companion animals. As Francione puts it, domestication is inherently unjust because it selectively breeds some sentient beings to be 'completely and perpetually dependent on us' (2021: 161). Humans have a responsibility to care for the cats, dogs, rabbits, sheep, chickens, cows, and other domesticated animals who are already alive. But humans also have a duty not to bring new such dependent animals into existence. Wild animals, by contrast, should simply be left alone.

Abolitionism further imposes demands on an individual level: everyone has a duty to become an ethical vegan. This means that, as far as practicable, one must no longer directly participate in the use or killing of animals; be it by eating meat, wearing wool, leather, or fur, using animals as mere tools (eg on farms), or by consuming other animal products. In addition, Abolitionism requires that one 'engage[s] in creative, nonviolent education focused on veganism as a moral imperative' (2021: 142).

What other practical steps do Abolitionists advocate to bring an end to animal exploitation? Specifically, considering that, as we will see below, Abolitionists view animal welfare reforms as counterproductive, are there any small-scale changes short of wholesale abolition that they endorse? For some time, Francione advised against but tolerated single-issue campaigns that abolish the exploitation of animals in specific areas, such as for example bans on using animals in circuses. However, to be tolerable such campaigns had to avoid as far as possible giving the impression that using animals in other than the targeted contexts (eg outside circuses) is justifiable and had therefore 'always [to] be explicitly linked with an [A]bolitionist message (Francione and Garner 2010: 78). More recently, Francione (2021: 140-41) and other Abolitionists such as Wrenn and Rob Johnson (2013) have adopted the view that single-issue campaigns should be rejected altogether because they perpetuate animal exploitation. We will return to this point in section IV below.

B. Critiques of Abolitionism

Considering the strong position it defends, it is no surprise that Abolitionism has been met with fierce opposition. We will briefly focus on four particularly salient criticisms, namely that Abolitionism downplays Welfarism's positive effects; is utopian; is strategically counterproductive; and engages in a risky bet.

Turning to the first objection, Abolitionism has been criticised for *downplaying the positive effects* of Welfarism. Robert Garner, who, as we will see in section IV, is the most prominent defender of New Welfarism, has argued that existing welfare improvements that have been achieved for animals are ethically desirable, even if they fall short of securing rights for animals. For example, he notes that 'a regulation that insists on environmental enrichment for all laboratory animals is, all things being equal, of greater worth than one that requires it only for particular species, which in turn is better than having no regulation at all' (Francione and Garner 2010: 132). In fact, given the large number of animals used, even if welfare reforms only lead to small improvements, such small improvements may still end up benefitting millions of animals. Another positive effect that animal welfare campaigns are said to have is the raising of awareness of the exploitation of animals, which is seen as a stepping stone for better legal protections in the future.

Second, Garner and others have challenged Abolitionism on the grounds that it is *utopian*. Abolitionism is a fundamentalist position, according to Garner, because it is unwilling to compromise with other political players such as Welfarists, let alone representatives of animal-use industries. As such, he holds, Abolitionism is best characterised as a 'moral crusade' (2010: 147) that is unlikely to fall on sympathetic ears. As we saw above, Abolitionism not only requires adopting a vegan lifestyle, but also putting an end to using animals for food, science, companionship, and other purposes. As Garner points out, such

> objectives are, at the present time, politically unrealistic. No country in the world has prohibited the use of animals for medical research or as a source of food ... Moreover, most consumers eat meat, and benefit from the production of drugs that have been developed and tested on animals (Garner 2008: 116).

The conclusion that critics such as Garner draw from this is that, rather than push for what they regard as utopian change that is unlikely to happen anytime soon, one should focus one's energies on (welfare) reforms that can realistically be achieved in the here and now.

Third, Abolitionism has been challenged on the grounds that it *alienates many* who would potentially be sympathetic to the plight of animals. The philosophers Sue Donaldson and Will Kymlicka have pressed this point, arguing that Abolitionism's objective to bring about the extinction of domesticated animals in particular has been 'a strategic disaster for the AR [animal rights] movement' because

> many people have come to their concern for animal rights precisely through their relationship with a companion animal, which has opened their eyes to the rich individuality of

animals' lives, and to the possibility of a relationship with animals that is not based on exploitation. To insist that support for AR requires condemning all such relationships is to alienate many potential supporters (Donaldson and Kymlicka 2011: 79).

Even aside from its requirement to end the keeping of domesticated animals, the uncompromising position that Abolitionists adopt has been criticised for complicating movement-building around animal rights – a point to which we will return in section V and chapter eight.

Fourth, Abolitionism could be accused of *engaging in a risky bet*: it assumes that refraining from bringing about welfare improvements now is worth it because this will facilitate abolition of animal exploitation in the future. As has been pointed out in the literature, however, there is little or no empirical evidence for Abolitionism's claim that welfare reforms make abolition less likely. In fact, one of the few studies that looks at this issue seems to support the opposite conclusion: that welfarist campaigns can drive down meat demand (Tonsor and Olynk 2011). However, even if Abolitionists were right that foregoing welfare reforms now makes it likelier that abolition will happen eventually, there is no guarantee that abolition will in fact occur. And if it does not occur, the objection goes, then Abolitionists will have gambled away welfare improvements that could have ameliorated the lives of countless animals. As Luis Chiesa has pointed out, Abolitionists are thus in a kind of 'dilemma' (2016: 557): if they oppose welfare reforms that would reduce suffering on the grounds that such reforms do not bring about abolition, they sacrifice animals' wellbeing without any certainty of abolition occurring down the road. On the other hand, if they embrace such welfare reforms, they jettison the fundamental tenet of their view that such reforms are problematic because they reinforce animals' property status (which we will discuss in section IV).

If you are interested in finding out more about these and other critiques – and in how Abolitionists have responded to them, you will find useful references at the end of the chapter and on the companion website.

Exercise 1: Abolitionism

1. Think about contexts where Abolitionism would change your personal relationship to animals. Would this change be good or bad in your view? Why?
2. Return to chapter one and look at existing animal welfare laws. Choose one of them and write a critical reflection of 300 words from an Abolitionist perspective.
3. Imagine you are the campaign manager of the animal advocacy organisation 'Abolition – Now!'. You are tasked with developing a new campaign. Which issue does your campaign focus on? What is the campaign slogan? What is the goal of the campaign? Which arguments

should your organisation put forward? Visualise your idea on a poster and present it to your peers at 'Abolition – Now!'.

4.   Your presentation is followed by a debate at 'Abolition – Now!'. Some new members (Group 1) have doubts about the campaign, the overall strategy, and goals of the organisation as a whole. Other members (Group 2) try to counter their criticisms. You can carry out this exercise with fellow students or think yourself about which arguments each group could make.

IV. New Welfarism

As we saw, Classic Welfarism was a particularly influential movement in the nineteenth and twentieth centuries and set the course for animal protection laws worldwide. Although it is still common in political discourse, since the 2000s it has amongst scholars increasingly been replaced by a revised version. Francione gave this revised version the label 'New Welfarism', which has been adopted by most authors and will also be used here, even though some, such as its main proponent Garner, prefer the term 'animal protectionism' (Francione and Garner 2010: 104).

New Welfarism shares with Classic Welfarism the first tenet of its philosophy: animals should be treated humanely because they can suffer. However, in contrast to Classic Welfarists, New Welfarists believe that not all human interests are morally weightier than animals'. They therefore argue that even the painless use and killing of animals for certain purposes must be limited, by giving animals rights where possible. Importantly, according to New Welfarists, welfare reforms that fall short of abolition are not incompatible with securing rights for animals. To the contrary, New Welfarists regard welfare reforms as a possible means of achieving the end of animal rights. How exactly do New Welfarists believe this could work? And what are some of the criticisms levelled against it? Let us address these two questions in turn.

A. First Bigger Cages, Then No Cages! New Welfarism's Hybrid Approach

Although New Welfarist ideas go back at least to the mid-twentieth century, it was in 2010 that Garner presented perhaps its most detailed defence yet. We will therefore primarily focus on his work here. Garner's New Welfarist position can best be described as a 'hybrid approach' (Taylor 1999: 27) that adopts the means of Classic Welfarism – small-scale welfare reforms – while still endorsing abolitionism's goal of ending animal exploitation. To construct this hybrid position, Garner contrasts his view with both Classic Welfarism and Abolitionism.

Starting with Classic Welfarism, Garner argues that it is based on a problematic belief in the moral superiority of humans, that is, the view that human interests always outweigh animals' interests. Garner challenges this in two ways. First, he takes issue with the Classic Welfarist position that animals have nothing to lose by death because they lack the ability to anticipate and plan for the future. As we saw, Bentham believed that for this reason, as long as it is done painlessly, killing animals is unproblematic. Garner, by contrast, argues that while killing humans is a greater wrong than killing animals, killing animals can nevertheless be wrong. The reason for this is that, even when killed painlessly, animals are deprived of future opportunities that would have been valuable to them, such as for example the opportunity to have offspring. According to Garner, that most animals may not understand what it means to die and therefore not have a conscious desire to remain alive does not change the fact that depriving these animals of opportunities by killing them is wrong. The lack of their desire to remain alive, he believes, is only a reason why animals' lives are worth *less* than humans' who have that capacity. It is however not a reason to think that their lives are worth *nothing*.

Second, Garner maintains that inflicting pain on animals for human benefit is generally wrong. According to him, humans and animals are equals when it comes to sentience, at least where the pain suffered by animals is as intense as that suffered by humans. Hence, although he does not grant animals a right to life as he believes humans' lives are worth more, he does argue that animals should have a right not to suffer, which would prevent humans from using animals even when it would be advantageous for humans to do so. As Garner emphasises, his approach is thus not one that opposes the animal rights idea as such, but only animal rights of a particular brand: Abolitionism, especially as defended by Francione.

Turning to Abolitionism, how exactly does New Welfarism depart from it? The most important way in which New Welfarists like Garner distance themselves from Abolitionism is in holding that animals' status as ownable things does not necessarily stand in the way of better treatment. Drawing on the work of the political philosopher Alasdair Cochrane (Cochrane 2009: 435–437), Garner argues that many animals do not have an intrinsic interest in liberty. While animals will generally have an *instrumental* interest in being free (eg because being free is a means for them to forage for food), they lack the capacity for making autonomous decisions about how they want to lead their lives, and therefore have no *intrinsic* interest in being free. If one accepts that many animals only have interests in not suffering, but not in being free per se, Garner argues, one can see why owning, keeping, and using an animal is not necessarily morally problematic, as long as the animal is not made to suffer. To be sure, Garner agrees with Abolitionists that most of the current owning, keeping, and using of animals violates their right not to suffer. However, in contrast to Abolitionists, he does not believe that animals need to be given a right not to be property for such exploitation to end. For Garner, welfare reforms are a perfectly suitable way of achieving the goal of animal rights. As he concludes: 'Abolishing animals' property status is not therefore a necessary condition for the achievement of animal rights' (Francione and Garner 2010, 130).

This, then, is the hybrid position of New Welfarism, which we can summarise as 'First bigger cages, then no cages!' What are the central implications of this position? According to Garner, New Welfarists should embrace 'unnecessary suffering' principles, which, as we saw in chapter one, exist in many animal protection laws. Garner agrees with Francione that these principles are not applied with sufficient rigour, as most countries allow the use of animals for purposes such as clothing or entertainment which are not 'necessary' because alternatives are readily available. Contrary to Francione, however, Garner believes that unnecessary suffering principles are strategically useful to have because they allow animal rights advocates to engage with opponents on the grounds of a principle accepted by all. Furthermore, unnecessary suffering principles are not static but can lend stronger protections to animals in the future. Garner gives the example of testing cosmetics on animals, which was considered 'necessary' some decades ago, but is now banned in many legal systems.

What about raising and killing animals for food? Garner believes that this practice would have to change radically, as it involves significant 'unnecessary' suffering in animals. He only foresees two exceptions to a ban on eating animals:

> One would be where depriving humans of the right to eat animals would be life-threatening, a scenario that does not exist now, at least in the developed world. The other would be an extensive system of animal agriculture where the suffering of animals is minimized. In an age of intensive animal agriculture, where factory farms are the norm, such a scenario is, at least at present, unlikely (Francione and Garner 2010: 118-19).

Similarly, scientific research on animals would still be allowed, but only under the conditions that the research would help protect human lives and that animals are not made to suffer in the process.

B. Critiques of New Welfarism

Classic Welfarism and New Welfarism have become the joint targets of criticisms in recent years, especially by Abolitionists, with Francione developing the most comprehensive critique. Let us focus on four of the most prominent objections to Classic and New Welfarism: that its means contradict its ends; that it has failed to deliver; that it makes people feel comfortable with animal exploitation; and that it employs problematic single-issue campaigns.

First, one of the key criticisms that Francione raises against Classic and New Welfarism is that it is *contradictory* to have abolition of animal exploitation as one's goal but to pursue animal welfare reforms as one's means. This is because, according to Francione, such reforms reinforce animals' status as things which we can exploit:

> The new welfarists are in error in that welfare reform does not move us away from the property paradigm; on the contrary, welfare reform relies on and reinforces the property status of animals (Francione and Garner 2010: 58).

Francione identifies two reasons why Classic and New Welfarism reinforce animals' status as property. First, they do not challenge the fact that animals can be used and killed. They only require that this be done painlessly and – in the case of New Welfarism – to protect human lives. As such, Francione argues, Classic and New Welfarism treat animals as little different from other ownable things. Second, while animals enjoy some welfare protections in some legal systems, Francione believes that such protections will rarely go beyond what is economically beneficial for producers and consumers. For example, he contends that gestation and veal crates were banned in some legal systems not primarily because of welfare reasons but because 'providing animals more space increases productivity and is economically efficient' (Francione and Garner 2010: 212).

Welfarism is sometimes also accused of having *failed to deliver*. Francione has been a prominent supporter of this objection. As he argues, Classic Welfarism has been the reigning paradigm for more than 200 years, 'and we are using more nonhuman animals in more horrific ways than at any time in human history' (Francione and Garner 2010: 49). While New Welfarism has not been around for that long, Francione believes it to be similarly unsuccessful because, like Classic Welfarism, it does not put an end to the using and killing of animals.

This holds true of course for all animals which do not fall under the scope of protection of animal protection laws. However, for Francione, it also holds true for those animals which are protected on paper. As he notes,

> even the most 'humanely' treated animals are subjected to what reasonable minds cannot disagree is, plainly put, torture. 'Humane' animal treatment is *nothing* more than a fantasy. Animals remain 'abandoned without redress to the caprice of a tormentor' – us (Francione 2021: 44).

Problematically, according to Francione, animal welfare organisations often play a role in supporting this status quo because they collaborate with animal-use industries, for example in the certification of 'happy' eggs, milk, or meat.

Third, some argue that all forms of Welfarism – including New Welfarism – have not only failed to meaningfully change animals' lot, but even made things worse. Welfare reforms are not backed up by any evidence that they work. If anything, the objection goes, such reforms have *facilitated public acceptance* of animal exploitation. As Francione has put the point, welfare reforms 'mak[e] humans who care about animals feel more comfortable about continuing to exploit animals rather than focus them on the idea that any animal use reflects an acceptance that animals are just things that have no moral value' (Francione 2021: 139). Like Francione, some therefore believe that welfare reforms serve at most as a sop to people's conscience, thus making abolition less likely.

Finally, Classic and New Welfarists alike have been challenged for pursuing what are viewed as *problematic single-issue campaigns*. As we saw above, such campaigns focus not on the wholesale abolition of animal exploitation, but rather on (often small-scale) abolitions of certain practices. Examples of single-issue campaigns include efforts to end the use of wild animals in circuses, ban the import of foie gras, or prohibit horse racing. Wrenn has been at the forefront of critiques of issue-specific campaigns. Using the metaphor of a tree representing animal exploitation, she argues that:

> Single-issue campaigns reinforce … irrational dichotomies by singling out specific uses of other animals as though they are worse than others. When campaigns seek to eliminate one branch of the tree, while ignoring other branches, they insinuate that certain forms of exploitation are worse than others. The movement thus presents a hierarchy of concern to the public (Wrenn 2016: 75).

For instance, on Wrenn's view, campaigns focusing on banning horse racing implicitly signal to the public that other cruel practices such as greyhound racing are less problematic, perhaps even legitimate. Rather than pruning single branches of the tree, Wrenn suggests that the only reasonable solution is to 'uproot and eliminat[e] the tree' (2016: 76). Like Francione, she believes this requires campaigns focusing on vegan education.

Readers interested in finding out more about these objections and Classic and New Welfarists' responses will find useful references at the end of this chapter and on the companion website.

V. Beyond the Dichotomy

Proponents of Abolitionism and Classic and New Welfarism actively exchanged views, especially in the early 2010s. Nonetheless, it seems that rather than resolve their debate, their positions have become more entrenched over the years. Perhaps for this reason, more recent scholarship has tended to steer clear of the welfare-abolition dichotomy, and some of it has even actively tried to move beyond it.

In the first category of scholarship trying to steer clear of the dichotomy are the many theories that promote a more open version of animal rights than Abolitionism, and that do not address Abolitionism or Welfarism explicitly. In this chapter, we have called these alternative rights accounts abolitionist accounts. For example, as we discuss in chapter four, theories such as Cochrane's (2009) or Visa Kurki's (2019) hold that animals can have certain legal rights despite being property, thus rejecting one of the key tenets of Abolitionism. Another example is Clare McCausland's (2014) theory. According to McCausland, the Five Freedoms (which we encountered in chapter one) can be viewed as rights among other reasons because they have all the marks of rights under the interest theory of rights (a theory we discuss in chapter four). For instance, squirrels may be said to have a right to be free from pain because they have an interest in being free from pain that is sufficiently weighty to impose duties on others not to inflict pain on the squirrels.

In this section, our focus is on the second category of scholarship, which directly engages with Abolitionists and Classic and New Welfarists to overcome the welfare-abolition dichotomy. We start by considering Donaldson's and Kymlicka's proposal for shared multispecies communities, before discussing Melanie Joy's plea for a multi-pronged strategy.

A. Cooperation Instead of Abolition: Sue Donaldson and Will Kymlicka's Theory of Shared Multispecies Communities

One of the central premises guiding the work of Donaldson and Kymlicka is that humans and animals do not live separately from each other. Rather, for thousands of years they have interacted with each other and sometimes lived in shared communities characterised by various forms of interdependency – and will likely continue to do so for the foreseeable future. Consider for instance domesticated animals such as dogs. While many of them have lived woeful lives dictated by human whim, others have participated in more beneficial relationships with humans, guarding homes, providing company, and receiving food, shelter, and company in return. Donaldson and Kymlicka believe that Abolitionists' proposal to bring about the extinction of domesticated animals is deeply problematic because it overlooks the possibility for such mutually beneficial co-existence.

According to Donaldson and Kymlicka, Abolitionism is furthermore problematic because it violates domesticated animals' intrinsic interests. Abolitionists rightly view the original domestication of animals – which often occurred and was carried on in coercive ways – as unjust. However, Donaldson and Kymlicka argue, this injustice does not mean that it would be better to put an end to domesticated animals. To believe that it would is to mistakenly think that one can 'turn back the clock to a time before domesticated animals existed in order to undo the historic wrongs' (Donaldson and Kymlicka 2011: 89). Drawing an analogy to abolitionism in the human context, they point out that:

> The original process by which Africans entered America was unjust, but the remedy to that historic injustice is not to turn back the clock to a time when there were no Africans in America. Indeed, far from remedying the original injustice, seeking the extinction or expulsion of African Americans compounds the original injustice, by denying their right to membership in the American community, and by denying their right to found families and reproduce themselves (2011: 79).

The Abolitionist proposal exacerbates the original injustice, according to Donaldson and Kymlicka, because abolition could not itself be achieved without violating the rights of domesticated animals. As they argue:

> The [A]bolitionist position implies that if humans stopped 'creating' domesticated animals, they would cease to exist. But this isn't the case. For domesticated animals to be 'phased out of existence' would not just require a cessation of human creation of animals, but a massively increased (and probably impossible) human effort to forcibly sterilize and/or confine all domesticated animals. It would mean not just limiting the procreation of domesticated animals, but preventing it entirely – denying them the opportunity ever to mate and raise a family. It would, in short, involve precisely the sort of coercion and confinement that [Abolitionist] theorists say makes domestication unjust, and in that sense compounds rather than remedies the original injustice (2011: 80–81).

Donaldson and Kymlicka's alternative approach tries not to 'turn back the clock' on domesticated animals but rather argues that, because they have been brought into human society, have been bred to suit our needs, and have few to no opportunities for leaving our societies, these animals deserve to be viewed as co-members of shared multispecies communities. Considering that domesticated animals are already part of our shared societies, justice requires reconstructing our relationships with them on fairer terms – not ending them.

How do Donaldson and Kymlicka propose to meet this challenge? Their approach is a complex one and we will discuss it in more detail in chapter three. There, we will also analyse how it deals with animals who are not domesticated. In a nutshell,

Donaldson and Kymlicka's argument is that domesticated animals should have citizenship rights that go beyond the universal rights such as the rights to life and to bodily integrity that all animals deserve. Concretely, they propose that all domesticated animals should have a right to residency in their home community; a right to have their interests count in determining the common good and to be viewed legally as part of the sovereign people; and have their agency in shaping the rules of cooperation recognised and promoted. Hence, on their approach, domesticated animals should not only be given rights and have their interests taken into consideration, but be viewed as active co-citizens with the ability to cooperate with humans and other animals and to co-create their political community.

What are some of the practical implications of this citizenship approach for domesticated animals? The answer to this, Donaldson and Kymlicka note, is contingent on how animals as co-citizens will ultimately shape their political arrangements. However, in broad terms, they propose that domesticated animals' citizenship would come with certain rights such as the right to be protected from harm, to medical care, and to political representation. However, as they emphasise, citizenship would also come with certain responsibilities. For instance, they believe that domesticated animals would need to be appropriately socialised. Dogs, for example, would 'need to be housebroken, to learn not to bite or to jump up on people, to be wary of cars, and not to chase the family cat' (2011: 124).

Importantly for our purposes, citizenship would also allow for the use of animals under certain circumstances. While Donaldson and Kymlicka argue that all animals have a right not to be owned, they believe that under the right conditions this would not prevent human use of animals. For example, they ask us to imagine a town in which sheep are full citizens and have access to ample pastures, healthy nutrition, shelter, protection from predators, and medical care. The humans in the town could not only benefit from the sheep's company, their manure, and their lawn-'mowing' services. According to Donaldson and Kymlicka, the humans would also be allowed to shear the sheep and use their wool as long as they shear them responsibly. Thus, like human citizens, the sheep would have to make their contributions to the community.

They believe the same applies in principle to using chickens' eggs and using animals for other purposes, such as using dogs as guard dogs or to sniff out dangerous substances. Regarding cows' milk, Donaldson and Kymlicka are more sceptical, arguing that even under ideal circumstances it would be difficult (albeit not impossible) to use them responsibly for more than just their companionship.

B. Dialogue over Debate: Melanie Joy's Plea for a Multi-Pronged Strategy

The social psychologist and author Melanie Joy criticises the welfare-abolition dichotomy from a different vantage point, by taking aim at the process of how proponents of Welfarism and Abolitionism have developed their claims and how they have communicated them. Put differently, Joy encourages us to consider the 'how' – not the 'what' – of the debate.

According to Joy, this shift in focus is necessary for two reasons. First, as we saw above, there is little empirical data available to conclusively confirm the truth of the central claims of either Abolitionism or Classic and New Welfarism. It is therefore reasonable to ask why the different camps have been locked in a 'stalemate' (Joy 2011). Second, the divisiveness and antagonism of the debate appears to be at odds with what Joy views as the core principles of 'compassion, reciprocity, justice, and humility' which she believes vegans and animal rights advocates to endorse (Joy 2011).

To break the stalemate, Joy proposes a change in consciousness: away from a model of debate and toward a model of dialogue. The debate-based model, according to her, is one that focuses on winning arguments by proving one's opponents wrong. It therefore encourages black-and-white thinking, which she associates with the 'speciesist-carnist culture' (Joy 2011) (with 'carnism' referring to a belief system based on meat eating), which animal rights advocates are trying to disrupt. By contrast, the model of dialogue welcomes diverse perspectives and the sharing of ideas. It also encourages reflecting on one's own position, recognising its limitations, and complementing it with alternative positions.

To move beyond the black-and-white welfare-abolition dichotomy, Joy urges the adoption of the dialogue model. Through dialogue, one can acquire what she calls a 'liberatory consciousness': a way of thinking that is in tune with the principles of veganism and animal rights as it 'requires curiosity, empathy, and compassion, and its objective is mutual understanding and collective empowerment rather than creating "winners" and "losers"' (Joy 2011). According to Joy, only such a liberatory consciousness is capacious enough to move animal rights forward:

> Achieving our objective of animal liberation depends on developing a comprehensive, complex, sophisticated, and flexible strategic approach to targeting a comprehensive, complex, sophisticated, and ever-changing form of institutionalized oppression. It is unlikely that the reductive, black-and-white rhetoric of debate can ever produce such nuance and analytical richness (Joy 2011).

Joy believes that such a change in consciousness would also help us realise that the debate has been wrapped up in 'ideology' (2011) in a way that has made it difficult to freely discuss strategy and that has imposed unhelpful labels on people – often against their will:

> When we debate whether it is more effective to campaign for institutional reform than to conduct vegan outreach (assuming these are mutually exclusive approaches, which they are not) the assumption is often that the disagreement is purely ideological, that one is either '[A]bolitionist' or '[W]elfarist'. However, most vegans do in fact share the goal of the abolition of animal exploitation and when we untangle ideology from strategy we can redirect the conversation to how best to bring about this end without getting sidetracked by moral argumentation (Joy 2011).

Hence, instead of buying into what Joy calls the 'The Myth of the Great Debate' (2011), animal rights advocates should shed unhelpful ideological commitments to camps that many may not even know or care about, and instead ask how, from a strategic point of view, an end to animal exploitation can be brought about most effectively.

VI. Conclusion

This chapter has provided an overview of the central tenets of Classic Welfarism, Abolitionism, and New Welfarism, and has analysed the arguments that have been made in favour and against these outlooks in the debate that consumed much of animal rights scholarship and advocacy for some time. Rather than taking sides in this debate, our aim here has been to present the different positions, shed light on the gap that sometimes exists between theory and reality, and draw attention to the unanswered empirical questions that make it difficult to dismiss either of these outlooks and strategies.

Given the uncertainties that remain about which – if any – of the outlooks gets things (more) right, it stands to reason that advocates of animal rights would do well to follow the call of Joy and others by keeping an open mind and trying to focus on how they can achieve their goals as effectively as possible. As we have argued elsewhere, there are many reasons speaking for what we call a 'pragmatic way forward' (Fasel and Butler 2020): an approach that moves beyond labels and focuses on achieving whatever concrete measures promote the legal status quo of animals in a way that takes them seriously as beings with vital interests similar to how humans' interests are protected. Not the least of these reasons is that internal rifts in a movement can be harmful to the causes that unite the movement: in this case, improving the wellbeing of animals. We will return to this issue in chapter eight.

Exercise 2: Welfarism vs Abolitionism?

1. 'Killing other animals … is nothing: the only harm is in tormenting them while they live'. (Bentham) Discuss.
2. Do you agree with Melanie Joy that the debate between Welfarists and Abolitionists is a 'myth'? Write a 500-words response explaining your view.
3. Can 'happy' eggs, milk, or meat ever exist? Defend your view by focusing on the different positions that Francione and Donaldson and Kymlicka take on this issue.
4. Consider the following claims describing Abolitionist and Classic and New Welfarist positions. Decide whether these claims are of a theoretical and/or empirical nature and think about whether and how they could be verified (ie proven right or wrong).

	Theoretical	Empirical	Verifiable
'Animals' status as ownable things does not in principle stand in the way of better treatment.'	☐	☐	☐

'Only if one has a right not to be property can one have any other fundamental rights.'   ☐   ☐   ☐

'Welfare reforms are a possible means of achieving the end of animal rights.'   ☐   ☐   ☐

'Welfarism has failed to deliver because we are using and killing more animals than ever.'   ☐   ☐   ☐

'Animal welfare protections rarely go beyond what is economically beneficial.'   ☐   ☐   ☐

'The "unnecessary suffering" principle is not static but can lend stronger protections to animals in the future.'   ☐   ☐   ☐

'Abolitionism alienates many who would potentially be sympathetic to the plight of animals.'   ☐   ☐   ☐

Useful References

Francione, GL and Friedrich, B, Vegan Debate Archive, available at www.youtube.com/watch?v=LOJWhs7fvnI.

DeGrazia, D (2002) *Animal Rights: A Very Short Introduction* (Oxford, Oxford University Press) 59–61.

Fischer, B and Milburn, J (2019) 'In Defence of Backyard Chickens' 36 *Journal of Applied Philosophy* 1, 108.

Korsgaard, CM (2018) *Fellow Creatures: Our Obligations to the Other Animals* (Oxford, Oxford University Press) 175–79, 233–37.

O'Sullivan, S (2019) 'The Abolitionist Approach with Gary L. Francione', Knowing Animals, available at knowinganimals.libsyn.com/size/25/?search=Gary+L.+Francione.

Svärd, PA (2011) 'Beyond Welfarist Morality: An Abolitionist Reply to Fetissenko' 1 *Journal of Animal Ethics* 2, 176.

Wrenn, CL and Johnson, R, 'A Critique of Single-issue Campaigning and the Importance of Comprehensive Abolitionist Vegan Advocacy' (2013) 16 *Food, Culture & Society* 4, 651.

3

Philosophical Foundations of Animal Rights

I. Introduction

Like any young discipline, animal rights law has drawn inspiration from work carried out in related fields. Arguably the most important such field has been philosophy, and moral philosophy (or ethics) in particular. Ethical treatises on how we ought to treat non-human animals go back thousands of years. For example, the philosopher Porphyry argued as early as the third century CE that it is absurd to think that 'no justice is due from us to the ox that ploughs, the dog that is fed with us, and the animals that nourish us with their milk, and adorn our bodies with their wool' (Porphyry 1999: 41).

Animal rights lawyers today are inspired by and often refer to more recent philosophical theories from the twentieth and twenty-first centuries. Focusing on these theories, this chapter will familiarise the reader with the four most influential philosophical approaches that support animal rights in the broad sense: Peter Singer's utilitarianism, Tom Regan's deontological approach, Martha Nussbaum's capabilities approach, and Sue Donaldson and Will Kymlicka's political approach. The chapter then turns to three philosophical critiques of the idea of animal rights or aspects of it: the Ecofeminist Critique, the Conservationist Critique, and the Contractualist Critique.

Before embarking on this philosophical journey, it is worth reminding ourselves that the philosophical landscape on animal rights is much broader than this chapter can map. If you are interested in any of the philosophical approaches that we do not discuss here (such as virtue ethics, Hinduist thought, or Māori and Mi'kmaq cosmologies), you will find useful references at the end of this chapter and on the companion website.

Central Issues

1. Philosophical theories dealing with animal rights go back millennia, but it is in particular theories from the twentieth and twenty-first centuries that animal rights lawyers have drawn on to develop their arguments.
2. Peter Singer's utilitarian approach to animal rights is one of the most well-known even though he only endorsed the concept of rights for political reasons. According to his approach, all sentient animals deserve equal consideration of their interests, but he allows the painless use and killing of most animals.
3. Developed as a critique of Singer's position, Tom Regan's deontological theory of animal rights argues that all animals that are 'subjects-of-a-life' have equal inherent moral worth and deserve moral rights against being used or killed.
4. According to Martha Nussbaum's capabilities approach, all sentient beings have a set of ten capabilities which should be promoted so as to allow these animals to flourish and live with dignity.
5. Following the so-called 'political turn', Sue Donaldson and Will Kymlicka developed a political theory of animal rights which draws on political concepts such as sovereignty, citizenship, and denizenship to explore the different relational duties humans have to domesticated animals, liminal animals, and wild animals.
6. Some philosophers have taken a more critical stance toward animal rights. Among the most important critiques have been those from ecofeminist scholars, conservationists, and contractualists.

II. Peter Singer's Utilitarianism

It is likely that even people who know little about animal rights have already heard of the work of the Australian philosopher Peter Singer, and in particular his book *Animal Liberation* (1975). With over half a million copies sold and translations in many languages, *Animal Liberation* has rightly been hailed as a milestone for the animal rights movement.

As this section shows, its success particularly with animal *rights* proponents is somewhat of a paradox because he follows the philosophical tradition of *utilitarianism*, which can broadly be defined as the view that one should act so as to produce the most utility (ie good). For most of his career, he has defended *preference utilitarianism*, according to which the utility that must be maximised are individuals' preferences, rather than simple pleasure (*hedonistic utilitarianism* – the view that Bentham held and

Singer later adopted (de Lazari-Radek and Singer 2014)). As a utilitarian, Singer does not primarily argue for animal *rights* but for considering animals as our moral equals.

To better understand his position, let us first consider his argument *that* we should consider non-human animals as worthy of moral consideration, and then turn to *how* he proposes to consider their interests.

A. Extending the Scope of Moral Concern to Animals

One of the key conclusions of Singer's *Animal Liberation* is that we should treat non-human animals as deserving of moral concern. To arrive at this conclusion, he adopted an argument that we have already encountered in chapter two when discussing Jeremy Bentham's approach. As we saw there, Bentham argued that it is not the colour of one's skin nor one's ability to talk that makes one deserving of moral consideration. Instead, he argued, it is one's ability to suffer, that is, to feel pain.

Drawing on and further developing Bentham's idea, Singer asked what the appropriate moral grounds are for considering someone as a moral equal, and for denying equality to others. Investigating the feminist case for women's equality, he found that factual equality between men and women cannot serve as a plausible ground because scientific investigation could potentially show that there are relevant factual differences between them. Nor should equality be based on how smart or strong or empathetic a person is. Instead, Singer proposes, we should understand equality as being based on sentience, which he defines as the capacity to suffer and/or experience happiness. Sentience is key, in his view, because it is both necessary and sufficient for having interests. That is, all and only those who are sentient have interests in not feeling pain and/or in being happy. Importantly, as Singer argues, not only humans are sentient and have interests, but so do many animals. The rational inference, for him, is that we must therefore extend our moral concern to these animals. He calls this the *equal consideration of interests principle*: the principle that if two beings have the same interests then they should be treated the same regarding those interests, regardless of who they are.

What if we fail to do so? To criticise arbitrary exclusions of animals' interests, Singer employed a term that was coined in 1971 and entered the Oxford English Dictionary in 1986: *'speciesism'*. Although the term was invented by psychologist and activist Richard Ryder (while 'ruminating in my bath about the human oppression of animals', as he later recounted (Ryder 2004)), he played a pivotal role in popularising the concept of speciesism. The term expresses a 'prejudice or attitude of bias in favour of the interests of members of one's own species and against those of members of other species' (Singer 2002: 6). As he notes, it is intentionally modelled on analogous terms such as sexism and racism:

> Racists violate the principle of equality by giving greater weight to the interests of members of their own race when there is a clash between their interests and the interests of those of another race. Sexists violate the principle of equality by favouring the interests of their own sex. Similarly, speciesists allow the interests of their own species to override the greater interests of members of other species. The pattern is identical in each case (Singer 2002: 9).

B. How Animals' Interests Ought to be Considered

Having retraced Singer's argument that sentient animals ought to be considered morally, we can now turn to *how* he proposes that we do so. At first glance, the equal consideration of interests principle might seem to suggest that we would have to treat all sentient beings equally in all respects. If this was so, we would have to give elephants the right to vote and bears the right to religious freedom because other sentient beings (humans) have these rights. However, as Singer notes, this would be absurd because elephants and bears do not have interests in those rights. Treating elephants, bears, and humans as equals, he emphasises, does not mean *treating them equally* in all respects, but *considering them as equals*. Practically, this means that we can owe different treatment to beings with different interests. For instance, considering as an equal a social animal like an elephant will require protecting their interest in being part of a herd. A solitary animal such a bear, by contrast, has no interest in being treated that way. Even where the interests of sentient beings are the same (eg their interest not to suffer), he argues that equal consideration may require different things. Consider for example how pain may be felt differently by different beings. According to Singer, a hard slap across the behind of a horse does not cause the horse the same amount of pain as a human baby who has a more sensitive constitution.

What if the blow was so hard that the horse or the baby died as a result? Would we have to conclude that the horse's death is just as morally problematic as the baby's? Singer believes not. As he observes, 'a rejection of speciesism does not imply that all lives are of equal worth' (2002: 20). To explain this, he again borrowed from Bentham who, as we saw in chapter two, claimed that non-human animals lack an interest in remaining alive because they do not have the ability to anticipate the future. In a similar vein, Singer argues that beings who have the capacity for self-awareness and to think ahead and plan for the future have an interest in 'continued existence' (1987: 8), that is, they prefer remaining alive. Beings who lack this preference only have an interest in not being killed in a painful way. In contrast to Bentham, however, Singer acknowledges that there are some non-human animals, such as for example great apes and whales, who possess an interest in continued existence. Still, because he thinks that most animals lack this interest, he argues that sacrificing the life of such animals to save that of a self-aware human is compatible with the principle of equal consideration of interests. This is not speciesist, according to him, because the principle can also cut the other way when the life of a self-aware animal such as a chimpanzee conflicts with that of a human being who lacks self-awareness due to, say, a mental disability. Although Singer has emphasised that the intention of his theory is not to level down marginalised humans but to level up animals, he has come under intense criticism by disability rights activists and others for this position (see eg Taylor 2017: 67–70).

The above would seem to suggest that Singer does not oppose the killing of non-self-aware animals for food. Indeed, he has argued that it is *theoretically* possible to ethically use and kill such animals for food as long as no pain is inflicted on them. However, he has also maintained that *practically* we still have a moral obligation to be vegetarians and to 'boycott all meat and eggs produced by large-scale commercial methods of animal production' (2020: 65). This is because, 'It is not practically possible to rear animals for food on a large scale without inflicting considerable suffering' (2002: 160).

Similarly, while Singer thinks that many experiments carried out on animals today are unjustified, he is not in principle opposed to animal experimentation. However, such experiments would only be justified if sufficiently many others benefited from them. For instance, he imagines that 'if a single experiment could cure a disease like leukemia, that experiment would be justifiable' (2002: 85). However, as he stresses, in such extreme circumstances the principle of equal consideration of interests would also justify experiments on human beings who lack self-awareness.

Before moving to Tom Regan's deontological approach and considering some of the weaknesses of Singer's utilitarianism, let us return to a point mentioned at the outset: that Singer does not defend animal *rights* in the strict sense. As this section has explained, he does not make the moral rightness of actions dependent on whether they further the rights of animals, but rather on whether they promote animals' preferences, in particular the preference not to suffer and to be happy. As we will see in the next section, furthering rights and promoting interests do not always overlap, specifically when it becomes necessary to infringe an individual's rights in order to promote the greater interests of others. As Singer noted,

> I certainly would never deny that we are justified in using animals for human goals, because as a consequentialist I must also hold that in the appropriate circumstances we are justified in using humans to achieve human goals (or the goal of assisting animals). I am not the kind of moral absolutist who holds that the end can never justify the means (Singer 1990: 46).

Yet, it would be wrong to conclude from this that he had as much disdain for rights as Bentham had for natural rights when famously declaring them to be 'nonsense upon stilts' (Bentham [1843] 2002: 330). As Singer already emphasised in *Animal Liberation*, the term 'animal rights' is a 'convenient political shorthand' (2002: 8). In later work, such as *The Great Ape Project* (1993) (which he co-edited with the philosopher Paola Cavalieri), Singer took the idea of political expediency of rights discourse even further when employing the concept of moral rights in the proposal for a declaration that recognises rights, such as the right to life and the right to liberty, for great apes.

III. Tom Regan's Deontological Approach

As the previous section has shown, Singer adopted the concept of rights primarily for political reasons. It was not until Tom Regan (1938–2017) in *The Case for Animal Rights* (1983) that a philosopher would for the first time make a comprehensive case for animal rights in the strict, moral sense. To develop his theory, Regan followed a philosophical approach that is diametrically opposed to Bentham's and Singer's. Instead of adopting utilitarianism, Regan made his case for animal rights on *deontological* grounds. Roughly speaking, deontology (Greek for the study (*logos*) of duty (*deon*)) is the philosophical position that the moral goodness or wrongness of an act depends on whether it follows certain rules. For instance, the Ten Commandments provide a classic example of such rules when decreeing that 'thou shalt not murder' or 'thou shalt not steal'. Importantly, deontologists argue that we are morally required to follow such rules even if we could increase overall utility by ignoring them. In other words, for deontologists, the consequences of an action do not determine whether it is morally right or wrong. There are certain actions that are wrong in principle, whatever the consequences.

Why did Regan adopt this approach, and under what circumstances did he think an action would be wrong in principle? Let us address these questions in turn.

A. Regan's Critique of Utilitarianism

To understand why Regan adopts a deontological approach, it is first necessary to consider why he rejected its philosophical counterpart: utilitarianism. The primary problem that he identifies with utilitarian theories is that they are *aggregative*. That is to say that such theories require us to calculate the sum total of good achieved across all sentient beings. The right course of action, on such theories, is that which maximises good overall, even if this requires ignoring the preferences of individual beings. To illustrate this, Regan gives the example of Aunt Bea:

> My Aunt Bea is old, inactive, a cranky, sour person, though not physically ill. She prefers to go on living. She is also rather rich. I could make a fortune if I could get my hands on her money, money she intends to give me in any event, after she dies, but which she refuses to give me now. In order to avoid a huge tax bite, I plan to donate a handsome sum of my profits to a local children's hospital. Many, many children will benefit from my generosity, and much joy will be brought to their parents, relatives, and friends. If I don't get the money rather soon, all these ambitions will come to naught. The once-in-a-lifetime opportunity to make a real killing will be gone. Why, then, not kill my Aunt Bea? ... There is *very* little chance of getting caught. And as for my conscience being guiltridden, I am a resourceful sort of fellow and will take more than sufficient comfort – as I lie on the beach at Acapulco – in contemplating the joy and health I have brought to so many others (Regan 1987: 185).

Assume he goes ahead and kills his aunt. We would think such an act immoral. Yet, Regan argues, utilitarian theories such as Singer's are unable to explain why it would be immoral. This is because, on Singer's approach, Aunt Bea's preference dissatisfaction would likely be outweighed by the aggregate good created in the many others who would benefit from her death. Far from forbidding it, Singer's theory would therefore even morally *require* the killing of Aunt Bea.

This example illustrates why Regan rejects utilitarianism on the basis that its aggregative character violates what is often called the 'separateness of persons'. As the philosopher John Rawls (1921–2002) noted, in holding that the greater good of the many compensates for the losses of the few, utilitarianism pretends that 'many persons are fused into one' (1971: 27). Regan, Rawls, and other critics of utilitarianism contend that such fusion ignores the fact that individuals are distinct from each other and that the protection of the interests of one cannot make up for the lack of protection of another. As this point is sometimes also put, individuals are mere 'receptacles' for utilitarians like Singer. The idea here is that utilitarians view individuals much like, say, bottles of wine. The bottles themselves have no value; only the wine itself (ie the preferences) does. To destroy a bottle is not per se a problem (the bottle itself has no value, after all), as long as another bottle is made that contains better wine (ie an individual with more satisfied preferences). Singer, who himself used the term 'receptacles', later distanced himself from it, emphasising that, unlike in the bottle example, experiences cannot be separated from the individuals experiencing them (1987: 6–13).

B. Inherent Value and Subjects-of-a-Life

According to Regan, the deontological approach is much better suited to protecting animals' interests than utilitarianism. This is because, on the deontological approach, animals have *inherent value*. Inherent value is value that attaches directly to its holders rather than simply to their preferences or experiences. As a result, even if one being has more satisfied preferences than another, this does not give it more inherent value than the other. Beings with inherent value, in other words, are not mere receptacles. To use our wine example: on the deontological approach, the wine bottle itself is what is valuable, not the wine it contains. Hence, an expensive bottle of wine, such as a Château Mouton Rothschild, would have just as much inherent value as a bottle of your neighbour's home brew. This is because inherent value, on Regan's theory, is 'incommensurate' (1983, 236), meaning that it cannot be compared with, let alone exchanged for the value of other beings with inherent value. Just as importantly, it is equal, meaning that everyone has the same inherent value.

Those with inherent value benefit from what Regan calls the 'respect principle': they have a moral *right* to be treated respectfully. This right requires not treating its holders as mere receptacles of value and not treating them as if their value depended on their instrumental usefulness to others. For instance, the killing of Aunt Bea would violate the respect principle because she would be treated as not having inherent value and as being a mere resource for the satisfaction of others' preferences. The respect principle also has a positive component in that it imposes on others a duty to actively help those with inherent value who are suffering from injustice.

This raises a crucial question: *who* exactly has inherent value? Regan proposes that being a '*subject-of-a-life*' is sufficient for having inherent value. It is important to note that being a subject-of-a-life requires more than simply being sentient. As he explains:

> Individuals are subjects of a life if they are able to perceive and remember; if they have beliefs, desires, and preferences; if they are able to act intentionally in pursuit of their desires or goals; if they are sentient and have an emotional life; if they have a sense of the future, including a sense of their own future; if they have a psychophysical identity over time; and if they have an individual experiential welfare that is logically independent of their utility for, and the interests of, others (1983: 264).

As this definition makes clear, being a member of a particular species (such as *Homo sapiens*) is not required to be a subject-of-a-life, nor is it enough. According to Regan, 'normal mammalian animals, aged one or more, as well as humans like these animals in the relevant respects' (1983: 247) are subjects-of-a-life and therefore have equal inherent value. He acknowledges that there can be disagreement about whether it is precisely at age one that one becomes a subject-of-a-life. However, he proposes that the line must be drawn somewhere around there because newborn infants of all species do not meet the requirements of being a subject-of-a-life.

The practical upshots of Regan's deontological theory are far-reaching, and it helped pave the way for the Abolitionist approach which we discussed in chapter two. As he argues, animal agriculture as it is currently practised would have to be abolished because it does not accord farm animals the respect they are due as subjects-of-a-life. This holds even for 'humane' farms because there, too, animals are killed prematurely to fulfil others' interest in eating them. According to Regan, we have a moral obligation to adopt a vegetarian way of life, just as we have a moral obligation not to eat human subjects-of-a-life.

For the same reason, hunting and trapping animals – whether for commercial gain or sport – and undertaking research on animals – no matter the purpose – would have to be eliminated. Equally for Regan, it is not sufficient to 'refine, reduce, and replace' (the so-called 3Rs) animal experiments which form the standard guideline in many countries today, nor can experiments be justified by the discovery of cures that will benefit the many (as in Singer's leukemia example). All experiments would have to stop altogether, at least as long as they involve animals that are subjects-of-a-life. Finally, as far as wild animals are concerned, he argues that all of them – regardless of whether they are endangered or not – have a right to respectful treatment, which in general will be met by not interfering with them.

To round off this discussion of Regan's deontological approach, let us return to the fact that he only considered mammals aged over one as subjects-of-a-life. Does this mean we can treat mammals aged below one in any way we please? No. According to him, they may be said to have inherent value on other grounds than being a subject-of-a-life. He also notes that because it is unclear where the line should be drawn, we may need to give such animals the benefit of doubt and treat them *as if* they were subjects-of-a-life. Finally, even in cases where this is difficult to justify, he argues that we would still have indirect duties (ie duties to protect them because doing so indirectly benefits those who are subjects-of-a-life). Hence, we would for instance have reason to protect new-born babies from being killed in order to protect the interests of their parents. His stance on humans and animals who are not subjects-of-a-life has been one of his critics' main targets (eg Donovan 1990). At the end of this chapter and on the companion website, you will find more references if you are interested in these critiques and in Regan's response to them.

Exercise 1: Utilitarianism vs Deontology

1.   Consider Regan's example of Aunt Bea. Do you think it would be morally right to kill Aunt Bea? Why (not)? If you agree with Regan that it would be wrong to kill her, would it make a difference if, instead of only benefitting one children's hospital, one could help *all* the sick children in the world by killing Aunt Bea?

2.   For Singer, the fact that most would intuitively think that killing Aunt Bea is wrong does not prove that it *is* wrong, but rather that our intuitions are misguided. As philosophers sometimes put this point, Singer would 'bite the bullet' (ie accept even the most radical implications of his theory) and tell Regan that we should ignore our intuitions, not change our theories. Do you think our intuitions and our everyday practices should influence whether we should adopt a certain moral theory?

3. Imagine that the government of your country funds a research project to find the cure for a new zoonotic disease that is likely to kill 1 million humans worldwide. The project requires infecting 100 million mice with the disease, which will cause them suffering and, in most cases, death. Using a utilitarian approach, discuss whether this experiment would be morally right. Test your arguments by considering deontological critiques of utilitarianism.

IV. Martha Nussbaum's Capabilities Approach

A third key philosophical approach to animal rights is the capabilities approach. Simply put, the capabilities approach holds that sentient beings have a set of capabilities which should be promoted so as to allow them to flourish and live with dignity. Originally conceived by the economist and philosopher Amartya Sen in the human context (1980), the capabilities approach has since been further developed and applied to non-human animals by the philosopher Martha Nussbaum. This section will focus on Nussbaum's theory.

The central book in which she defends the capabilities approach is *Frontiers of Justice: Disability, Nationality, Species Membership* (2006). In contrast to some other philosophers who focus primarily on individuals' duties, her aim in this book is to develop a theory of justice that helps us frame political principles on what basic entitlements that society owes to individuals. To understand this approach, let us first consider why she rejected alternative theories, and then shed more light on the capabilities approach.

A. Nussbaum's Critique of Other Approaches

To develop her account, she first considers and dismisses three other philosophical approaches to animals: Singer's utilitarianism, Kantianism, and contractualism in the Kantian tradition.

Starting with utilitarianism, Nussbaum, like Regan before her, criticises its aggregative nature. However, she also puts forth another criticism: utilitarianism's one-dimensional focus on pleasure and pain flattens our moral landscape. As she points out, 'there may be goods they [animals] pursue that are not felt as pain and frustration when they are absent' (2007: 345). For example, animals can find value in moving around freely, having physical achievements, sacrificing themselves for kin, or grieving for a dead child or parent. It is arguable that Singer's preference utilitarianism is not as vulnerable to this critique as hedonistic utilitarianism because it can identify free movement, sacrifice, and so on as preferences. However, its focus on whether preferences are either 'satisfied' or 'dissatisfied' may still leave some people wanting for a richer moral approach.

Kantianism is the philosophy of the German thinker Immanuel Kant (1724–1804). Nussbaum reproaches Kant for his position that humans do not owe any direct moral duties to animals. Kant's argument was that animals lack self-consciousness and there-fore cannot be ends-in-themselves and have dignity. They are, as Kant put it, a 'mere means' to humans ([1785] 1998: 37). For him, the only duties we can have toward animals are indirect (ie of the same sort as the duties Regan applies to beings who are not subjects-of-a-life). That is, we ought to protect animals not for their own sakes, but because it helps us better protect humans. As Kant explains,

> If a man shoots his dog because the animal is no longer capable of service, he does not fail in his duty to the dog, for the dog cannot judge, but his act is inhuman and damages in himself that humanity which it is his duty to show towards mankind. If he is not to stifle his human feelings, he must practice kindness towards animals, for he who is cruel to animals becomes hard also in his dealings with men ([1784] 1997: 212).

In addition to criticising Kant for failing to explain that animals can be owed direct duties, Nussbaum also takes issue with contemporary contractualist approaches that build on Kant's theory. We will address one of her main criticisms of Kantian contrac-tualism in section VI below. For now, let us turn to the alternative approach that she proposes.

B. The Capabilities Approach

Nussbaum's capabilities approach starts from the assumption that different animals have different capabilities (ie abilities and needs) that must be fulfilled so that they can flourish and live in a dignified way. To meet the demands of justice, Nussbaum argues, it is sufficient if everyone's capabilities are adequately met. They do not, however, need to be met fully or equally in everyone. The general idea behind Nussbaum's theory goes back to Aristotle, according to whom certain entities have an inherent purpose or goal (Greek *telos*). If that purpose is realised, then these entities can be the best version of themselves. If it is not realised, then we are faced with tragedy and waste. Consider emperor penguins. Emperor penguin parents are famous for going months without food to lay and keep their eggs warm in the harsh Antarctic climate. Although this is perhaps painful, emperor penguins can nevertheless only flourish if they can take care of their eggs and, once hatched, their young. It would therefore be a tragedy if someone stole their eggs. To avoid this tragedy, she would argue, one should protect emperor penguins' capability to look after their young.

But how do we know which animals have which capabilities? According to Nussbaum, every species has what she calls a 'species norm' (2007: 179), that is, abili-ties and needs that are characteristic of that species. Individuals should be treated according to the species norm. For instance, tending to their eggs and young is part of emperor penguins' species norm, whereas the norm of some species of cuckoo is notoriously to let other birds take care of the parenting. Unlike Singer and Regan, then, she thinks that one's species membership ought not be irrelevant for moral and political purposes.

This raises an important question: do we have to protect *any* ability and need that is natural to a species? For instance, do we have to promote lions' ability to hunt and kill gazelles? Nussbaum thinks not. The capabilities approach, as she puts it, does not amount to 'nature worship' (2007: 366). This is because determining what forms part of the species norm requires evaluation, that is, normative judgement. According to her, only capabilities that are *good* and *central* to an animal's life should be protected as basic entitlements of justice. *Good* are the capabilities which do not cause harm to others. This means that lions' capability to hunt and kill gazelles would not be protected. But would this not undermine lions' flourishing? Nussbaum rejects this, arguing that the lions' needs could be met in other ways, such as by providing them with toys that simulate real gazelles. *Central* are the capabilities that are essential to allowing a being to flourish. For example, it is central for gorillas' ability to flourish that they have their bodily integrity respected. However, it is not central that they can speak American Sign Language – as some gorillas such as Koko learned to do.

Does this mean that *all* animals – even the ones who are not sentient – have basic entitlements of justice? Nussbaum is more open to this idea than Singer as she acknowledges that, theoretically, any being capable of having emotions, thought, affiliation, or any of the other capabilities listed below would qualify for basic entitlements. However, she claims that, practically, animals who have such capabilities tend to also be sentient. As a result, she argues that sentience can be seen as a 'threshold condition' (2007: 361) for counting morally.

What, then, are the capabilities that are both good and central? Nussbaum presents a list of ten basic capabilities, which is the same she developed for humans (see Figure 1).

Figure 1 The ten capabilities

Life	Bodily health	Bodily integrity	Senses, imagination, thought	Emotions
Practical reason	Affiliation	Other species	Play	Control over environment

Animals first have an entitlement to *life*. In contrast to Singer, Nussbaum argues that even those animals who lack an interest in continued existence possess this entitlement. Concretely, it requires a ban on the killing of animals for sport and for luxury items such as fur. However, unlike Regan, she does not rule out killing animals for food as long as it does not involve 'cruel practices and painful killings in the process of raising animals' and does not affect 'more complexly sentient animals' (2007: 393). According to Nussbaum, euthanasia and the painless killing of animals for the purpose of population control are also compatible with this basic entitlement.

Bodily health means that animals have a right to lead a healthy life. This demands the enactment of anti-cruelty laws and laws requiring the provision of adequate nutrition and space to animals.

In addition, animals have an entitlement to *bodily integrity*. This requires protecting them even from painless violations of their physical integrity. Positively, it also entitles animals to opportunities for sexual satisfaction and reproduction. However, Nussbaum argues that sexual choice is not as important for animals as it is for humans, which is why she claims that sterilisation can be legitimate if it is done to benefit the individual animal or others.

Senses, imagination, and thought: this capability requires ensuring that animals have sufficient access to spacious environments with enough light and shade and opportunities to engage in species-characteristic activities. In the case of some animals, society also has a duty to provide them with education. For example, companion animals would have a right to be toilet trained.

Further, we need to respect animals' *emotions*, understanding that these can be as diverse as 'anger, resentment, gratitude, grief, envy, … joy' and even 'compassion' (2006: 397). Animals must for example not be kept in isolation or be subjected to experiments that induce fear.

Practical reason describes the entitlement (especially of humans) to choose their own goals in life and to pursue them. Nussbaum argues that, to the extent that some animals may have the same capacity, it requires supporting the provision of room to move, and activities to select from.

Additionally, animals possess an entitlement to have *affiliations*, that is, to form attachments and bonds with other members of their species. What is more, animals have a right to 'self-respect and non-humiliation' (2007: 398). According to Nussbaum, this means that animals 'are entitled to world policies that grant them political rights and the legal status of dignified beings' (2007: 398–99).

Animals not only have an entitlement to form bonds with members of their own species, but also with members of *other species*. Furthermore, they should be allowed to form bonds with the rest of nature.

Play is another key capability of all animals, and Nussbaum argues that it would require protection through some of the mechanisms already mentioned: provision of adequate space, light, and the presence of other animals to play with, for example.

Finally, animals have a basic entitlement of *control over their environment*. This has a political and material component. Politically, it requires ensuring that animals are 'part of a political conception that is framed so as to respect them, and is committed to treating them justly' (2007: 400). This gives animals rights to have human guardians who can defend their basic entitlements in court. Materially, it requires protecting the territorial integrity of animals' habitats and, in the case of working animals, the right to 'dignified and respectful labour conditions' (2007: 400).

The fact that Nussbaum's ten capabilities are the same as the ones she developed in the human context could be viewed as a strength because it reflects the fact that humans too are animals. However, it could also be criticised for not being an ideal fit for many animal species. For instance, the capability of *practical reason* does not seem to play any role for most animal species. As Nussbaum herself admits, her list of capabilities is 'tentative' (2007: 392). Indeed, because the species norm is ultimately what should drive lists of protected capabilities, it is to be expected that different species will have at least partially different lists of capabilities.

V. Sue Donaldson and Will Kymlicka's Political Theory

As we saw above, Nussbaum's capabilities approach advocates that animals should have some form of political control over their environment. However, according to her, animals would not be granted citizenship and rights to political participation which humans with that capability are due. In this section, we turn to a theory that offers citizenship and political rights to at least some animals: the theory of political philosophers Sue Donaldson and Will Kymlicka.

They first presented their theory in the influential book *Zoopolis: A Political Theory of Animal Rights* (2011). As the book's title indicates, the authors develop a theory that views animals (Greek *zoon*) as part of political communities (Greek *polis*) with humans. In what follows, we first discuss the so-called 'political turn' in animal ethics that forms the backdrop of Donaldson and Kymlicka's work, before analysing their political theory in more detail and filling some gaps we left open in chapter two where we first encountered their account.

A. The Political Turn in Animal Ethics and Animal Studies

Donaldson and Kymlicka's account forms part of a broader trend in animal ethics and animal studies scholarship referred to as 'political turn'. This turn describes the shift away from focusing on individuals' moral duties, and toward the duties of *society* to govern humans and animals justly. This shift is sometimes expressed as one away from 'morality' and toward 'justice' (see eg Garner and O'Sullivan 2016: 2).

As we saw in the previous sections, Singer's work is primarily concerned with individuals' moral obligations, not questions of justice in the institutional sense. Likewise, although Regan employed the term 'justice' (1983: 232) and criticised 'the system that allows us to view animals as *our resources*' (1987: 179), his focus was on individual moral obligations. Among the first works to shift to a more political approach was Nussbaum's capabilities approach, which she conceived in terms of a theory of justice that helps us frame political principles. Others thinking about the political turn include Robert Garner (2005), Alasdair Cochrane (2010), and Eva Meijer (2019).

Although they are therefore not the only or first ones to theorise animals in political terms, their theory and its focus on political relationships have become particularly prominent. What has motivated them to centre political relationships in their work? As we saw in chapter two, they reject the Abolitionists' aim of bringing an end to domesticated animals. Positions such as Francione's, they hold, ignore the reality that humans and animals coexist in manifold and complex ways. However, that does not lead them to reject the idea of animal rights. Instead they adopt an abolitionist approach: one that promotes the abolition of animal exploitation in a way that diverges from Francione's 'extinctionist' (Donaldson and Kymlicka 2011: 79) approach. As they point out, they endorse one particular aspect of what they identify as the current animal rights approach, and reject another.

The aspect they endorse is animal rights' focus on protecting individuals' inviolable rights. Like Regan and other rights proponents, Donaldson and Kymlicka maintain that we need to recognise that animals are not mere means to our ends, but have rights that need to be respected. Drawing on Cavalieri who sees animal rights as an extension of human rights (which we discuss in chapter five), they argue that rights for animals are just like universal human rights in that their aim is to protect the basic interests of vulnerable beings, which they take all sentient animals to be. A consequence of this rights approach is that they conclude that practices such as 'farming, hunting, the commercial pet industry, zoo-keeping, animal experimentation, and many others' (2011: 49) would have to be banned.

The aspect of animal rights theory they criticise is what they regard as its narrow focus on so-called 'negative rights'. Negative rights are rights *against* interference, such as the 'right *not* to be owned, killed, confined, tortured, or separated from one's family' (2011: 5–6, emphasis added). The problem with this negative focus, they believe, is that animal rights theorists have said little about the positive rights that animals have *to* certain things. For example, instead of only having a right not to be interfered with, animals could have a positive right to be provided with a suitable habitat, safe neighbourhoods, and care. In addition, Donaldson and Kymlicka identify a lack of engagement with the question as to what *relational duties* are owed to animals. These are duties that do not arise from a being's inherent capacities, but rather 'from the more geographically and historically specific relationships that have developed between particular groups of humans and particular groups of animals' (2011: 6), such as between humans and domesticated animals. It is only by adopting a different framework that focuses on such positive relational duties, they argue, that we can tackle questions like: what do we owe to animals as members of our communities? And what should a just political and legal system more generally look like?

B. *Zoopolis*'s Differentiated Theory of Animal Rights

To develop their framework, Donaldson and Kymlicka draw on citizenship theory: the theory that deals with political relationships between humans and operates with categories such as sovereignty, citizenship, and denizenship. Employing these categories, they distinguish three different types of animals: wild animals who form sovereign communities, liminal animals who are denizens akin to human migrants, and domesticated animals who are to be regarded as co-citizens.

Take *wild animals*, which they define as animals 'who avoid humans and human settlement, maintaining a separate and independent existence (insofar as they are able to) in their own shrinking habitats or territories' (2011: 156). According to Donaldson and Kymlicka, wild animals have an interest in and the competence to self-regulate on their territory, and should therefore be regarded as '*sovereign* communities'

(2011: 157, emphasis added). The relation between different sovereign communities – including human communities – should be determined by the same norms that govern international relationships between states. As they tell us, this requires recognising that wild animal communities (and not humans) govern these territories. A consequence of this is that it would be illegal for humans to colonise wild animals' territories or relocate those animals (although they allow that humans could still travel to and even live in such territories, as they can today in other countries). In most cases, wild animals' sovereign status would require leaving them alone – a duty we have already encountered above. However, they emphasise that humans also have positive duties to intervene on a small scale, such as by rescuing a drowning animal, as well as on a large scale, for example by 'halt[ing] an aggressive and systemic new bacterium which is about to invade and devastate an ecosystem' (2011: 178). Such large-scale interventions are morally required if they serve to promote wild animals' self-determination. By contrast, interventions that would compromise self-determination – which they believe to be the case for attempts to end predation – are not allowed.

Donaldson and Kymlicka distinguish such 'truly wild animals' (2011: 217) from *liminal animals*, for which they propose the status of *denizens*. Liminal animals are animals who are neither entirely wild nor domesticated, and instead live among humans or near human dwellings, albeit without seeking their company. This includes rats, foxes, squirrels, raccoons, sparrows, deer, coyotes, mice, and many other species. They propose to view these animals in a similar way as human groups such as refugees, seasonal migrant workers, or religious communities such as the Amish, which are neither foreigners nor fully integrated into a given political community. According to them, although liminal animals would not have a right to enter our cities, once they are here, they have a right of residency and may not be treated as aliens or pests. Hence, we must respect their basic rights by not interfering with them, as well as take their interests into account positively when building roads, constructing buildings, or planning developments. For instance, Donaldson and Kymlicka propose that we should create animal corridors that allow liminal animals to move around without facing the danger of crossing roads. Equally, we should change pesticide policies to ensure that liminal animals are not killed and instead promote more effective policies such as proper garbage disposal, discourage unnecessary feeding, erecting fences or other physical barriers, setting up deterring sound systems, or take house-proofing measures.

Finally, *domesticated animals*. As we saw in chapter two, Donaldson and Kymlicka argue that these are the animals that have the closest relationships with humans and should therefore be regarded as *citizens*. As citizens, domesticated animals are 'co-members of a shared human-animal political community' (2011: 74). As we discussed in chapter two, they have the most extensive rights of all animals (eg the right to have their interests counted in political decisions on the common good), but also have to reciprocate by fulfilling certain obligations (eg not harming others).

Donaldson and Kymlicka's theory has been widely applauded for its inclusive and imaginative approach to animal rights. However, it has not remained without critics. For instance, one criticism launched at it has come from philosophers who, like Singer and Regan, take the view of so-called 'cosmopolitanism', according to which all should have equal rights, regardless of their citizenship or other political affiliations. For instance, Cochrane (2013a) has criticised Donaldson's and Kymlicka's approach on this ground, arguing that it overstates the importance of group-membership and neglects the primary role played by individuals' interests. If you are interested in finding out more about this and other criticisms, you will find more references at the end of this chapter and on the companion website.

VI. Critical Approaches to Animal Rights

As the previous sections have shown, not all philosophers who advocate the protection of animal rights do so on the same grounds. Whereas for Singer animals' interests in not suffering should be considered equally, for Regan animals' inherent equal value must be respected, for Nussbaum a species' capabilities are what matters, and for Donaldson and Kymlicka group-membership partly determines what rights an animal has. However, they all agreed that animal rights are, in one way or another, a good thing.

In this section, we outline three philosophical approaches that are critical of the animal rights idea – either as a whole or some aspects of it. We can call them, respectively, the Ecofeminist Critique, the Conservationist Critique, and the Contractualist Critique.

A. The Ecofeminist Critique

The first approach, the ecofeminist approach, is one that has an ambivalent relationship with animal rights. Some of its proponents reject animal rights outright, while others find animal rights useful because of its emphasis on individuals' needs or because they think that rights language is politically expedient. One of the things that unites its proponents, however, is a critical take on standard theories such as Singer's and Regan's. In contrast to these theories, the ecofeminist approach holds that one cannot rely on reason alone to identify universal moral duties that bind everyone everywhere – to the extent that universal duties are taken to exist at all. Instead, ecofeminists draw primarily on moral emotions such as love and empathy to underscore the value of caring relationships between embodied beings. Take for instance the caring relationship between two friends. This relationship comes with certain reciprocal responsibilities such as the responsibilities to listen to the other and support them. Importantly, such responsibilities are not universal but always context dependent. For instance, a stranger does not have the responsibility to support you in the same way as a friend does.

First developed in the human context by the psychologist Carol Gilligan (1982) and the philosopher Nel Noddings (1982), the ecofeminist approach was later applied to animals by the literature scholar Josephine Donovan and the activist and writer Carol Adams. In powerful works such as *Animals and Women: Feminist Theoretical Explorations* (Adams and Donovan 1995) and *The Feminist Care Tradition in Animal Ethics* (Donovan and Adams 2007), these authors explore what they see as the interlocking nature of different forms of oppression such as sexism, racism, and speciesism. The idea that systems of oppression are interconnected and can therefore only be tackled together is sometimes referred to as 'intersectionality' – a concept we will return to in chapter eight.

Importantly for our purposes here, while some ecofeminist theorists support the idea of animal rights at least in part (eg Slicer 1991; Adams 1991), others reject it. This is because they view it as being rooted in a problematic liberal and male view of atomistic and disembodied individuals, that is, individuals who do not depend on others to flourish and who are driven by their mind, not their bodies. Such individuals, the classic liberal view goes, only require negative rights not to be interfered with.

Even more problematically, some ecofeminists argue, animal rights proponents perpetuate logics of domination when attempting to *extend* rights from humans to animals. To understand this argument, it is necessary to see why ecofeminists reject ethical theories that are based on so-called 'dualisms' (Plumwood 1993: 2). Speciesist theories, for example, are based on the human/animal dualism, where the left side of the binary is seen as the dominant one – the one that gets rights – and the right side is its oppressed opposite. The same dualistic logic can be found in sexist theories (eg man/woman), racist theories (eg white/black), as well as intersectional dualisms such as reason/instinct, which is seen as mapping onto the aforementioned dualisms (eg stereotypic correlations between gender, race and traits). In all these dualisms, an 'other' (Adams 1994: 52) is created who is regarded as lacking the beneficial traits of the binary's left side, and is therefore excluded from it. The logic of animal rights, ecofeminists believe, can reproduce this dualistic structure if animal rights proponents do not abandon dualisms, but simply draw the line elsewhere. For instance, extending rights to primates creates a primates/non-primates dualism, and extending rights to all sentient beings a sentient/non-sentient dualism. The result is one of 'othering' and excluding some animals. The logic of domination is still there, just in a different place.

Because of this, some ecofeminists, such as the philosopher Val Plumwood (1939–2008) (2002: 152–159), have rejected the idea of animal rights altogether. In fact, Plumwood and others, such as the philosopher Kathryn Paxton George, have even gone as far as to reject arguments for ethical veganism. George, for instance, does so on the ground that such arguments 'presuppose a "male physiological norm" that gives a privileged position to adult, middle-class males living in industrialized countries' (1994: 19), whom George views as having fewer health and economic risks than women and the poor.

To be sure, as noted, other ecofeminists like Adams and Slicer support veganism and find some value in the idea of animal rights insofar as it rejects the instrumentalisation of animals. However, their goal too is to go beyond animal rights and to promote a care-based theory of animal protection that is no longer based on what they see as problematic rationalist and dualist assumptions. To avoid setting up new binaries which are all-too-often dominated by human interests, ecofeminists urge us not to focus on what makes animals human-*like*, as this risks overlooking the value that can lie in animals' *difference*. Furthermore, ecofeminists adopt a holistic view of the world in which animals (and humans) are seen as vulnerable, embodied beings who are dependent on and connected with each other, rather than being independent atomistic individuals (see Figure 2).

Figure 2 Traditional ethics vs ecofeminist ethics

	Traditional Ethics	**Ecofeminist Ethics**
Scope of Obligations	Universal	Context-based
View of the Individual	Atomistic, disembodied	Dependent, embodied
View of Systems of Oppression	Separable or negligible	Key and interconnected
What is Valued	Similarity, individualism	Difference, holism

We mention the critical legal scholar Maneesha Deckha (2020), who has drawn on the feminist care tradition to develop an account of 'legal beingness' that aims to avoid the problems of liberal animal rights approaches. And chapter eight will return to the relevance of ecofeminists' critique for animal rights activists.

B. The Conservationist Critique

What all the philosophical traditions discussed in the previous sections have in common is the fact that they value individual animals for their own sakes because they are sentient beings or subjects-of-a-life. However, not everyone shares that view. According to many conservationists, what ultimately matters morally is not the individual animal, but the biological community. One of the first to defend such an alternative ethical theory was the author and ecologist Aldo Leopold (1887–1948). According to Leopold, our morality should evolve to extend not only to humans and animals, but also to nature more generally. This 'land ethic' (1949: 201), as he called it, 'enlarges the boundaries of the community to include soils, waters, plants, and animals, or collectively: the land' (1949: 204).

At first glance, Leopold's land ethic may seem to be in tune with the ethical theories considered in this chapter, but simply be more ambitious in its call for an extension of our moral scope of concern. However, this affinity hides a fundamental conflict between animal rights theories and the land ethic. As the environmental philosopher J Baird Callicott has pointed out, the land ethic differs from animal rights theories in that it is based on a different conception of the good. Whereas in animal rights theories *individuals'* interests determine what is right, in the land ethic 'the good of the biotic *community* is the ultimate measure of the moral value, the rightness or wrongness, of actions' (Callicott 1980: 320). In a similar vein, conservation biologist Michael Soulé argues that '[b]iotic diversity has intrinsic value, irrespective of its instrumental or utilitarian value. This normative postulate is the most fundamental' (1985: 731). Put simply, in the land ethic and other conservationist ethics, an action is right if it has a positive effect on the ecosystem, or on biodiversity, and it is wrong if it has a negative effect.

This holistic ethical approach has radical implications. For instance, it rejects the commitment of animal rights theories to consider the basic interests or capabilities of all animals equally. In the land ethic, domesticated animals would have a significantly lower status than wild animals, if they deserve any protection at all. This is because, for the land ethicist, wild animals tend to have a positive effect on the ecosystem, whereas domesticated animals are seen as either lacking such effect or even being positively harmful to nature. As Callicott puts it, '[f]rom the perspective of the land ethic a herd of cattle, sheep, or pigs is as much or more a ruinous blight on the landscape as a fleet of four-wheel drive off-road vehicles' (1980: 330). But not only would land ethicists place some animals above others in the moral hierarchy, they would even place some plants above animals. Consider again Callicott:

> Certain plants, similarly, may be overwhelmingly important to the stability, integrity, and beauty of biotic communities, while some animals, such as domestic sheep (allowed perhaps by egalitarian and humane herdspersons to graze freely and to reproduce themselves without being harvested for lamb and mutton) could be a pestilential threat to the natural floral community of a given locale (1980: 320).

If taken to its logical conclusions, the land ethic would have an even more far-reaching ramification: it would sanction the confinement and potentially even killing of *human* animals if that is what it took to benefit the ecosystem or biodiversity. Although most conservationists shy away from this conclusion (see eg Soulé 1985: 731), it cannot be rejected outright that, given the great damage that humanity is causing to nature, the land ethic could not only put plants above animals, but also above humans.

Does this mean that animal rights proponents and conservationists will never see eye to eye? Not necessarily. First, the two already often join forces when it comes to projects such as combating wildlife trade, zoos, and the killing of members of certain species such as orangutans and whales. Second, and more importantly, an alternative approach has emerged that combines the insights of conservation and animal rights: *compassionate conservation*. As a group of adherents of this view have recently summarised it, '[c]ompassionate conservationists strive to embody 4 overarching tenets: first, do no harm; individuals matter; inclusivity; and peaceful coexistence' (Wallach et al 2018: 1260). Because they recognise the inherent value of all sentient individuals, compassionate conservationists for instance oppose the killing of members of invasive species where compassionate alternatives such as sterilisation are available.

C. The Contractualist Critique

Finally, let us turn to another influential philosophical tradition – contractualism – from which some have argued against animal rights. What is contractualism? Broadly, it can be defined as the view that morality is based on a contract or agreement. This contract is generally viewed as a hypothetical one, with the question becoming: what rules and principles *would* contractors *rationally* agree to? The answer to that question determines what the contract would look like, and thereby defines what is morally right and wrong. This tradition of moral thinking goes back to Kant who, as we saw above, rejected the idea that humans have direct moral duties to animals. More recently, the philosopher Peter Carruthers further developed what we can call the Contractualist Critique in his book *The Animals Issue* (2011).

According to Carruthers, contractualism presupposes that the contractors are rational *agents*. This is because, to determine what contractual rules and principles they should agree to, contractors are required not only to have general knowledge about the world but also to be able to reflect rationally on their own needs and desires. What is more, underlying this idea of rational agents is that contracting parties must be capable of reciprocating other parties' rights and duties. Animals, Carruthers claims, are not rational agents because they lack these abilities. This has drastic implications: if, as Carruthers suggests, animals do not have the rational agency required to be parties to the moral contract, they cannot benefit directly from the contract. This is because contracting parties only owe direct duties and rights to other contracting parties, but not to non-contracting outsiders.

Does this mean that animals do not deserve any moral protection in Carruthers's theory? Not quite. Following in Kant's footsteps, Carruthers argues that contracting parties (ie humans) could have at least indirect duties to animals. This is the case in two types of circumstances: first, if not protecting animals would cause offence to rational agents or, second, if not protecting animals makes us worse persons toward rational agents (this, it will be recalled, was also Kant's point).

What is the practical upshot of this approach? As Carruthers maintains, 'there is no basis for extending moral protection to animals beyond that which is already provided. In particular, there are no good moral grounds for forbidding hunting, factory farming, or laboratory testing on animals' (1992: 196). Carruthers thus pronounces a sweeping verdict: 'those who are committed to any aspect of the animal rights movement are thoroughly misguided' (1992: 196).

Even if one grants that no animals qualify as agents – an assumption that has become increasingly contested (see eg Blattner 2019b) – Carruthers's theory is debatable. For instance, it appears to put the moral status of humans who are not rational agents on a precarious footing. His assurances that such humans would still have to be treated like rational agents rather than animals, because not doing so would create a slippery slope undermining rational agents' rights and/or lead to social instability, have not convinced everyone. What is more, Nussbaum has criticised contractualist approaches like his for conflating two questions that need to be kept separate: who frames the contract, and who gets to benefit from it. Contractualists often assume that the answer to these questions is identical, but it need not be. Moved by similar considerations as Nussbaum, there are proponents of contractualism who have developed contractualist approaches to animal rights. For example, Tom Huffman has emphasised the potential offered by the contract's hypothetical nature, essentially asking: if the contract is hypothetical anyway, why not extend it to animals? As he put it: 'All we need ask is what *would* a nonrational being bargain for *if* it were temporarily able?' (Huffman 1993: 25). Another objection arises from the work of political thinkers like Donaldson and Kymlicka who try to show that at least domesticated animals are capable of reciprocating duties – a view we discussed in the previous section and in chapter two.

Despite the sustained criticism that the Contractualist Critique has received, it continues to be influential in contemporary animal rights discourse. As we will see in chapter six, some courts have employed contractualist arguments concerning the reciprocity of rights and duties (sometimes calling them 'social contract' arguments) to deny rights to animals.

VII. Conclusion

As this chapter has illustrated, philosophical accounts differ in how they justify animals' moral status, with utilitarians like Singer emphasising equal consideration of interests, deontologists like Regan rights, capabilities-theorists like Nussbaum capabilities, and political thinkers like Donaldson and Kymlicka group-differentiated rights. What is more, there are philosophical traditions like the ecofeminist, conservationist, and contractualist approach, from which critiques have been directed against the idea of animal rights.

Despite these critiques, however, there appears to be a growing consensus in recent decades that especially sentient animals are deserving of some moral consideration (Birch 2017). As the next chapters will show, there is also increasing debate in law and politics as to how this moral recognition of animals' interests can be translated into legal form. As we will see there, the simple recognition that animals have certain moral rights does not yet tell us which legal rights they have and how such legal rights could be operationalised. For this, we need to turn to legal theory.

Exercise 2: Philosophical Foundations of Animal Rights

1. Which of the philosophical positions discussed in this chapter do you agree with most? Why? Can you anticipate objections to your position from those who adopt the other approaches we discussed?
2. Take an animal of your choice and try to identify the good and central capabilities that belong to its 'species norm'. How does your list compare with Nussbaum's list of ten capabilities? And how could your animal's capabilities be promoted in practice?
3. According to Donaldson and Kymlicka, domesticated animals' right to political representation involves 'representation in the legislative process, but it will also require representing animals in, for example, municipal land planning decisions, or on the governance boards of various professions and public services (police, emergency services, medicine, law, urban planning, social services, etc)' (2011: 154). Taking the example of dogs, try to imagine – in groups or alone – what representation in these various processes and services could involve.
4. Some years ago, in an effort to save tortoises and rare plants in the Galapagos Islands, conservationists chartered helicopters with machine guns and reportedly shot around 140,000 goats (a species introduced by humans) (Marris 2018). Applying what you have learned in the previous section, what philosophical arguments could be made in favour and against this? What is your position?

Useful References

Adams, CJ and Gruen, L (2014) 'Groundwork' in CJ Adams and L Gruen (eds), *Ecofeminism: Feminist Intersections with Other Animals and the Earth* (London, Bloomsbury).

Korsgaard, CM (2018) *Fellow Creatures: Our Obligations to the Other Animals* (Oxford, Oxford University Press).

Palmer, C (2010) *Animal Ethics in Context* (New York, Columbia University Press).

Wadiwel, D (2013) 'Zoopolis: Challenging our Conceptualisation of Political Sovereignty Through Animal Sovereignties' 52 *Dialogue* 749.

Dunn, K (2019) 'Kaimangatanga: Maori Perspectives on Veganism and Plant-based Kai' 8 *Animal Studies Journal* 1, 42.

Steiner, G (2010) *Anthropocentrism and its Discontents: The Moral Status of Animals in the History of Western Philosophy* (Pittsburgh PA, University of Pittsburgh Press).

Schaler, JA (ed) (2009) *Peter Singer Under Fire: The Moral Iconoclast Faces His Critics* (Chicago, Open Court).

Gruen, L (2011) *Ethics and Animals* (Cambridge, Cambridge University Press).

Regan, T and Singer, P (1976) *Animal Rights and Human Obligations* (Hoboken, Prentice Hall Inc).

Calarco, M (2015) *Thinking Through Animals* (Boston, Stanford University Press).

4

The Legal Theory of Animal Rights

I. Introduction

As animals' moral rights are increasingly being cast into legal form, some challenges have arisen. One of these challenges is whether the idea of animal rights is sound from the point of view of legal theory. Sceptics believe that speaking of legal animal rights is a kind of 'loose talk': well-intentioned, perhaps, but with no more legal purchase than other disputed rights claims such as, for example, claims to a right to be loved or to charity. This chapter responds to the sceptics' challenge by shedding light on three key legal theoretical debates in animal rights law: first, are animals fit to have legal rights? Second, do they already have legal rights? And third, would they need to become legal persons to have legal rights, or can they remain property?

There is growing awareness that these questions cannot be answered simply by drawing on philosophical arguments. This is because legal animal rights are not just copied and pasted moral rights. Rather, they are rights with uniquely legal features that require a legal-theoretical toolbox to be understood properly. In this chapter, we consider the emerging legal-theoretical literature to acquire these tools. As you will see, more often than not there will be several possible answers to the three above-mentioned questions. The aim of this chapter is not to resolve any of these debates in a final way, but rather to provide readers with an overview of the central arguments. As will emerge from this discussion, there are plausible arguments for conceiving of animals as actual or potential legal rights-holders.

> **Central Issues**
>
> 1.   Sceptics believe that animal rights claims are simply 'loose talk' that do not withstand legal-theoretical scrutiny. However, there are plausible arguments showing that animal rights are a sound legal-theoretical project.

2. There are two broad theories on the functions of rights: the choice- (or will-) based approach (on which rights serve to protect the sphere of autonomy of individuals who are capable of making legal choices) and the interest-based theory (which says that rights serve to protect the interests of individuals). While both theories are subject to debate, the interest-based theory can explain more easily why animals can have rights.

3. Some argue that animals already possess certain legal rights because they are the beneficiaries of legal duties and other constraints imposed on human beings. Others argue that these constraints might entail rights, but not rights in the special or meaningful sense normally envisioned by 'rights', which we call 'thick rights'.

4. Legal personhood is widely believed to be a necessary condition for any being to have legal rights. This traditional view holds that animals, given that they are property, cannot have any legal rights. The traditional view of legal personhood has recently come under attack by authors who hold that, even as property, animals can and do have legal rights.

II. Are Animals Fit to have Legal Rights?

The first hurdle that animal rights law needs to clear is establishing that animals are capable of having legal rights. Legal rights for animals would be a non-starter if it turned out that animals – like bikes or books – are simply not the kind of beings that can have such rights. We therefore need to begin by asking if rights are *right* for animals. Whether an entity can hold legal rights is usually assessed in light of the 'function' of rights. There are two main theoretical accounts of the functions of rights. According to the first, the choice-based approach, rights protect individuals' choices. The second, the interest-based approach, sees rights as protecting individuals' interests.

A. The Choice-Based Approach to Rights

Let us first consider what the function of rights is according to the choice-based approach and how that approach applies to animals. This will then allow us to evaluate the approach.

According to the choice-based approach, legal rights serve the *function* of expressing and protecting the choices made by autonomous individuals. Take, for example, the prominent choice theory of the legal theorist HLA Hart. On his theory, someone (call her X) is a rights-holder if she can determine by her own choice whether someone else (Y) should act in a certain way, and thereby restrict his freedom. For instance, Sophie is a rights-holder on the choice-approach if she is capable of choosing whether Kenzo must return her copy of the Animal Rights Law textbook which she lent him. If she chooses that he must return the book, Sophie limits Kenzo's freedom as he can now no longer use the book himself.

An important point to note is that it does not matter on the choice-based approach whether Sophie actually *benefits* from Kenzo returning the book. Her right to demand (or to waive) that Kenzo perform his duty is meant to protect her standing as an autonomous individual. Whether she gains or loses anything by demanding or waiving performance is neither here nor there for her possession of the right. As Hart puts it, on the choice-based approach, her right makes her a 'small-scale sovereign' (1982: 183): free to choose as she pleases within her sphere of autonomy. As we will see below, this differs from the interest-based approach, where a right must be in the interest of its holder.

Can the choice-based approach apply to animals? Due to its focus on individual autonomy, the choice-based rights approach is widely believed to stand in the way of granting legal rights to animals. Only human beings, the common view goes, have the capacity to choose how they want to lead their lives, and to decide whether and how others are to discharge their legal duties toward them. Hart explicitly drew this conclusion: he believed that while it is wrong to ill-treat animals, they cannot have legal rights against ill-treatment because they lack the ability to choose how to exercise their rights. Saying that they have a 'right' not to be ill-treated, he argued, would be meaningless because it adds nothing to the already existing obligations that humans have not to ill-treat animals (Hart 1955: 180–81). Like the sceptics we mentioned at the outset of this chapter, Hart thus seemed to think that animal rights claims are 'loose talk'.

Not everyone agrees with Hart and others that all (non-human) animals lack the ability to choose. As we have seen in chapter three, there is a growing trend in animal rights scholarship to view animals as beings who are able to make decisions for themselves and/or who can participate in shared human-animal communities. Could one use this scholarship to argue that animals do, in fact, have a legally sufficient capacity to choose, and are therefore suitable for legal rights-holdership according to the choice theory? For instance, one might argue that when Dante the dog sits in front of the door – his tail wagging – he *chooses* that his owner perform his duty to go for a walk with him. Not just dogs, but many other animals could be said to have agency and the ability to choose in the sense suggested by this example.

But does this suffice to prove Hart and other choice-theorists wrong? Not quite. For the question is not only whether non-humans have the ability to choose, but whether they have the ability to choose *legally*. When Dante insists on going for a walk, he may plausibly be said to exercise a choice to want to go for a walk rather than, say, play with his toys. However, that does not necessarily mean that Dante has the ability to choose legally whether his owner should perform his legal duty to go for a walk with him. This is unlike Sophie who can insist that it is her legal right to get the book back from Kenzo, if need be by enforcing it in court.

B. Evaluating the Choice-Based Approach

While it may be possible to show that at least some animals possess the ability to exercise legal agency in the sense required, animal rights lawyers have arguably more promising ways of challenging choice-based rights theories. One problem with these theories is that they struggle to account for so-called 'absolute rights', such as the right not to be tortured. Absolute rights are rights that cannot be limited (in contrast to 'relative' or 'qualified' rights). It is also commonly accepted that absolute rights cannot be waived. This has an odd consequence under the choice-based approach: if the holder of the right not to be tortured cannot exercise his or her choice by waiving that right, then the right not to be tortured would not be a right.

Another problem with choice-based theories is the difficulties they face with explaining distributions of legal rights among human beings. Perhaps the greatest challenge of the choice-based approach is that it would seem to lead to the counterintuitive conclusion that human beings who lack the relevant capacities to make legal choices – such as infants, humans in a coma, or humans with severe cognitive impairments – lack legal rights. In fact, Hart (1955: 181) himself acknowledged that it would be just as meaningless to talk of a human baby's legal rights as it would be of animals' rights. Like non-human animals, human babies as well as some other human beings either temporarily or permanently lack the ability to make legal choices and would therefore not be eligible for legal rights on the choice-based approach.

Many choice-based theorists see this as a virtue rather than a vice of their approach. This is because these thinkers believe that limiting legal rights to those who have the ability to choose how to structure their lives, legally helps protect the special character of these rights and the dignity of their holders. And, as we saw above, choice-based theorists do not take the absence of legal rights to mean that the relevant beings would lack protection from ill-treatment.

However, other choice-based theorists (including Hart later in his career) are less comfortable with the implication of excluding certain human beings from rights-holdership – not least because human infants and other human beings who lack legal agency are widely accepted to have legal rights. For instance, the United Nations Convention on the Rights of the Child (1989) and the Convention on the Rights of Persons with Disabilities (2006) enshrine legal rights for humans who would seem to be ineligible for rights under choice-based approaches. Some choice theorists have therefore tried to solve this problem by pointing to the need for human guardians who possess agency to *exercise* (eg Hart 1982: 184), or even to *hold* (eg Steiner 1998: 261) the rights on behalf of those who lack agency. There may be some merit to these solutions. However, they would also seem to lend themselves to justifying legal rights for non-human animals. Like human infants or humans with severe cognitive disabilities, they could be provided with a guardian to exercise or hold their legal rights, and would therefore no longer be excluded from rights-holdership under the choice-based approach.

C. The Interest-Based Approach to Rights

The second theory about the function of legal rights is the interest-based approach to rights. As with the choice-based approach, we can first ask what the function of rights is on this approach and how it applies to animals. This will then allow us to evaluate the approach.

The interest-based approach is the most popular approach among animal rights thinkers, and also some human rights proponents. According to this approach, the *function* of legal rights is quite a simple one: to protect the interests of their holders. This means that rights have the aim of promoting the wellbeing of their holders.

How does the interest-based approach apply to animals? There are numerous different formulations of the interest-based approach, but a particularly influential one is that of Joseph Raz. According to Raz, a being X has a right if three conditions are met: (1) X is the kind of being that can have rights; (2) the right is based on X's interest; and (3) X's interest is a sufficient reason to hold others (A, B, C, ...) under a corresponding duty (1984: 195). For example, in Raz's interest theory, I have a right not to be tortured by you if I can have rights, if my right is based on my interest in not being tortured, and if my interest is reason enough to impose a duty on you not to torture me. Let us consider each condition in turn.

Who exactly can have rights, condition (1)? According to Raz, only entities whose wellbeing is important, or valuable for its own sake – who have 'ultimate value', as he puts it – qualify for rights-holdership. Their interests are not important because they benefit other persons, but because they benefit themselves. Take Bao the dog and his owner, Chen. Chen might love Bao and insist that Bao's welfare is important. Raz believes, however, that the value of animals like Bao derives from their owners' – here Chen's – concern for them, and from how animals enrich human lives. In other words, Bao is valuable *because Chen values him*. Conversely, Raz would say that Chen's wellbeing is valuable intrinsically, or 'non-derivatively': not depending on whether Chen benefits others, and indeed remaining important even if others disregard Chen's wellbeing.

However, one need not agree with Raz on this point to adopt his interest-based approach. In fact, most interest-based theorists (eg Cochrane 2012: 16) disagree with Raz and consider that the wellbeing of dogs and other animals is important in itself, that is, regardless of whether others value it. There is widespread consensus that sentience is a sufficient ground to hold that sentient animals are intrinsically valuable. As a result, most interest theorists believe that sentient animals have ultimate value and pass the first condition of Raz's test.

What about plants and other entities such as rivers and mountains: do they have intrinsic value and interests in their own wellbeing? This is a more contested matter. According to some environmental ethicists, plants have intrinsic value in the sense that there are things – such as water and sunlight – that are good for them and other things – such as herbicides and goats – that are bad. The good things are things plants can be said to have an interest in, whether or not they are sentient. Some believe that even larger entities such as ecosystems can have intrinsic value and interests. According to the Te Awa Tupua (Whanganui River Claims Settlement) Act (2017) in New Zealand, for instance, the Whanganui River has intrinsic value. The legal theorist Matthew Kramer has suggested that even inanimate objects like a listed building (ie one that is protected from development) could conceptually be said to have interests (eg in not being torn down). But, as Kramer (2001) notes, moral reasons (such as the fact that inanimate objects are not sentient) can justify limiting interest-based rights to sentient creatures. The political philosopher Alasdair Cochrane (2013b) arrives at a similar conclusion, arguing that only sentient beings can have intrinsic value and interests relevant for the interest-based rights approach. Whatever one's views are on the interests of plants and other entities, there is wide agreement today that at least all sentient animals possess the intrinsic value and interests required to meet condition (1) of Raz's test.

Condition (2) of the test holds that a being's rights must actually be based on their interest(s). In other words, a being's own interests must be the ground or justification of their rights. It is therefore not sufficient that *any* interest be promoted by the right. For example, your friends may have an interest in you being alive and well. Yet, your right to life is not grounded in their interest in your life and wellbeing, but in your own interest. When does a being have an interest in a particular right? When fulfilling that interest generally promotes the wellbeing of the being: that is, when meeting the interest generally makes the being fare better rather than worse. For instance, most human and non-human animals fare better when their interest in eating food is being met.

However, not every interest of a being justifies a right. Suppose that my wellbeing would be significantly enhanced if I was a millionaire. Does this mean that I have a right to be a millionaire? This is where condition (3) of Raz's theory comes into play. According to this condition, I can only have a right to be a millionaire if this interest is reason enough to impose a duty on others to make me a millionaire. As important as my interest may be to myself, it would demand too much of others if they had to turn me into a millionaire. It would in all likelihood also be impossible to give everyone the same right to become a millionaire, as no practicable system could be established that places duties on everyone to make everyone else a millionaire.

This raises a question. Could one not challenge animal rights on the ground that giving legal rights to animals would be as difficult as granting me a legal right to become a millionaire? Yes and no. Many interest theorists believe that it is true that not all interests of all animals are reason enough to impose legal duties on others to promote these interests. For instance, dogs' interests in having their bellies rubbed would hardly be sufficient reason for imposing legal duties on humans to rub dogs' bellies. But many also agree that there are at least some animal interests that will generally be sufficient to impose corresponding duties. The interest in not suffering bodily harm, for instance, is regarded as sufficient reason for imposing duties on humans not to inflict bodily harm on animals.

D. Evaluating the Interest-Based Approach

As this shows, the interest-based approach can explain animals' rights more easily than the choice-based approach. If we apply Raz's theory, for example, we can say that non-human animals possess rights if and to the extent that: (1) they possess intrinsic value, such as in virtue of being sentient; (2) their own interests serve as the grounds for their rights; and (3) protection and promotion of their interests is reason enough to impose legal duties on others. Importantly, on the interest-based approach, the justification for animals' rights is no different from how human rights are justified. We will return to this point in chapter five.

To be sure, interest-based theories are not without their shortcomings either. Two common objections are worth considering briefly. First, interest theories are sometimes criticised for causing an 'inflation' of both rights and rights-holders that would ultimately undermine human rights. As some believe, there is nothing in the interest theory preventing it from recognising, for example, a legal right to wear a hat or to use TikTok if these rights met the three conditions mentioned above. Would recognising such trivial rights as genuine rights not undermine the special status of core human rights such as the right to life and to freedom from slavery? Similarly, would extending rights to non-human beings, such as animals and perhaps even plants, mountains, and rivers, not devalue what it means to have rights? If everyone has rights to everything, no one has rights to anything – or so the objection goes.

A second objection is that by making rights dependent on whether they are reason enough to impose duties on others, the interest-based approach requires us to engage in a balancing exercise to identify which rights a being has and what the scope of these rights is. However, this is said to deprive rights of their absolute character which forbids such trade-offs with other people's or the community's interests. As the choice theorist Nigel Simmonds points out, for example, it is problematic to make individuals' rights subject to a weighing of interests as this denies rights the 'peremptory force' (2016: 251) that makes them so desirable.

Interest theorists have proposed responses to meet these objections. For example, some have turned the tables on the first objection, and argued that inflating rights in these ways is not a weakness but a strength of the interest-based approach as it allows the extension of rights to beings who need them. What is more, suggestions have been put forward as to how to create a threshold of importance that an interest must meet in order to be considered a right and to eliminate rights to trivial things such as hats and TikTok. In response to the second objection, it has been suggested that even human rights are subject to balancing and that very few, if any, rights are peremptory. We return to the question of balancing rights in chapter five.

If you are interested in these criticisms, and the responses that interest theorists have developed, you will find useful references at the end of the chapter and on the companion website. For the purposes of our section here, it is sufficient to note that, with the interest-based approach, there are plausible arguments that suggest that non-human animals are indeed suitable for rights-holdership.

Exercise 1: Choice and Interest Rights Theories

1. Consider the following entities with the choice and interest-based rights approaches in mind and use the check boxes to indicate whether the relevant entity would qualify for rights-holdership under the choice-based approach, the interest-based approach, both, or neither.

	Choice Theories	Interest Theories
Michelle Obama	☐	☐
Bob the Street Cat	☐	☐

X Æ A-12 Musk	☐	☐
Mount Everest	☐	☐
The Taj Mahal	☐	☐
Nim Chimpsky	☐	☐
A Giant Sequoia Tree	☐	☐
Stephen Hawking	☐	☐
The River Nile	☐	☐

2.   Which of these entities do you consider typical rights-holders? Which *should* be? Which theory explains your answers better?

3.   What issues could arise if (some of) these entities were rights-holders?

III. Do Animals Already have Legal Rights?

Having established that there are good reasons for believing that, at least under the interest-based rights approach, some animals *can* have rights, we now need to address another debated issue: Do animals in fact *already* possess some legal rights? Or are they yet to be granted such rights? These questions have arisen particularly in the context of existing animal protection laws, which we surveyed in chapter one. Can the protection laws we discussed there be said to grant legal rights to animals? And, if they do, are these legal rights in any way different from the rights that human beings possess?

In this section, we address these questions by first focusing on what we call the Thin Conception of rights, according to which animals already possess legal rights. We then contrast this with the Thick Conception of rights, according to which animals currently lack legal rights in the relevant (thick) sense.

A. Animals Already have Legal Rights: The Thin Conception

It is common for people to speak of animals as having 'rights'. For instance, when Harambe the gorilla was shot in the Cincinnati Zoo in 2016 after having grabbed a small child who climbed into his enclosure, there were claims on social media that Harambe's 'right to life' had been violated. But not only non-lawyers believe that animals already possess legal rights. Some laws specifically refer to animals as having rights. Consider, for example, the following provision from Bolivia:

Article 3 – Law for the Defence of Animals Against Acts of Cruelty and Abuse (2015)

Animals as subjects of protection have the following rights:

(a)   to be recognized as living beings;
(b)   to a healthy and protected environment ...

There is also a tradition in legal theoretical thinking that holds that many animals have rights as a matter of law. The legal scholar Cass Sunstein, for example, has argued that 'legal rights' should simply be understood as legal protections that animals have from being harmed, and to which they have a moral right. Sunstein points out that the laws of many countries provide animals with legal protections from harm. As we saw in chapter one, these generally take the form of prohibiting the infliction of unnecessary or unreasonable suffering on animals, or outright bans on harmful practices. Sunstein also suggests that there is widespread agreement that animals morally deserve this kind of protection. As a result, he says, animals already possess legal rights against being harmed.

Kramer reaches the same conclusion as Sunstein, but through a different route. To develop his argument, Kramer (1998; 2001) draws on the analysis of the jurist Wesley Newcomb Hohfeld (1879–1918), who presented a framework of rights in the early twentieth century that is still frequently used today. Hohfeld believed that our understanding of rights is clouded because we use the term 'right' indiscriminately to express many different things. To bring order into rights talk, Hohfeld identified eight different concepts (also called 'legal positions') that the term 'right' denotes. According to Hohfeld, these legal positions stand in 'jural relations' with each other, meaning that they are best understood as pairs that stand in opposition to or correlation with each other. Figure 1 shows legal positions that *correlate* with each other.

Figure 1 Jural correlatives in Wesley Hohfeld's framework of rights

claim-right	privilege	power	immunity
↕	↕	↕	↕
duty	no-right	liability	disability

Consider first the correlation between 'claim-right' and 'duty'. According to Hohfeld, to say that Sophie has a claim-right that Kenzo return her Animal Rights Law textbook simply means that Kenzo has a duty to return that book to her. Whenever there is a claim-right, there is a duty, and *vice versa*. The same holds true for 'privileges' and 'no-rights'. If I have a privilege (sometimes also called a 'liberty') to do something, such as to ride my bicycle, then someone else lacks the right that I do *not* ride my bicycle (they have a 'no-right' in Hohfeld's terminology). When Hohfeld talks of correlativity, then, he simply means that the two respective legal positions always come together.

The relations between 'power' and 'liability', and 'immunity' and 'disability', are also correlative in this sense. The only difference here is that these are, in some sense, meta-legal positions that alter the four other positions (claim-rights, duties, privileges, and no-rights). Let us illustrate this with an example. On Hohfeld's account, the manager of a supermarket can have the 'power' to change the legal situation of her employees. This means that her employees are 'liable' to have their legal situation changed. The manager can, for example, order an employee to fill the shelves, thereby imposing on that employee a *duty* to fill the shelves and removing his *privilege* not to fill the shelves. Suppose, however, that that employee has a clause in their contract stating that they do not have to fill the shelves. In this case, Hohfeld would say that the employee has an 'immunity' from having his legal status changed in this way. The manager, in turn, would have a 'disability', meaning that she lacks the ability to change the employee's legal situation in this way.

These, then, are Hohfeld's 'jural correlatives': legal positions that describe a legal relationship between two or more persons. 'Jural opposites' involve the same legal positions, but are focused on the legal situation of one and the same person. Figure 2 illustrates legal positions that are *opposites* of each other.

Figure 2 Jural opposites in Wesley Hohfeld's framework of rights

right	privilege	power	immunity
↕	↕	↕	↕
no-right	duty	disability	liability

For example, if Sophie has a right that Kenzo return her book, this means that Sophie does not lack the right (or, in Hohfeld's terminology, that she does not have a 'no-right') that Kenzo return her book. Likewise, if I have the privilege to ride my bicycle, then I do not have a duty not to ride my bicycle. If the manager has a power to change her employee's legal situation, then she does not have a disability to change his legal situation. And if the employee has an immunity from having his legal situation changed, then he does not have a liability to have his legal situation changed.

Equipped with Hohfeld's framework, we can now return to the question of how Kramer and others use it to argue that animals already possess certain legal rights. They do so, quite simply, by looking for concrete instances in the law where animals have legal positions that Hohfeld would qualify as rights: claim-rights, privileges, powers, or immunities. In most legal systems, the richest deposit of such legal positions can be found in animal protection laws. Take, for example, the legal *duty* many of these laws impose on humans not to inflict unnecessary suffering on sentient animals. Because, as we saw, legal duties are always correlative with claim-rights in Hohfeld's framework, it can be argued that animals who are protected by such laws possess a *claim-right* not to have unnecessary suffering inflicted upon them. Or take, for instance, the *disability* of states to change the federal animal protection laws in their country: on Hohfeld's account, this disability correlates with an *immunity* on the part of the animals not to have their federal protections changed by states.

Note that, on Hohfeld's account, in order to possess claim-rights (or privileges, powers, and immunities), animals need not be able to bear legal duties. Rather, it is human beings who will in most instances bear the legal duties that correlate to animals' claim-rights. However, as we will see in the next section, animals' capacity to bear legal duties remains an important issue in debates on whether animals are 'legal persons' or not.

B. The Thin Conception: A Review

Many have been critical of Sunstein's and Kramer's rather narrow definition of what makes a right – which we called the Thin Conception of rights. Of its apparent short-comings, one has been pointed out in particular: the thin rights that animals possess as a matter of law do not protect their fundamental interests such as in life. This raises the question as to whether they should be called 'rights' at all. As some have suggested, they are not 'fundamental rights' but rather what one can call mere 'animal welfare rights' – terms that the animal rights scholar Saskia Stucki (2020) has recently taken up and further developed.

As is widely believed, thin rights may grant some legal protections to animals but they do not protect animals' interests in the ways that human rights protect humans' basic interests. For example, whereas all human beings possess (at least on paper) fundamental rights to life and to bodily and mental integrity, no non-human animals currently possess any such thick rights to protect their basic interests. As we saw in chapter two, according to the Abolitionist scholar Gary Francione, the reason for this is that animals' thin rights are premised on the idea that animals do not have intrinsic value deserving of fundamental rights protection.

That is also why, according to Francione, even to the extent that the thin rights contained in animal welfare laws do protect animals' basic interests, they generally do so only in a limited way. For instance, in numerous countries, sentient animals possess a thin right against being slaughtered without prior stunning. However, not only do animals lack a right not to be killed at all, but their right against being slaughtered without prior stunning is in many of these countries inapplicable if they are slaughtered for religious purposes. Hence, animals in these legal systems are left with a narrow right not to be killed without prior stunning for non-religious purposes. Similarly, while animals may not have unnecessary suffering inflicted upon them in many legal systems, this falls far short of the standard of the right to bodily and mental integrity that human beings enjoy. As we saw in chapter one, as long as the suffering of animals is regarded as 'necessary' or 'reasonable', animals' interests in not being harmed are not protected. This is the case, for example, with regard to the production of food, which is considered necessary even in countries where suitable alternatives are readily available. Here, too, animals are left with a narrow right not to be made to suffer unnecessarily except when that suffering serves a trivial culinary or economic purpose.

It is, of course, possible to say that animals already possess thin rights and to argue that they should *also* have thick rights. However, as we will see in the next section, many proponents of the Thick Conception prefer not to call thin rights 'rights' at all.

To be sure, the Thin Conception may have certain advantages. According to its proponents, one of its strategic virtues is that it lowers the stakes in debates on animal rights (see eg Kurki 2021). If animals already possess certain legal rights, then giving them more rights is not the paradigm change or legal revolution that some proponents of the Thick Conception often make it out to be. For example, the animal rights lawyer Steven Wise suggests that granting animals legal personhood and rights would amount to an historic breach in the 'thick legal wall [that] separates all humans from all nonhumans' (2010: 5). However, if the adherents of the Thin Conception are right, then that wall has long been breached, and ongoing efforts to secure rights for animals (which we analyse in chapters six and seven) are simply efforts to give *more* rights to animals. According to advocates of the Thin Conception, this realisation makes it easier for judges and politicians to support animal rights efforts, as they will not be seen as renegades for doing so.

Proponents of the Thin Conception could thus argue that even those who prefer thick rights for animals may benefit from being able to point to existing thin rights as a legal (or at least rhetorical) basis on which to advocate the adoption of more and stronger animal rights. For example, animal rights groups in the UK could use the fact that the Animal Welfare Act (2006) already grants a thin right to dogs not to have their tails docked as a springboard for requesting that similarly painful practices in other animals (such as the debeaking of chickens) be banned for the sake of legal consistency.

Exercise 2: King Louis's *Code Noir* (1685)

In 1685, the French King Louis XIV decreed the so-called *Code Noir* (Black Code) to regulate the conditions of slavery in the French colonies. In addition to upholding chattel slavery as such, the Code contained numerous articles that were detrimental to the slaves, such as provisions determining that any child born in a marriage between slaves is itself a slave, or that any slave who strikes a member of their master's family is to be punished by death. However, it also contained some provisions that served the slaves' interests. Consider, for example, the following articles:

Article IV

Let us enjoin all our subjects, of whatever quality and condition they may be, to observe Sundays and holidays which are observed by our subjects of the Catholic, Apostolic and Roman religion. Let us forbid them to work, and to make their slaves work on said days, from midnight until the following midnight, either in the cultivation of the earth, in the manufacture of sugars, and in all other areas of work, on pain of fine and arbitrary punishment against the masters ...

Article XI

Let us forbid the parish priests to marry slaves when it is not apparent that they have the consent of their masters. Let us also forbid the masters to use any constraints on their slaves to marry them against their will ...

Article XXVII

Slaves who are infirm due to old age, disease or otherwise, whether the disease is incurable or not, will be fed and maintained by their masters; and in case they abandon them, said slaves will be admitted to the hospital, and the masters will be condemned to pay six sols per day, for the food and maintenance of each slave.

1. Does the *Code Noir* grant legal rights to slaves, according to the Thin Conception of rights? If so, which rights does it confer on them?
2. Applying Hohfeld's framework, can you identify specific claim-rights, privileges, powers, and/or immunities in the *Code Noir*?
3. 'The Code Noir was a proto-"Bill of Rights" for slaves'. In a group or alone, reflect on whether you agree with this statement. You may find it useful in your discussion to reflect on the similarities and differences between the articles listed above and those in human and constitutional rights documents you may be familiar with.
4. Are animal protection laws comparable to the *Code Noir*? If yes, in which respects? In which respects are they different?
5. Some believe that comparisons between the legal situation of (former) slaves and animals are problematic (we will return to this issue in chapter eight). Do you agree?

C. Animals do not Yet have Legal Rights: The Thick Conception

Because of what they regard as the shortcomings of thin rights – in particular their widespread failure to protect animals' basic interests in more than just narrow ways – some scholars and practitioners have advocated for thicker animal rights. In their view, which we can call the Thick Conception of rights, at present animals do not possess any legal rights.

Consider, for example, Wise's statement that he and the Nonhuman Rights Project (NhRP) – a US-based animal rights organisation which he leads – want to breach the wall separating humans from non-humans. On Wise's view and that of many other animal rights practitioners and scholars, there is still a wall to be breached. This is because, according to them, while animals may be said to already have thin 'rights', they still lack rights that are worthy of their name. That is, animals lack *thick rights*.

What exactly is a thick right? Views on this differ, but it is possible to distil at least five elements on which there is broad convergence in the literature, and which are inspired by the characteristics of human rights. A thick right: (1) is complex and made up of a set of Hohfeldian legal positions; (2) protects individuals' fundamental interests; (3) has a high threshold for justifying limitations; (4) is directly enforceable by the individual or their representatives; and (5) has a dynamic character allowing it to enhance its protection over time.

(1) Thick rights are characterised by the fact that they do not merely consist of single claim-rights, privileges, powers, or immunities, but of a *complex set of such legal positions*. These combinations are sometimes referred to as 'clusters' of Hohfeldian positions. Take, for instance, the human right to bodily integrity, which is such a cluster right. This right consists of numerous legal positions, including claim-rights not to have one's physical integrity violated without one's consent by others (who have corresponding duties not to violate one's physical integrity); privileges to determine what to do with one's body, such as getting piercings or tattoos; powers to change one's own and others' legal positions, such as by consenting to medical surgeries; and immunities from having one's claim-rights and privileges removed by others, including the state.

To be sure, some animal protection provisions can also be understood in terms of Hohfeldian clusters. For example, according to section 9 of England and Wales's Animal Welfare Act (2006), '[a] person commits an offence if he does not take such steps as are reasonable in all the circumstances to ensure that the needs of an animal for which he is responsible are met to the extent required by good practice'. This provision imposes not only duties on individuals responsible for an animal, but also confers privileges on them to take steps to ensure that the animal's needs are met. However, thick rights will generally comprise *larger* clusters of Hohfeldian positions, as exemplified by the right to bodily integrity.

(2) What is more, the kinds of clusters that are characteristic of thick rights contain Hohfeldian positions that *protect the right-holder's fundamental interests*. Human rights again serve as a useful illustration. The rights to life, integrity, free speech, religion, health, education, or political participation, for example, all protect and promote fundamental human interests. As we saw in the previous subsection and chapter one, existing thin rights in animal protection laws either fail to protect the fundamental interests of non-human animals altogether, or they protect these interests in only marginal ways. Recall, for instance, that many animal protection laws serve animals' interest in life only to the extent that they prohibit the killing of animals if it is carried out without prior stunning, and if the absence of stunning is not required by religious exceptions. Hence, when animal rights advocates urge that certain animals should have a right to life, what they mean is that animals' fundamental interests in actual life should be protected. That is, their interest in life should be protected in a similar way to how humans' interest in life is protected through a general right to life.

(3) Proponents of the Thick Conception also advocate for legal rights that *cannot be easily infringed* whenever there is a countervailing interest. Take the example of animal protection provisions that prohibit unnecessary suffering. As we noted earlier, these provisions are often thought problematic because they make protection of animals' integrity conditional on what counts as 'necessary' suffering. We saw that the rearing and killing of animals in industrial and often dire conditions is regarded as 'necessary' suffering, with 'necessity' being understood as human convenience, profit, or culinary pleasure. The same holds true for the use of animals in scientific experimentation, where their subjection to bodily harm and death is generally considered 'necessary' even in cases where the countervailing human interest in scientific knowledge is relatively trivial.

It is important to note that, while some believe that animal rights should have some inviolable (ie absolute) core content, many animal rights advocates do not take issue with the fact that there often has to be *some* balancing between an animal's interests and the interests of humans and other animals. With the possible exception of the US, where a more absolute approach is taken to rights thinking, it is widely accepted that not only animals' rights but even human rights can in many instances be limited (and are therefore 'relative' or 'qualified'). That is, they are subject to being balanced against countervailing interests (with the aid of the so-called proportionality test, about which we say more in chapter five). Your right to free speech, for example, protects your interest in speaking your mind freely. However, your right is not absolute and must be balanced against other people's interests in not being slandered. Similarly, an animal's right to, say, life could be limited in cases where that animal poses a threat to the lives of others.

The claim of the Thick Conception, then, is not that thick rights should generally be absolute, but, as Stucki (2020) has emphasised, that the threshold for allowing infringements of animals' rights should be much higher than it is for thin rights. Whether or not the threshold would have to be as high for animal rights as for equivalent human rights is a matter of controversy to which we will return in chapter five.

(4) Another central feature of the Thick Conception is that animals' legal rights should be *directly enforceable* by the individual or their legal representatives. As chapter one noted, in many legal systems the enforcement of animal protection laws leaves much to be desired. More often than not, underfunded state agencies that have other priorities are in charge of investigating and prosecuting violations of these laws. In only some legal systems are private organisations allowed to help enforce animal protection laws.

This again stands in stark contrast to the enforcement of human rights. Human beings are allowed to enforce their rights directly and have standing to bring violations of their rights to the attention of courts and other state organs. What is more, humans who lack the ability to claim their rights themselves – such as for example infants or humans with severe cognitive impairment – can have most of their rights represented and defended by legal guardians. Proponents of the Thick Conception advocate for similar enforcement of animals' rights through human guardians (an issue we return to in chapter eight). These guardians would have the power to bring cases to court to contest the violation of their animal client's rights; they could appeal decisions, and potentially also receive and administer compensation in the interest of the animal.

On the Thick Conception, animals' ability to have their rights enforced through designated guardians is not only of practical importance; it also has symbolic significance. It expresses the fact that their rights are what are sometimes called 'subjective rights', that is, rights whose purpose is to protect the intrinsic interests of their holders, who are conceived of as legal persons (we return to this in the next section). In other words, thick animal rights are not merely the reflex of duties, disabilities, and other Hohfeldian positions imposed on humans, but legal entitlements that are granted directly to animal subjects to protect their intrinsic interests, and that are enforceable by them or their guardians.

(5) Finally, in order to ensure that the protection of animals' interests does not wane over time, thick rights are regarded as having a *dynamic character* that allows them to increase or at least maintain the level of protection as circumstances change. This point has been emphasised, for example, by Anne Peters (2016b). Advocates like her of the Thick Conception draw parallels with human rights. The European Court of Human Rights (ECtHR), for example, has interpreted the European Convention on Human Rights (ECHR) as a so-called 'living instrument', meaning that it has changed

its interpretation of ECHR rights in light of evolving moral views. For example, the ECtHR changed its interpretation of Article 8's right to respect for private and family life as including protection not only for heterosexual couples but also same-sex couples (eg *Oliari and others v Italy* 2015). In practice, the 'living instrument' interpretation has invariably served to enhance the level of protection enjoyed by the holders of ECHR rights.

The dynamic character of rights is also connected with the fact that they are often seen as 'principles' rather than 'rules'. According to the legal philosopher Ronald Dworkin (1997: 40–45), who introduced this distinction, rules are binary in that they either apply or do not apply. For instance, if the road traffic laws of a country set 120 km/h as the maximum speed limit on motorways, the rule applies if someone exceeds the limit, and it does not apply if they do not. Principles are considered different in that they come in degree. They are vague standards that do not make it immediately clear what their weight or legal consequences are. As such, they are considered particularly useful for expressing general values. An example of a principle is human dignity, which we can find at the beginning of numerous modern constitutions. Many scholars (eg Alexy 2010) regard rights as principles because they do not apply in a binary fashion but rather express general values that courts need to weigh and interpret to determine their consequences (we return to this in chapter five). Such weighing and interpreting can lend a dynamic quality to rights.

Proponents of the Thick Conception follow a similar approach and argue that – when they exist – animals' legal rights should not be seen as set in stone. Rather, they should evolve over time and justify stronger protection for animals as society gains better awareness of their needs and of the ways in which these needs are neglected. Thick rights, then, are not immutable clusters of legal positions, but clusters (or principles) that grow over time and in ways that favour animals' fundamental interests. While it may be said that even thin rights can be interpreted dynamically, thick rights offer more opportunities for this because of their more comprehensive protection of animals' interests.

According to advocates of the Thick Conception, animals currently lack legal rights that manifest most, if not all, of these five elements. That is, on their approach, there is still an important legal wall between humans and animals that has not yet been breached. As we saw, proponents of the Thick Conception need not reject the view that animals already possess thin rights. However, they believe that these rights are insufficient and, in many ways, do not amount to genuine 'rights'.

Exercise 3: Thin and Thick Rights

1. What are the main characteristics of the Thin and Thick Conceptions of rights?
2. 'The Thick Conception of rights is incompatible with the Thin Conception'. Do you agree with this statement? Why (not)?

3.   Why do animals currently lack thick legal rights in most legal systems? Is this due to moral, legal, and/or practical reasons?
4.   Should legal animal rights be absolute or relative? What are the respective advantages and disadvantages (you may find it helpful to consult chapter five on this)?
5.   From a strategic point of view, is it better to argue that animals already have legal rights? Or is it better to argue that they currently lack legal rights?

IV. Would Animals Need to Become Legal Persons?

Let us now turn to the final issue that has given rise to much discussion: Would animals need to become legal persons (sometimes also called 'legal subjects') to hold legal rights? Or can animals have legal rights even without being legal persons? Specifically, can they remain legal property or things and still have certain legal rights?

As with the concept of legal rights, there are many different accounts of the concept of legal personhood that disagree on what it takes to become a legal person, and what having legal personhood entails. The legal theorist Ngaire Naffine (2009) has proposed that 'legal person' may best be viewed as an answer to the general question *who is law for?* As Naffine tells us, legal personhood can serve different purposes, depending on one's view. It can serve a rhetorical purpose in highlighting the special worth of its holders, and/or it can serve as a marker for entities that hold legal rights, duties, or other legal positions.

Regardless of what we take its purpose to be, one of the central characteristics of legal personhood is that it is often viewed as the conceptual opposite of property. That is, many believe that one cannot be a legal person *and* property. This conceptual bifurcation, which – as we saw in chapter one – can be traced back to Roman Law, is at the heart of debates on animal rights, as animals have traditionally been placed in the category of property or thing rather than of legal person.

This section discusses this categorisation with a particular focus on animals' legal rights-holdership. In the first subsection, we address the prevailing view – which we call the Traditional View – that animals need to be recognised as legal persons in order to have any legal rights. In the second subsection, we discuss the Unorthodox View, according to which animals need *not* have legal personhood to hold legal rights. On this View, animals' general exclusion from legal personhood is not a problem, or at least not one that should be animal rights lawyers' primary focus.

It is worth noting that there are also voices in the literature that criticise the use of the concept of legal personhood for animals. Maneesha Deckha (2020), for instance, proposes to replace legal personhood with the alternative concept of 'beingness'.

In a similar vein, Will Kymlicka (2017) has argued that placing domesticated animals in legal categories such as 'workers' or 'family members' may be a more fruitful way forward than legal personhood. The section here will focus on the more dominant strands in the discussion which employ the concept of legal personhood.

A. The Traditional View: Legal Personhood is Necessary for Rights-Holdership

A majority of animal rights scholars and practitioners either explicitly or implicitly defend the view that only legal persons (or, synonymously for our purposes, legal subjects) can hold legal rights. While this is not always expressly stated, the type of rights that the proponents of this Traditional View seem to have in mind are what we called thick rights in the previous section. Animals, on this View, would thus have to be legal persons, rather than property, to hold any thick rights.

Arguably the most prominent defender of the Traditional View is the animal rights scholar Gary Francione, whose theory we examined in chapter two. As we saw there, Francione's account insists that there is a dichotomy between legal persons and property. According to Francione, this dichotomy regards legal persons as entities with intrinsic interests, whereas property is only valued instrumentally, that is, insofar as persons have an interest in it. Because only persons have intrinsic interests, only they are granted thick legal rights – or 'respect-based rights' (1995: xvi), as he calls them. Being placed in the category of property, Francione argues, practically ensures that animals' interests will be dominated by the interests of human beings. Whenever there is a conflict between the two, the weakly protected interests of animals almost always give way to the respect-based rights of human legal persons. Hence, Francione's Abolitionist approach argues that we can only save animals from being exploited by granting them a basic right not to be property, that is, by turning animals into legal persons holding thick legal rights.

Steven Wise (2013) also defends the Traditional View of legal personhood. Like Francione, Wise believes that there is a dichotomy between legal persons and property/legal things. As Wise defines the term, a 'legal person' is an entity with the capacity to have legal rights. By contrast, an entity that is property or a legal thing lacks this capacity. Wise uses the metaphor of a rights 'container' to explain how he understands legal personhood: legal personhood is like an empty container and legal rights are 'drips' that go into the container (2013: 1281). Unless one is a legal person (a container), there is no place for legal rights (the drips) to go.

On Wise's account, the division between legal personhood and property expresses a hierarchy of entities, with persons being those who have rights over property, whereas property has no such rights. Things that are property, in other words, are the objects of rights, not the subjects of rights. Even though Wise is sometimes not explicit about this, he too seems to have *thick* legal rights in mind – 'dignity rights' (2010: 6) in his terminology – when stating that only legal persons currently have 'legal rights'.

In his writings, Wise draws explicit analogies between the legal status of non-human animals and that of former slaves, who were also categorised as legal things rather than persons and whose commodity-status facilitated their exploitation. In fact, as we will see in chapter six, Wise and the NhRP have built their legal strategy on the assumption that, like former slaves, some animals could also make the leap from legal thinghood to legal personhood with the aid of *habeas corpus* petitions. This, then, is the legal 'wall' that Wise wants to breach.

As Wise acknowledges, however, there are limited respects in which animals are already treated as legal persons rather than legal things. For example, under the New York Pet Trust Statute (1998), domestic animals can be the beneficiaries of trusts. Because only legal persons can be trust beneficiaries in New York state law, Wise argues, the statute implicitly recognises animals as legal persons.

Wise's intimation that not all areas of law need to operate with the same definition of 'legal person' is an important one that was also confirmed in a 2020 decision by the Swiss Federal Supreme Court, which chapter six explores in more depth. The Court was asked to adjudicate on the legality of the primate rights initiative (discussed in chapter seven), which aimed to grant constitutional rights to life and bodily and mental integrity to non-human primates. In its ruling, the Court suggested that the definition of legal subjecthood in the Swiss Civil Code (which is based on an idea of persons who can have private law rights *and* duties) is not applicable in all areas of Swiss law. Swiss public law operates with a different notion of the legal subject that is open to extending rights to non-human primates.

The Swiss Court thus implicitly concluded that someone can be a legal person without bearing legal duties. Is that correct? Or does one require *both* the capacity to have legal rights *and* bear duties in order to be a legal person? This question has turned out to be a stumbling block for the NhRP's attempts to have chimpanzees and elephants recognised as legal persons for the purposes of *habeas corpus*. Setting a precedent that other US courts followed, the Appellate Division of the New York Supreme Court (Third Department) turned down one of the NhRP's petitions on behalf of chimpanzees, arguing that

> unlike human beings, chimpanzees cannot bear any legal duties, submit to societal responsibilities or be held legally accountable for their actions. In our view, it is this incapability to bear any legal responsibilities and societal duties that renders it inappropriate to confer upon chimpanzees the legal rights – such as the fundamental right to liberty protected by the writ of habeas corpus – that have been afforded to human beings (Appellate Division, New York Supreme Court 2014: 6).

As we saw in section III, Hohfeld's theory does not lend support to the conclusion that rights-holders must also be able to bear legal duties. But the Third Department tried to justify its decision by using a different argument. Drawing on the work of the animal rights sceptic Richard Cupp (2012), which we discuss in chapter five, the Court argued that the reciprocity of rights and duties *in the same person* follows from contractualist theories according to which rights-holdership is connected to one's ability to accept social responsibility – which it believed only human beings can do. However, as a group of 17 philosophers have argued in response, this argument stands on shaky ground, not least because many humans lack the ability to accept social responsibility and to reciprocate duties (Proposed Brief 2018) – an issue that readers will recall from chapter three's discussion of contractualist theories. We do not want to deprive these humans of legal rights, so how do we explain that they have legal rights but animals do not? These questions are a matter of ongoing debate, but many animal rights scholars believe that the conventional social contract argument ultimately fails, and that animals can have legal personhood (and legal rights) even if they cannot bear legal duties.

B. The Unorthodox View: Legal Personhood is not Necessary for Rights-Holdership

The Traditional View remains the dominant position in legal theory, doctrine, and practice. However, it is not uncontested. In recent years, an alternative view has gained traction according to which legal personhood is not actually necessary for rights-holdership (or for the capacity to have legal rights, as Wise puts it). In other words, animals can have rights despite being property. On this Unorthodox View, legal personhood may still be an important status, but it is far from being the Holy Grail that animal rights lawyers of the Traditional View take it to be.

The political philosopher Alasdair Cochrane has been among the most prominent defenders of the Unorthodox View. According to Cochrane (2009), the dichotomy between property and legal personhood is not as strict as advocates of the Traditional View believe. Not only are there certain entities – like corporations – that can be both legal persons and property, but there are also entities that have rights despite not being legal persons. Focusing specifically on the question of ownership, Cochrane argues that animals can possess legal rights while remaining ownable things. Challenging the position of Abolitionists such as Francione, Cochrane proposes that we would not need to abolish all forms of animal ownership in order to be able to protect their interests.

Cochrane's argument takes as its point of departure the finding that ownership is not absolute. If I am the owner of a listed building, then there are certain things I must not do with the building. For example, I must not tear it down or remodel its front. Drawing on the work of the jurist Tony Honoré (1961), Cochrane argues that ownership should thus be understood not as a right of absolute control over a thing, but rather as a bundle of 'relations' (or legal positions) that apply to the owner of the thing in most instances. Among the standard relations are, for example, the rights to possess, use, manage, and transfer the thing, the right not to be expropriated or to receive compensation for expropriation, and the duty to not use the thing in ways that are harmful to others. Importantly, on Honoré's bundle conception of ownership, not all of these legal relations need to be present for someone to have ownership; it is possible that some relations are present in one instance, and absent or modified in another. For instance, that I own a car does not necessarily mean that I can use it, because I may have hired it out for someone else to use.

This variability of ownership positions forms the crux of Cochrane's challenge to the Traditional View. For once we realise that ownership is not absolute, it is possible to show that at least some of the legal relations that make up ownership of animals are compatible with animals' rights in two respects.

First, we can show that some ownership relations can conceptually co-exist with animals' possession of legal rights. For example, as Cochrane notes in alignment with the Thin Conception, existing animal protection laws already confer a legal right on animals not to be treated cruelly – despite the fact that humans have a right to *use* these animals. The protection laws simply limit the ownership right in a way that imposes duties on humans not to use their animals in a cruel way.

Second, we can demonstrate that the existence of certain ownership relations respects animals' rights from a moral point of view, such as by securing equal consideration of their interests (a notion we discussed in chapter three). For instance, Cochrane argues that the right to *possess* animals – which he defines as the right to exercise physical control over them – need not violate their rights. While possession of wild and autonomous animals like primates would violate the rights of these beings, Cochrane argues that the same does not hold for domesticated animals. This is because, as Cochrane claims, domesticated animals lack an intrinsic interest in not having their liberty curtailed by their owners. Much like human children have a general interest in being under the physical control of their parents, Cochrane suggests, domesticated animals may benefit from being under the control of caring owners. Hence, in contrast to what authors like Francione argue, Cochrane believes that the ownership right to possess domesticated animals is not incompatible with respect for their rights because owning these animals is not the same as owning human slaves.

A similar conclusion is reached by the legal scholar David Favre who has proposed to categorise animals as so-called 'living property' (2010) – a fourth type of property next to personal, real, and intellectual property (eg a bike, a house, and a piece of music, respectively). Like Cochrane, Favre does not see a problem in principle with the fact that animals are possessed and used by their human owners. We simply need to legally limit this ownership to protect the intrinsic interests that animals have as living sentient things.

As Favre points out, by virtue of being living property, animals could possess a variety of legal rights, including rights to be cared for, to have a place to live, not to be used for certain purposes or be harmed, and even a right to own property themselves. To exercise these rights, animals would be afforded legal guardians.

Another recent proponent of the Unorthodox View who shares Cochrane's and Favre's conviction that animals can be owned but still possess certain legal rights is the legal theorist Visa Kurki (2019). According to Kurki, it is a mistake to equate legal persons with legal rights-holders. Adopting the Hohfeldian rights framework, Kurki argues that there are categories of beings that hold legal rights, despite being property. Slaves, for instance, were regarded as legal things, not persons, but still had certain legal rights (think, for example, of the *Code Noir* which we discussed in the previous section). Animals, Kurki believes, are in a similar position today. They, too, have certain legal rights in virtue of being the beneficiaries of correlative duties imposed on humans. Hence, like Cochrane and Favre, Kurki concludes that the binary division between legal persons who hold rights and legal things that do not is not as strict as proponents of the Traditional View believe.

In response to the Traditional View, Kurki has developed what he calls the 'Bundle Theory of legal personhood' (2019: 91). Kurki's Bundle Theory is similar to Honoré's and Cochrane's theories of ownership, but focuses on legal personhood to argue that this concept is best understood as a bundle or cluster of different legal positions that do not always all have to be present. Legal personhood, on this view, is not a binary concept, but one that can come in different degrees and shapes.

Specifically, Kurki distinguishes what he calls 'passive legal personhood' from 'active legal personhood' (2019: 138). The former is made up of 'passive' legal positions which include, among others, fundamental protections of life, liberty, and bodily integrity, the capacity to own property, the immunity from being property, standing, and victim status under criminal law. According to Kurki, having enough of these passive positions is necessary for anyone to count as a legal person. Active legal personhood, by contrast, consists of 'active' positions such as the capacity to exercise other legal positions without the help of a guardian, and the capacity to be held responsible under criminal and tort law. According to Kurki, passive legal personhood best describes the legal situation of human infants and humans with severe cognitive disabilities, whereas active legal personhood best captures that of adult human agents (who in paradigmatic cases also possess passive legal personhood).

Kurki believes his theory to be superior to the Traditional View because, among other reasons, it can make better sense of the legal status of slaves and animals. For example, according to him, the Bundle Theory can accommodate the fact that slaves held legal positions such as rights without however counting as proper legal persons. This is because while slaves had some legal positions that pointed toward legal personhood, they lacked *sufficient* passive legal positions to fully count as legal persons. Among other things, they lacked immunity from being property and protections of their liberty. Animals also lack most passive legal positions. For example, they can be owned and lack fundamental protections of life and, in most cases, of liberty and bodily integrity. As a result, they are not currently full legal persons.

Note that, in contrast to the Traditional View, Kurki's Bundle Theory does not explain the fact that animals lack legal personhood by claiming that animals lack legal rights. Kurki in fact believes that animals already possess legal rights. Instead, his theory explains animals' lack of legal personhood by pointing to the insufficient passive legal positions that animals have to count as legal persons.

C. Evaluating the Traditional and Unorthodox Views

Although Kurki's account is intended to be primarily analytical, it can also be regarded as yielding some practical lessons. One of these lessons is that an overemphasis on legal personhood can take away resources from where some think them more urgently needed: in the struggle for important passive legal positions such as protections of fundamental interests to life, liberty, and bodily integrity. While defenders of the Traditional View may believe such struggles to be inextricably linked with the struggle for legal personhood (and for animals not to be property), opponents of that view regard the obsession with legal personhood as a red herring.

As suggested above, advocates of the Unorthodox View also believe that courts would be more likely to afford stronger legal protections to animals if such decisions were not viewed as revolutionary breaches of legal walls – which judges, conservative by nature, prefer to avoid. The NhRP at the time of writing has lost all its cases – and advocates of the Unorthodox View may be inclined to suggest that this is in no small part due to the exaggeration of the personhood/property binary.

Whether this is correct, however, is an empirical question that is difficult to test. As proponents of the Traditional View could retort, their account may be just as (if not more) likely to be successful in practice. Judges' and other lawyers' adoption of the personhood/property dichotomy could, after all, be based on a centuries-long tradition, rather than on personal preference. As a result, most judges and lawyers may be disinclined to embrace the Unorthodox View, regardless of its potential merits.

Finally, we can ask whether the Traditional and Unorthodox Views are necessarily at odds with each other. While this is not always made explicit, Traditional accounts argue primarily that animals cannot have any *thick rights* without being legal persons, whereas Unorthodox accounts hold primarily that animals can and do have *thin rights* despite being property. It would therefore appear that the two Views are simply different sides of the same coin. To be sure, proponents of the Unorthodox View could defend the stronger claim that animals can also have thick rights while remaining property. However, the question this raises is whether ownership of animals with thick rights still bears any resemblance to the concept of property as we know it, or whether it would become indistinguishable from the animal legal personhood that Traditional accounts are after.

Exercise 4: Traditional and Unorthodox Views of Animal Legal Personhood

1. Do animals require legal personhood to have: (a) thin rights; (b) thick rights?
2. Is the debate between proponents of the Traditional and Unorthodox Views meaningful, or are they simply focusing on different questions, and therefore talking past each other?
3. Is there a practical difference between treating animals as legal persons (as Wise proposes) and treating them as property but with far-reaching legal rights and legal guardians (as Favre proposes)?

V. Conclusion

The guiding question of this chapter has been whether the idea of legal rights for animals is sound from the point of view of legal theory, or whether it is simply 'loose talk'. To answer this question, we have analysed three theoretical debates in animal rights law: whether animals are suitable for legal rights-holdership, whether they already hold legal rights, and whether they require legal personhood for legal rights-holdership. Although views diverge on all these issues, the relevant discussions have revealed plausible reasons for thinking that legal animal rights are indeed a sound legal theoretical concept.

To arrive at this conclusion, the chapter took seriously the insight that legal animal rights are not the same as moral animal rights. While we saw connections between the two, we principally employed legal-theoretical tools rather than philosophical ones to make sense of animals' legal rights. In the subsequent chapters, we will be able to build on the legal-theoretical foundation that this chapter has laid, and will spell out the practical implications of animal rights theory.

Exercise 5: The Legal Theory of Animal Rights

1. 'Rights, personhood, and property are abstractions that are hard to understand, especially for laypeople.' Do you think this is true? If so, how can animal rights proponents make their case to the general public?

2. Imagine you are a judge sitting in a last-instance court and have to decide on whether the fundamental right to liberty that the constitution of your country safeguards should be applied to a zoo elephant. Using the scales, indicate how important the facts listed below would be in inducing you to decide in favour of the elephant.

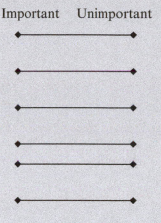

Important   Unimportant

Elephants are protected against cruelty in your country's animal protection act.

Elephants are recognised as legal persons in your country's law of succession.

There is ample scientific evidence that elephants have an interest in liberty.

Elephants cannot reciprocate legal duties.

No country has so far recognised any animals as holders of the right to liberty.

No country has so far recognised any animals as legal persons in all areas of law.

Useful References

Bernet Kempers, E (2022) 'Transition Rather than Revolution: The Gradual Road Towards Animal Legal Personhood through the Legislature' *Transnational Environmental Law* [online view] 1.

Bilchitz, D (2012) 'When Is Animal Suffering "Necessary"?' 27 *Southern African Public Law* 1, available at papers.ssrn.com/sol3/papers.cfm?abstract_id=2319419.

Edmundson, WA (2015) 'Do Animals Need Rights?' 23 *Journal of Political Philosophy* 345.

Feinberg, J (1974) 'The Rights of Animals and Unborn Generations' in W Blackstone (ed), *Philosophy and Environmental Crisis* (Georgia, University of Georgia Press).

Kurki, VAJ (2015) 'Why Things Can Hold Rights: Reconceptualizing the Legal Person', *University of Cambridge Faculty of Law Research Paper No. 7/2015* 1, available at papers.ssrn.com/sol3/papers.cfm?abstract_id=2563683.

Sandler, R (2012) 'Intrinsic Value, Ecology, and Conservation' *Nature*, available at www.nature.com/scitable/knowledge/library/intrinsic-value-ecology-and-conservation-25815400/.

Sztybel, D (2001) 'Animal Rights: Autonomy and Redundancy' 14 *Journal of Agricultural and Environmental Ethics* 259.

5

Animal Rights and Human Rights

I. Introduction

In February 2022, the citizens of the Swiss canton of Basel-Stadt went to the ballot box to decide on a proposal that made international headlines: amending the constitution to extend the rights to life and bodily and mental integrity to non-human primates. The cantonal authorities advised the citizens against adopting this so-called 'primate rights initiative', arguing that '[i]f fundamental rights were also granted to non-human primates, this would blur the line between humans and animals and our fundamental and human rights would be watered down and relativised' (Abstimmungserläuterungen 2021, our translation). The primate rights initiative, which we will study in more detail in chapter seven, raised fundamental questions about the relationship between animal rights and human rights: are they conflicting projects that undermine each other, as the cantonal authorities suggested? Or are they ultimately cut from the same cloth and thus mutually supportive?

This chapter addresses these questions, first, by considering some of the common justifications for the view that only humans should have human rights. Following our definition in chapter four, in this chapter human (and animal) rights means *thick* legal rights, that is, complex legal entitlements that protect the fundamental interests of their holders in a way that is dynamic, privately enforceable, and not easily infringeable. Second, the chapter discusses more harmonious ways of thinking about human and animal rights that animal rights proponents have put forward. Lastly, we address how conflicts arising between human and animal rights could be resolved.

Central Issues

1. With animal rights becoming a more salient topic around the world, the question arises as to the relationship between animal rights and human rights. While some believe that the two are in tension, others argue they are mutually supportive.

2.   Those who believe the two are in tension have resorted to two different approaches to explain that only humans should have human rights: the foundationalist (which builds on empirical features of humans), and the anti-foundationalist (which builds on political practices and decisions).
3.   Animal rights thinkers have rejected such views and have argued that human and animal rights flow from the same source and are mutually supportive projects.
4.   Even if human and animal rights are mutually supportive, conflicts between them can still arise. However, there are legal tools – such as the proportionality test, the prioritisation of minorities' interests, and the Species Membership Approach – that could help resolve such conflicts.

II. Should Only Humans have Human Rights?

The question as to whether non-human animals should have human rights seems to invite an obvious answer: as the name makes clear, *human rights* are rights for *humans*. Hence, anyone who is not human should by definition not have those rights. Although superficially compelling, this answer begs the question: what exactly makes humans special and justifies their exclusive possession of human rights? In other words, what justifies excluding animals from such thick legal rights that are traditionally afforded to human beings? This section sheds light on the answers given to that question by proponents of the two most popular approaches in human rights scholarship and practice: the foundationalist approach, which grounds human rights in features that are characteristic of humans, and the anti-foundationalist approach, which bases human rights on political practices and decisions.

A. Are Human Rights Grounded in Human Properties? The Foundationalist Approach

The first common way of explaining why only humans should have human rights tries to identify specific features in human beings that make humans special and deserving of human rights. This approach is sometimes called *foundationalist* because it tries to explain rights by referring to (or, as it is sometimes put, 'grounding' rights in) empirical characteristics of humans. These characteristics are thus viewed as the foundations, or grounds, of such rights. This approach can be found, for instance, in human rights treaties such as the American Convention on Human Rights:

Preamble – American Convention on Human Rights (1969)

Recognizing that the essential rights of man are not derived from one's being a national of a certain state, but are based upon attributes of the human personality.

It is possible to distinguish between two different foundations – or 'attributes', as the American Convention puts it – that are often offered as the ground for human rights: membership of the human species, and the possession of characteristically human capacities.

Starting with the first one, the view that humans' rights are grounded in their *membership in the species Homo sapiens* is perhaps the most common justifications for human rights. It traces its origins back at least as far as the Enlightenment when rights-holding was widely seen to be intimately connected with the idea of being human. Consider, for example, the French Declaration of the Rights of Man and of the Citizen (1789):

Article 1 – Declaration of the Rights of Man and of the Citizen (1789)

Men are born and remain free and equal in rights. Social distinctions may be founded only upon the general good.

This position has increasingly come under criticism, however. At least since Peter Singer's influential work *Animal Liberation* (1975), the argument that someone deserves a moral or legal right or status simply because of their species membership has become regarded as suspect. The reason for this, as we discussed in chapter three, is that Singer and many others hold that one's belonging to a specific species is an arbitrary ground for distributing rights and other protections. If two beings are alike in their interests but only differ in their species, then why give one more protection than the other? To do so would be to engage in speciesism, similar to how it would be racist or sexist to give someone better protection only because of their ethnicity or sex.

Perhaps partly motivated by this problem of speciesism, some human rights proponents have put human rights on a different foundation: the *possession of characteristically human capacities*. The theories that follow this second approach have been almost as varied as the proposed capacities themselves. Among the suggested candidates for characteristically human capacities are features such as language (Kateb 2014), culture (Rolston 2008), agency (Gewirth 1996), personhood (Griffin 2008), needs (Miller 2012), and rationality (MacDonald 1984). For the purposes of our discussion, we can focus on two of these theories: Griffin's personhood account and Miller's human needs account.

The moral philosopher James Griffin developed a theory that influenced an entire tradition of human rights thinking focused on characteristic human capacities, often referred to as the 'orthodox' or 'naturalistic' human rights tradition (Etinson 2018: 1). According to Griffin, human rights protect something that is characteristic about human beings: their *personhood*. Personhood, on his understanding, is the capacity of autonomy, which he defines as the ability to 'choose one's own path through life – that is, not be dominated or controlled by someone or something else' (Griffin 2008: 33). On this account, the capacity of autonomy needs to be real in the sense that one needs to have a minimum provision of resources to be able to act on one's choices. What is more, others must not be allowed to stop one from pursuing one's conception of the good life – a criterion he refers to as 'liberty'. Importantly, according to Griffin, non-human animals differ from humans in that they lack personhood and therefore human rights:

Human life is different from the life of other animals. We human beings have a conception of ourselves and of our past and future. We reflect and assess. We form pictures of what a good life would be … And we try to realise these pictures. This is what we mean by a distinctively *human* existence … Perhaps Great Apes share more of our nature than we used to think, though we have no evidence that any species but *Homo sapiens* can form and pursue conceptions of a worthwhile life … And we value our status as human beings especially highly, often more highly than even our happiness. This status centres on our being agents – deliberating, assessing, choosing, and acting to make what we see as a good life for ourselves (2008: 32).

Miller, whom we have encountered above, has proposed another capacity on which human rights are based: *human needs*. According to Miller, we can distinguish between social needs that are contingent on the society we live in and universal needs that all humans have. The need to have a broadband Internet connection, for instance, is contingent on living in modern societies, whereas the need to be physically intact is shared by all humans. As he argues, if a person lacks the opportunity to fulfil their universal needs, 'this threatens her ability to lead a decent life, understood in terms of a core set of activities' (Miller 2012: 414). According to Miller, among the most important human needs are: the need to plan and organise one's life securely (giving rise to the rights not to be enslaved, tortured, or arbitrarily arrested), to communicate (justifying the rights to freedom of expression, association, and conscience), and the need for recognition (grounding the rights to legal personhood status, to an effective remedy, and the protection against arbitrary treatment).

Other scholars have followed a similar path as Miller but prefer to talk of 'interests' (Tasioulas 2015), 'well-being' (Talbott 2010), or 'capabilities' (Nussbaum 2006) instead of 'needs'. Regardless of the precise terminology used, foundationalist accounts that focus on characteristic human capacities rather than species membership have an advantage in that they cannot easily be accused of speciesism. However, they run into a different problem: they struggle to explain why *all and only* humans have human rights. For those who, like Nussbaum, support animal rights, this is a welcome conclusion (see chapter three). For others who, like Griffin, try to exclude animals from their accounts, it is not.

To understand this, consider Griffin's criterion of personhood. It is true that many humans are persons in the sense of being able to choose their own path in life. But not *all* humans are persons in this sense: infants are too young to be persons, people who are senile may no longer be persons, and people with severe mental disabilities may never have been persons in the first place. This is what one of us has called the 'problem of underinclusiveness' (Fasel 2018: 474): the problem that the chosen capacity that is supposed to serve as the foundation for human rights may turn out not to include all humans.

But even if a capacity can be identified that all humans have, there is still the inverse problem: the 'problem of overinclusiveness' (Fasel 2018: 474). Take for example Miller's criterion of having needs, which has a better claim than personhood to being possessed by all humans. The issue is that although all humans may have the relevant needs, not *only* humans have them. For instance, the needs to communicate and to lead a secure life are not exclusively human but are also important for many animals. Hence, if the goal is to create a foundation for human rights that excludes all other animals, such inclusive foundations will prove problematic.

The philosophical literature on human rights contains some interesting answers to these challenges. For instance, some have argued that although not all humans are currently persons, they have at least the *potential* of becoming persons (see eg Rawls 1971: 509), the *genetic basis* for moral agency (Liao 2010), or belong to a species whose members *usually* have the relevant features (Foreman 2014: 69). If you are interested in finding out more about these answers – and rejoinders to those answers – you will find additional references at the end of this chapter and on the companion website.

B. Are Human Rights the Outcome of Political Practices and Decisions? The Anti-Foundationalist Approach

As we saw in the previous subsection, deriving human rights from human species membership or characteristic human capacities is a more difficult task than it may seem at first glance. In response to that difficulty, a different approach to explaining human rights has emerged. According to this approach, the reason why humans have human rights should not be sought in their empirical properties, but rather in political decisions and practices that protect human rights. This approach is *anti-foundationalist* in that it avoids grounding rights in empirical foundations. Many different variations of this approach have emerged in the past decades. We can focus here on two particular variations: political and decisionist accounts of human rights.

According to *political accounts* of human rights, human rights are rights that play a key role in the practice of international politics. Take for example the philosopher John Rawls's account. According to Rawls, a state's fulfilment of human rights is 'sufficient to exclude justified and forceful intervention by other peoples, for example, by diplomatic and economic sanctions, or in grave cases by military force' (1999: 80). In other words, human rights describe the limits of what a state is allowed to do; limits that, if overstepped, enable the international community to intervene. For Rawls, then, to understand what human rights are, our focus should not be on moral justifications of the sort we have encountered above. Rather, it should be on studying how human rights create reasons for political action on the international plane. For instance, the right not to be enslaved is a human right, on this theory, not because it is grounded in any human features, but because when states allow slavery to happen on their territory, other states can carry out a humanitarian intervention to stop the human rights violation.

Applied to the question of animal rights, the political approach would seem to yield the conclusion that animal rights cannot count as human rights. The reason for this is that no similar political response is available when animals' interests are being infringed. For instance, when an animal is 'enslaved', the international community could not (and would not) permit interference to stop this. Even the World Organisation for Animal Health (OIE) – the international body tasked with animal health – could not intervene as its mandate is primarily concerned with preventing animal disease and ensuring that animals are safe for human consumption (see OIE 2022).

To be sure, Rawls does not offer the only political human rights account. Other accounts, such as for example Charles Beitz's (2009), focus on a broader range of actors and responses rather than simply international interferences with state sovereignty. Such accounts may be more capable than Rawls's to show that not only humans have rights. However, they still run into the problem that political practice does not respond to animal rights violations in nearly the same way as it does to human rights violations. Even authors such as Alasdair Cochrane and Steven Cooke (2016) – who argue that international interventions to protect animals are justified in principle – find that they are impossible in practice at the moment.

Political accounts are not without their own problems, however. One of the criticisms made against some of these accounts is that they only allow the recognition of a narrow list of rights which does not accommodate many of the rights that are ordinarily regarded as human rights (see eg Buchanan 2006). This is because not all such rights trigger international political responses when violated. Another difficulty is that political accounts give us little indication as to what rights (if any) ought normatively to be protected as human rights if the international practices are not yet in place to do so.

The second anti-foundationalist approach tries to anchor human rights not in political practices but *political decisions*. Arguably the most prominent version of this approach is defended by the political theorist Anne Phillips. Phillips explicitly rejects foundationalist accounts that try to ground human rights in human capacities. Even if such accounts may be well-intentioned, she warns, they create the danger of undermining human rights and people's equal status:

> If we link the entitlement to human rights to characteristics like vulnerability to pain or capacity for conscious planning, the empirical evidence may well lead to the conclusion that some of the great apes qualify for at least some of the so-called human rights. But it may also lead … to the conclusion that some humans who currently qualify – day-old infants who have not yet developed consciousness; those in a coma who have lost it – are not entitled (2015, 40).

To avoid the issue of making human rights and equality contingent on empirical facts, Phillips instead proposes to explain them as entitlements and statuses that we simply *decide* humans – and only humans – should have. As she puts it pithily, '[p]eople assert, rather than prove, their claims to be regarded as human' (2015: 9). Such decisions and assertions, she notes, are most common in response to violations of human rights, when humans have been denied equal status and rights – think for example of the human rights atrocities committed in the Holocaust – and the human rights documents created as a result. In moments of such violations, the boundary between those who have equal status and rights (ie humans) and those who do not (ie all non-humans) becomes blurred. According to Phillips, the only way to prevent this and to 'insulate us from the insidious distinctions still widely made between different kinds of humans' (2015: 132–33) is to draw a clear line between humans and non-humans.

Decisionist accounts like Phillips's are designed to avoid the threats posed by foundationalist accounts, but they are not immune to some other challenges. One problem that decisionist theories face is that they risk being based on arbitrary distinctions that unjustly exclude certain beings. For instance, considering the increasing understanding we have about animals' capacities and their interests in some of the same things (eg life, bodily integrity, family) that are protected by rights in humans, how can decisionists justify excluding them from such rights? If their answer is 'to protect human beings' rights', then the broader question becomes: should we be allowed to sacrifice some for the good of others? As Phillips herself admits, this is a 'somewhat uncomfortable position to arrive at' (2015: 131) because the same logic was – and in certain respects continues to be – applied to exclude marginalised human groups such as indigenous communities, women, or humans with disabilities.

The references at the end of this chapter and the companion website allow you to further explore these challenges.

III. Should Animals have Similar Rights to Humans?

Not convinced by the arguments we explored in the previous section that only human beings should have human rights, some animal rights scholars have recently developed theories proposing that animals ought to have similar rights. This section first presents two of the most prominent such accounts: Paola Cavalieri's and Alasdair Cochrane's. We then consider a challenge that has been raised against accounts like theirs and address it by looking at empirical research that is used to support arguments that human and animal rights are indeed aligned projects.

A. Do Human and Animal Rights Flow from the Same Source?

In her book *The Animal Question: Why Nonhuman Animals Deserve Human Rights* (2001), Paola Cavalieri was one of the first to make the case for what she calls an 'expanded theory of human rights' (2001: 139, emphasis removed). According to Cavalieri, the reason why humans matter morally cannot be their species membership because this would run into the problem of speciesism. Nor do they matter because they are rational or have personhood because that would exclude human beings who lack these capacities. Instead, she proposes, humans matter because they possess *consciousness*. As she defines it, consciousness is the capacity that allows its holders 'to have experiences and to care about these experiences' (2001: 38, emphasis removed). Importantly, because not only humans are conscious in this sense but also many animals, she argues that they too should be included in the moral community.

With this inclusion in the moral community comes the entitlement to certain human rights. Human rights, on Cavalieri's definition, are negative rights held against the state. To enjoy such negative rights, a being simply needs to be alive, have wellbeing, and the ability to live freely. Of course, not only humans but also some non-humans meet these criteria. For this reason, as Cavalieri holds, 'it is the same justificatory argument underlying [the doctrine of human rights] that drives us toward the attribution of human rights to members of species other than our own' (2001: 139). According to her, human rights constitute the 'minimal cohabitation rules' (2001: 125) in society, which should protect not only humans but also animals.

A similar argument was more recently put forward by the political philosopher Alasdair Cochrane. As Cochrane points out, human rights doctrine and practice are not as inclusive as they seem. The reason for this is that they exclude all non-human animals from their protection. In a similar vein as Cavalieri, Cochrane reasons that the only non-arbitrary justification for human rights is *sentience*. According to him, only beings who are sentient have inherent interests in their own wellbeing and therefore matter morally. As we saw in chapter four, Cochrane follows an interest-based approach to rights, which says that all sentient beings with interests that are sufficiently weighty to impose duties on others possess rights to have those interests protected. Because the feature that justifies human rights on this approach – interests and sentience – cannot only be found in humans, Cochrane proposes that we should abandon the term 'human rights' and instead talk of 'sentient rights' (2012: 656). As he puts it, 'the basic rights of sentient humans and non-humans are neither conceptually nor ethically distinct ... they are part of the same normative enterprise' (2012: 656).

Cavalieri and Cochrane are not the only ones to argue that human and animal rights flow from the same source. Other traditions of thinking that have emphasised the interconnection of human and animal rights include the vulnerabilities-based approach (eg Turner 2006), the feminist approach (eg Robinson 2003), the capabilities approach (Nussbaum 2006), and the 'One Rights' approach (Stucki 2022). Regardless of the precise approach taken, however, arguments trying to link animal rights with human rights have come under fire.

One of the chief contemporary critics of the idea of connecting human rights with animal rights is the legal scholar Richard Cupp. In amicus curiae briefs that were discussed by US courts dealing with animal rights cases, Cupp has contended that arguments for extending rights to animals based on their consciousness, sentience, or other abilities puts vulnerable human beings – in particular humans with serious cognitive impairments – at risk (2016: 17; 2022: 26). Focusing on the Nonhuman Rights Project (NhRP)'s efforts to have animals such as chimpanzees and elephants recognised as legal persons, Cupp warns that

> going down the path of connecting individual cognitive abilities to personhood would encourage us as a society to think increasingly about individual cognitive ability when we think about personhood. Over the course of many years, this changed paradigm could gradually erode our enthusiasm for some of the protections provided to humans who would not fare well in a mental capacities analysis (2017: 503).

The worries of Cupp and other sceptics are at least threefold. First, they are concerned that human beings who are not autonomous agents, conscious, or sentient (eg because their brains are damaged) would not have any rights under some of the proposed frameworks. As we saw, their belonging to the human species alone is not seen as sufficient by many. Second, there is the related worry that if empirical capacities such as consciousness or autonomy are taken to determine who has rights and to what extent, then human beings with cognitive impairments get the short end of the stick because they may have those capacities to lesser degrees. The legal scholar Laurence Tribe, who is otherwise supportive of the NhRP's lawsuits, put this point starkly:

> If your theory is that simply being human cannot entitle you to basic rights, although it might be nice if they were given to you, I think you are on an awfully steep and slippery slope that we would do well to avoid. Once we have said that infants and very old people with

advanced Alzheimer's and the comatose have no rights unless we choose to grant them, we must decide about people who are three-quarters of the way to such a condition. I needn't spell it all out, but the possibilities are genocidal and horrific and reminiscent of slavery and of the holocaust (2001: 7).

Finally, there is the practical worry that if animals are recognised as holders of thick rights, then some of the scarce resources currently used to protect human rights will be diverted away to protect animals. One such resource is the availability of courts to litigate rights violations. As Cupp claims, 'extending legal personhood to all animals capable of suffering could open the courts to billions of potential plaintiffs' (2017: 515). The thrust of all these concerns, then, is that animal rights would cause a 'levelling down' (Wills 2020: 203) of human rights.

B. Are Human and Animal Rights Mutually Supportive?

Proponents of animal rights have developed different answers to counter the above-mentioned levelling down concerns. In this subsection, we focus on one response that has gained considerable traction. Far from jeopardising the rights of vulnerable humans, this response goes, animal rights bolster them. Put another way, animal rights and human rights are not mutually exclusive but mutually supportive.

Among the scholars who have developed this response are Will Kymlicka (2018), Joe Wills (2020), and Anne Peters (2021). These scholars have drawn on empirical research in moral psychology and sociology to suggest that excluding animals from rights protection would *harm* rather than benefit marginalised human beings. Three of the empirical concepts that stand out in this respect are Social Dominance Orientation, Dehumanisation, and Moral Expansiveness.

Social Dominance Orientation is a concept that describes people's desire to bring about and maintain inequality and dominance among social groups. Previous studies showed that people with strong Social Dominance Orientation in one context (eg men who are sexist) are more likely to express such views also in other contexts (eg be racist). Recent research has found that this also translates beyond purely human contexts to human-animal relationships. Specifically, studies have found that speciesist attitudes are correlated to discriminatory attitudes toward social out-groups (see eg Dhont et al 2014). This means that people who are speciesist are more likely to also discriminate against vulnerable human beings.

Dehumanisation is the related phenomenon of denying humans their humanness and instead considering them as non-human (more subtle expressions of this are sometimes described as 'infrahumanisation') (Haslam 2006). As the legal scholar Peters notes, 'it is a recurrent feature of intra-human conflict that the rivalling ... groups dehumanise each other by animal names. Nazis called the Jews rats; Europeans and Americans referred to Blacks and Japanese as monkeys; Hutus called Tutsis cockroaches' (2021: 477). For this reason, scholars like Peters argue that emphasising the divide between humans and animals facilitates discrimination of human groups who are sometimes characterised as 'animals' rather than 'humans'. As she cautions: 'Verbal dehumanisations of human groups can prepare the legal and finally the physical exclusion of the "Other" from human society and serves to exculpate crime' (2021: 477).

Finally, *Moral Expansiveness* describes the enlargement of people's moral boundaries, usually measured on a scale reaching from one's family and friends to more remote entities such as plants or villains. Empirical studies have shown that people who extend moral concern to a wider range of entities (eg not only to family and friends but also to stigmatised humans, out-groups, or animals) tend to be more willing to uphold others' rights and to make personal sacrifices for them (eg Crimston et al 2016). In other words, people who defend animal rights are more likely to also defend the rights of marginalised human beings.

According to the above-mentioned authors, research such as this shows that levelling down concerns are misplaced. In fact, not only would promoting animal rights *not* undermine the human rights project, but it would *actively support* it. For example, as the legal scholar Wills argues regarding Moral Expansiveness, 'individuals who highly value chimpanzees, including up to the point of campaigning for their legal personhood, are more, rather than less, likely to have moral concern for cognitively disabled human beings, suggesting precisely the opposite of Cupp's fears' (Wills 2020: 218–19). Or take Social Dominance Orientation: advocating a speciesist position that excludes animals from right-holdership might increase rather than decrease discrimination against people with cognitive disabilities and other vulnerable human beings. And the same may hold true for fears about Dehumanisation. Protecting the rights of animals, it turns out, may strengthen safeguards against the dehumanisation of vulnerable humans. As Peters observes:

> the malign force of … 'dehumanisation' cannot be mitigated by entrenching and deepening the human/animal divide but rather by upgrading non-human animals. For example, when humans become accultured to more respect and appreciation of pigs and rats, calling others by those names loses some of its depreciating and tension-fuelling power (2021: 477).

Exercise 1: Applying the Foundations of Human and Animal Rights

1. Consider the following human beings: Astrid (a new-born baby); Petro (who suffers from anencephaly, meaning that major parts of his brain are missing); Yana (a 35-year-old mother); and Bai (who suffers from late-stage dementia). Drawing on what you have learned in the previous sections, use the check boxes to indicate whether these humans would possess human rights based on the listed criteria. Then ask yourself whether these criteria are good explanations for human rights.

	Astrid	Petro	Yana	Bai
Personhood	☐	☐	☐	☐
Rationality	☐	☐	☐	☐
Language	☐	☐	☐	☐

Culture	☐	☐	☐	☐
Sentience	☐	☐	☐	☐
Homo sapiens	☐	☐	☐	☐
Protected through international human rights law	☐	☐	☐	☐

2.   Now consider whether Tim (an adult chimpanzee), Fuad (a calf), Orla (an octopus), and Kora (a bee) would qualify for rights on these criteria. Do your own research to find out more about the capacities that are typical for their species.

	Tim	Fuad	Orla	Kora
Personhood	☐	☐	☐	☐
Rationality	☐	☐	☐	☐
Language	☐	☐	☐	☐
Culture	☐	☐	☐	☐
Sentience	☐	☐	☐	☐
Homo sapiens	☐	☐	☐	☐
Protected through international human rights law	☐	☐	☐	☐

3.   'Human and animal rights are a zero-sum game. By promoting the rights of one, we diminish the rights of the other.' Write a 500-word essay discussing this statement.

IV. How Could Human and Animal Rights be Reconciled Legally?

The previous two sections have analysed the conflicting views of those who argue that human rights should belong only to human beings, and those who argue that we should understand human and animal rights as being mutually supportive projects that are conceptually cut from the same cloth. This latter view is becoming more and more accepted, but even under it, human rights and animal rights do not always align. In this section, we consider some of the potential tensions that could arise if animal and human rights co-existed in a given legal system, and the tools that the law offers to resolve them. We begin by considering rights conflicts and discuss the proportionality test that is generally employed to address them. Second, we consider proposals to prioritise human minorities' interests in cases of conflicts, before addressing the Species Membership Approach for extending rights and other protections to animals.

A. Rights Conflicts and the Proportionality Test

On approaches such as Cavalieri's and Cochrane's, it may appear at first glance that human and animal rights are in perfect harmony with each other. After all, human and animal rights are both said to arise from the same source: consciousness or sentience. Hence, some scholars (eg Colb 2018) have proposed that protecting human rights and promoting animal rights should not be seen as a zero-sum game. However, there is an obvious way in which rights are not always in perfect harmony: rights can and do conflict. In fact, such conflicts could be an inevitable side-effect of animal rights: the very purpose of granting animals rights to bodily autonomy, integrity, and life, for instance, is to limit humans' right to property in these animals. This conflict can only arise once we recognise that animals have countervailing rights.

However, such conflicts need not necessarily be seen as something undesirable or uncommon. In fact, conflicts occur regularly in human rights law. Take, for instance, a journalist's right to free speech and a celebrity's right to privacy. The journalist in principle has the right to take photographs and print information about the celebrity, but if this is done too intrusively then the celebrity's right to privacy is infringed and the two rights conflict. Because such conflicts are common, the law has developed ways of resolving them.

In most legal systems, the way the law resolves such conflicts is by employing a so-called *proportionality test*. Some animal rights scholars (eg Bilchitz 2016, 141) have proposed that this test could also apply to conflicts between human and animal rights. To understand the proportionality test, it is helpful to start with the key assumption on which it is based, namely that most rights are not 'absolute', but rather 'relative' or 'qualified' (concepts we already encountered in chapter four). What does this mean? Absolute rights are rights that are inviolable, that is, they cannot legitimately be limited or infringed, whatever the circumstances. For example, even in situations of war, one's right not to be tortured cannot be limited. By contrast, relative or qualified rights are rights that can be limited if there are sufficiently weighty countervailing interests. For instance, the above-mentioned celebrity's right to privacy is a relative right because it can justifiably be limited if, for example, the journalist's interest in printing a story about the celebrity is considered more important and/or if there is large public interest in the story. Importantly, just because a right can be justifiably limited or qualified in a given situation does not mean that the right ceases to matter. Rather, courts will try to minimise limitations of the right to the greatest extent possible, and the right may win out against other rights in future conflicts. Most human rights are considered relative rights, and so would likely most animal rights.

How does the proportionality test resolve conflicts between relative rights, exactly? While not all courts operate with the same version of the proportionality test, many adopt a three-pronged test according to which limitations of a right must: (1) be a suitable means to promoting a legitimate aim (suitability); (2) not exceed what is necessary to achieve that aim (necessity); and (3) be more important than the interest they limit (balancing). In cases where one right conflicts with another right (rather than with the action or policy of a public authority), balancing is the relevant prong, so let us consider it in more detail.

Balancing – sometimes also called proportionality in the narrow sense – describes the process of weighing the competing interests in a rights conflict. The image that is often used in this context is that of scales. In one pan, we have the right of the first party (eg the journalist), in the other pan the right of the second party (eg the celebrity). The question then becomes: which side weighs more and should therefore win out in the balancing exercise? There is some disagreement as to how best to assess the weight of the conflicting rights, but one prominent approach is that of Aharon Barak, a former President of the Supreme Court of Israel and a proportionality scholar. According to Barak, the weight is determined, first, by the '*social importance*' (2012: 745, emphasis added) of the benefit of realising the purpose of protecting one right compared to the social importance of avoiding a limitation of the countervailing right. The social importance of a right is determined by a society's social and cultural history, as well as by the role the right plays among other rights. For instance, human dignity plays a key social and cultural role in South Africa given its apartheid history, and it is seen as the foundation of other rights. Second, in determining the weight of a right it is also important to consider the *severity of the limitation*; that is, it has to be determined whether the right is only marginally affected or whether its core is touched. For example, if the celebrity is photographed on their front porch, their right to privacy is likely only marginally affected, whereas if they are involuntarily placed in a 'Big Brother'-type setting, the core of the right may be affected.

Let us now consider an example to see what this means for conflicts between animal and human rights. Imagine that Louis, a scientist, would like to exercise his right to engage in scientific inquiry by testing the strength of family bonds in bonobos. To do so, he proposes to separate Therese, a mother bonobo, from her one-month-old child, Joseph for two months, to see how they both respond to the separation. Applying the balancing test, we would have to weigh the respective social importance of Louis's right to scientific inquiry and Therese and Joseph's right to family life, as well as consider the severity of the limitation of the rights. The outcome of this balancing exercise would ultimately depend on the facts of the given case. However, it seems plausible to say that, in this example, Louis's right to scientific inquiry, despite its important social role, is less important than the right to family life of a mother and her young child. Furthermore, Louis's right would only be marginally affected because he could still conduct less invasive experiments such as observational research. For these reasons, assuming that a court would take seriously Therese and Joseph's right to family life as a thick right, their right would win out in the proportionality test. It would, as this is sometimes put, 'outweigh' Louis's countervailing right, and the state would have to make sure that Louis does not infringe Therese and Joseph's rights.

B. Prioritising the Rights of Minorities?

The availability of the proportionality test and of balancing in particular can be seen as reassuring: where conflicts between animal rights and human rights arise, the law already has a tried and tested method of resolving conflicts. However, some scholars have taken issue with the idea of applying the proportionality test to such conflicts because it could, in their view, lead to human minorities' interests being outweighed by animals' interests. In fact, some argue, minorities' interests could be outweighed even while majorities would continue to use animals, giving rise to the concern that majorities are using animal rights (or animal welfare) as an excuse to dominate minorities.

Consider the example of ritual slaughter. Certain religious groups, such as Jewish and Muslim communities, have rituals surrounding the slaughter of animals. For some, it is a requirement that animals must not be stunned before their throat is cut with a sharp knife and their blood is drained. As we have seen in chapter one, while numerous countries provide exemptions to religious groups and only mandate stunning for non-religious slaughter, several European countries have banned non-stun slaughter. The concern that has been raised in these countries – and other countries where similar efforts are under way – is that such bans protect animals' interests not because of a genuine concern for animals, but because of prejudices against minority groups. For instance, as Peters puts it,

> There is a real risk that the protection of animals targets minority practices (such as Muslim ritual slaughter or indigenous seal and whale hunting), although these practices are in numerical terms insignificant in comparison to the majority's 'normal' massive use and killing of animals. This targeting manifests and fuels majority prejudices against the singled out groups, and can pave the way for intervention and domination (2018, 358).

To avoid majorities applying a double standard at the expense of minorities, some scholars have proposed that minorities' interests should be prioritised. For instance, the political scientist Alison Dundes Renteln has argued that a 'principle of maximum accommodation' (2004: 112) should be applied in such contexts. This entails that there would be a presumption in favour of the religious groups and that exemptions would have to be granted for practices such as ritual slaughter in order to ensure that minorities' religious claims are taken seriously. More recently, the legal scholar Iddo Porat has coined the term 'starting at home principle' for a similar proposal: 'members of a minority (a minority in terms of power relations) have a right not to be subjected to more stringent moral criteria than the majority is willing to subject itself to' (2021: 32). Porat draws on animal rights scholarship and undercover investigations to argue that animal suffering is greater in majority practices like the industrialised raising and killing of animals for non-religious food, where slaughter also often happens without proper stunning. As he points out, '[c]oncentrating campaigns against religious minority practices rather than against majority practices that result in much greater harm and pain to a greater number of animals is an indication of majority-based bias and the targeting of minorities' (2021: 48). According to Porat, only once a majority is willing to consistently apply and enforce the same protections to all animals – regardless of whether they are used by a minority or majority – will it be permissible to ban practices such as non-stun slaughter.

Proposals such as Renteln's and Porat's could help ease potential tensions between human and animal rights in at least two ways. First, they can incentivise animal rights scholars to focus on numerically more harmful majority practices such as the raising and killing of animals for non-religious food where there is less danger of fuelling prejudices and domination. Second, they can serve as a legal tool to resolve conflicts in favour of minority groups when such conflicts arise.

However, these proposals are not devoid of problems either. Consider again Porat's argument that one should start with majorities, not minorities – categories which he defines in terms of power relations. Interestingly, he does not consider that animals can also be categorised as a minority in these terms. This raises a critical question: why should one prioritise religious groups' interests over those of another group that is oppressed not because of its religion but its species? The political scientist Claire Jean Kim has put this issue powerfully when asking:

> Why should disadvantage along one dimension (race/culture) translate into relative immunity along another (… species)? This only makes sense if one assumes without argument that the dimension of race/culture is so much more important than the others that we must refrain from critique about … species for fear of aggravating racial/cultural marginalisation (2015: 196).

Kim rejects proposals such as the above-mentioned ones, arguing that 'minorities' disadvantages do not earn them *a place at the end of the reform queue*' (2015: 195–96). Instead, she proposes the adoption of a 'multi-optic vision'. This vision rejects automatic presumptions in favour of certain groups and instead requires that judgments are made in a way that is 'informed intellectually and affectively by the experiences of others' (2015: 198) – regardless of whether they are dominated based on religious, ethnic, sex, species, or other grounds. Only in adopting such a vision, she suggests, can one put an end to the oppression of minorities by majorities.

C. The Species Membership Approach

The last proposal we consider is one that is not aimed at addressing rights conflicts per se, but at the question as to how rights and other protections can be extended to animals in the first place without undermining the legal status of marginalised human beings. The proposal is the so-called Species Membership Approach (SMA), which one of the authors of this textbook has developed (Fasel 2019). The SMA is the view that, in law, fundamental rights (and similar legal protections and statuses such as personhood and dignity) should be extended to deserving animals based on *species membership*, not individual sentience or interests.

The idea of extending rights and other protections on the basis of an animal's species may appear unorthodox because it would seem to go against the widespread rejection of using species membership as a criterion for deciding who matters. As we saw in chapter three, Singer has popularised the term speciesism to describe views that discriminate against animals based on their species. However, the SMA does not in fact reject this philosophical critique of speciesism. Instead, it focuses purely on the legal domain and argues that, while speciesism may need to be rejected when deciding on animals' *moral* rights, that does not necessarily mean that the law should avoid operating with species-based criteria when distributing *legal* rights. Fasel provides two reasons to support this view.

First, there are *pragmatic reasons* for extending rights and other protections based on species. As Fasel points out, the SMA helps overcome the problem of judges' lack of expertise in zoological matters that makes it difficult for them to decide whether a particular animal before them possesses the relevant interests required to have a certain right. In addition, the SMA helps judges decide cases more efficiently because it saves them from having to spend time studying the characteristics of the animal before them, and instead allows them to rely on the more widely available general studies about the species of the relevant animal. Further, the SMA serves as a precautionary principle, allowing judges to err on the safe side and assume that the animal before them has the relevant characteristics of 'normal' adult members of its species. This avoids the risk of withholding rights from animals, such as for example animals with mental disabilities, who may have the relevant characteristics to a lesser degree or lack them altogether.

Second, Fasel argues that there are *political reasons* why the SMA is preferable to the dominant animal rights approach that distributes rights based on the capacities of individual animals. Fasel refers to this as the 'Meritocratic' approach because it justifies individuals' rights based on their possession of relevant capacities. For example, if an individual has the ability to anticipate the future, it is seen by some as 'deserving' the right to life. If it lacks that interest, it does not 'deserve' the right. The problem with this individualistic approach, Fasel contends, is that it runs the risk of denying certain rights to vulnerable humans who are seen as lacking the relevant capacities that ground these rights. This would go against the egalitarian commitment to indivisibility of human rights – that is, the idea that all human beings have an equal legal status and the same human rights – which underpins human rights law. The SMA avoids this problem because – heeding Phillips's call which we discussed above – it does not make rights-holdership contingent on individuals' empirical capacities. Rather, to have rights, one only has to be born into a species whose rights are recognised. This is the dominant approach to human rights, which Fasel calls the 'Aristocratic' approach. As he contends, the SMA is politically desirable not only because it manages to preserve humans' equal status and rights in this Aristocratic way. It is also desirable because it is simultaneously able to explain why rights and other protections should be extended to other deserving animal species, as Meritocratic animal rights accounts require. The SMA can do that because, in contrast to prevailing human rights approaches, it does not hold that only the *human* species matters for holding rights. *Non-human* species whose members possess relevant interests for holding rights should also be granted these rights.

If correct, Fasel's proposal would for example entail that legislative strategies to extend rights to animals may be preferable to certain litigation-based strategies insofar as statutes can confer rights on whole species (or groups of species) of animals. By contrast, animal rights litigation that focuses on individual animals' rights and their corresponding interests, could be seen as being more problematic, as highlighted by the above-discussed critique of Cupp. To decide which species should receive which rights, Fasel proposes that lawmakers should take into account both whether a species possesses the relevant capacities for particular rights ('merit'), and whether extending rights to that species is politically and practically feasible ('feasibility'). The stronger the merit and feasibility for extending rights to a particular species, the stronger the case for applying the SMA to it. For example, Great Ape species would rank high on this scale because their capacities make them deserving of numerous rights and because many cultures do not have significant cultural or economic interests in them, thus making it more feasible to extend rights to them (we return to the strengths and weaknesses of the SMA in chapter eight).

V. Conclusion

Would human rights be 'watered down and relativised' if animals were granted thick rights, as the authorities of the canton of Basel-Stadt claimed in response to the primate rights initiative? As this chapter has shown, answering this question is more complex than what the authorities suggest. While there are human rights scholars who would support the authorities' claim by arguing that only human beings can or should have human rights, there is also an increasing number of animal (and human) rights theorists who emphasise the commonalities between human and animal rights. Far from relativising human rights, these thinkers argue that protecting animal rights can help bolster human rights and lead to a less oppressive approach to rights protection more generally that also benefits vulnerable human beings. Finally, the chapter addressed legal tools that can help resolve or alleviate conflicts that could arise between animal and human rights. Tools such as the proportionality test, the prioritisation of minority interests, and the Species Membership Approach – although limited in their own ways – help show that the feared relativisation of human rights is less problematic than often believed.

Equipped with this insight, in the next chapter we can turn to the cases that animal rights lawyers have brought to achieve animal rights through litigation, and then in chapter seven consider animal rights legislation that has been proposed on the domestic and international level.

Exercise 2: Animal Rights and Human Rights

1. '[T]he essential rights of man are not derived from one's being a national of a certain state, but are based upon attributes of the human personality'. Critically assess this statement from the Preamble of the American Convention on Human Rights by drawing on what you learned in section one.
2. In groups or alone, discuss how the law should approach minority practices such as ritual slaughter or seal hunting, which involve harm to animals? What counterarguments could be made against your view, and how would you address them?
3. Assume you initiated *habeas corpus* proceedings on behalf of a chimpanzee. How do you convince the Court that granting fundamental rights to non-human primates is not going to water down or relativise human rights? Write a brief of 500 words.

Useful References

Fasel, R (2019) 'The Old "New" Dignitarianism' 25 *Res Publica* 531.

Glock, JH (2012) 'The Anthropological Difference: What Can Philosophers Do to Identify the Differences Between Human and Non-Human Animals?' 70 *Royal Institute of Philosophy Supplements* 105, 127–28.

Nickel, J (2021) 'Human Rights', in E Zalta (ed), *The Stanford Encyclopedia of Philosophy*, available at https://plato.stanford.edu/archives/fall2021/entries/rights-human/.

Stucki, S and Sparks, T (2020) 'The Elephant in the (Court)Room: Interdependence of Human and Animal Rights in the Anthropocene', EJIL Talk, available at www.ejiltalk.org/the-elephant-in-the-courtroom-interdependence-of-human-and-animal-rights-in-the-anthropocene/.

The Nonhuman Rights Project (2022) Response to Amicus Curiae Brief of Richard L. Cupp, Jr., 6 May, available at www.nonhumanrights.org/content/uploads/NhRP-Response-to-Cupp-CoA-Happy.pdf.

Valentini, L (2011) 'In What Sense Are Human Rights Political? A Preliminary Exploration' 60 *Political Studies* 1, 180–94.

Waldron, J (2018) 'Human Rights: A Critique of the Raz/Rawls Approach', in A Etinson (ed), *Human Rights: Moral or Political?* (Oxford, Oxford University Press) 117–38.

Wills, J (2020) 'The Legal Regulation of Non-stun Slaughter: Balancing Religious Freedom, Non-discrimination and Animal Welfare' 41 *Liverpool Law Review* 145.

6

Animal Rights in Litigation

I. Introduction

Since the turn of the millennium, courts around the world have been witnessing a new phenomenon: cases that are being brought on behalf of animals to argue that existing laws designed for the protection of humans could be extended to provide protection for some non-human animals.

In this chapter, we discuss the most important cases (so far) that domestic courts from both common law and civil law legal systems have had to decide on. Our focus will mostly be on litigation in which lawyers have attempted to claim thick rights for animals – ie rights which are akin to those held by humans, like the rights to life and to liberty. In many of these cases, the claim for thick rights was closely intertwined with a claim for legal personhood for animals. The principal animal rights cases that have been brought so far can be considered in three groups, and the chapter will discuss them in this order:

(a) cases where the primary issue is whether the (animal) applicant is able to bring a case at all, that is, whether the applicant has legal standing;
(b) cases where the court is asked to issue a writ of *habeas corpus* on behalf of an animal; and
(c) cases where the court considered whether animals have constitutional or other fundamental rights that go beyond *habeas corpus*.

Although interesting in their own right, we will not concentrate on cases that deal solely with animal protection laws. As chapter four has shown, views differ as to whether such laws give rights to animals. While we will encounter some cases that involve animal protection claims, we will focus on cases that more explicitly deal with animals' thick rights and legal personhood. As we will see, much of the animal rights litigation so far has been unsuccessful in the courts. However, in recent years there have been some important breakthroughs, with an increasing number of courts being willing to decide in favour of animals, and extend some thick rights to them. With the exception of section four which follows a thematic order, the following sections discuss these court cases in chronological order.

Central Issues

1. Across the world, lawyers have attempted to use existing laws to secure thick legal rights for animals through litigation. Such cases are often brought on behalf of individual animals who, the lawyers argue, share relevant qualities with humans.
2. A critical hurdle in many animal rights cases is the issue of legal standing: the requirement that a claimant must be a person with sufficient interest in the case. Animals would have sufficient interest but are generally not considered persons, whereas humans who try to bring cases on their behalf are persons but are generally not considered to have sufficient interest.
3. To avoid the issue of standing, some lawyers are bringing *habeas corpus* claims on behalf of animals. This is a medieval common-law instrument that challenges unlawful detention of persons, and has relaxed standing requirements.
4. Finally, there are cases concerning the extension of fundamental rights that go beyond *habeas corpus*. These cases have dealt with animals' rights to life, to bodily and mental integrity, to liberty, and to food, as well as legal personhood.

II. Animals and the Issue of Legal Standing to Bring an Action

In most legal systems, cases can generally only be brought to a court by an applicant with legal standing, that is, with a sufficient interest in the issue or the outcome. This is the case, for example, when applicants have personally been affected by an activity (eg injured or damaged) or when they will directly stand to benefit from a successful outcome of the case. In cases involving animals, the problem is that legal standing is difficult to obtain. This is because, with the exception of owners, animals are often the only victims.

Assume, for instance, that your neighbour beats his dog. In most legal systems, courts would not hear a case brought by you because your interests are not directly affected (you are not the one who is beaten, after all). As the dog's owner, your neighbour would have standing but, of course, would be unlikely to turn himself in. If state agencies do not bring a case, then there is no one that can legally help the dog. The concrete legal consequence of failing to show standing is that the court will reject the case without addressing the substance of it. Hence, in our example, the court would dismiss the case without discussing whether your neighbour actually treated his dog cruelly. Let us consider some of the main cases that illustrate the problem of obtaining legal standing for animals.

A. Cetacean Community (2003)

'Cetacean Community' was the name adopted by a US lawyer claiming to act for the world's whales, porpoises, and dolphins. The lawyer argued that the US Navy was damaging the animals' hearing and health by using sub-sea sonar and was therefore in breach of various US animal protection laws, including the Endangered Species Act (ESA; 1973), which aims to protect endangered species from extinction. The action brought by the lawyer was for several injunctions, which would require the Navy to stop using the sonar and mandate the government to prepare an environmental impact statement to assess possible harm to the animals.

However, the issue arose whether whales, porpoises, and dolphins could bring a legal action in the first place – that is, whether they had standing. The US District Court of the District of Hawaii dismissed the case in 2003. It held that, in this situation, the relevant statutes would only give 'persons' standing, which it argued excludes non-human animals (US District Court, District of Hawaii 2003, 1210).

On appeal, the US Court of Appeals (Ninth Circuit) (2004) upheld the District Court's dismissal of standing for the animals as well as for the 'Cetacean Community'. Like the District Court, it found that, despite statements it had made in an earlier decision, non-human animals cannot bring suit under the ESA:

> It is obvious both from the scheme of the statute [the ESA], as well as from the statute's explicit definitions of its terms, that animals are the protected rather than the protectors ... Animals are not authorized to sue in their own names to protect themselves. There is no hint in the definition of 'person' in §1532(13) [ESA] that the 'person' authorized to bring suit to protect an endangered or threatened species can be an animal that is itself endangered or threatened (US Court of Appeals, Ninth Circuit 2004: 1177–78).

However, the Court suggested that Article 3 of the US Constitution (which empowers courts to hear cases under federal law) does not in principle exclude the possibility of granting standing to animals. But it would be for US Congress (ie the national parliament) to take that step in its legislation, and it has not done so in this instance:

> If Congress and the President intended to take the extraordinary step of authorizing animals as well as people and legal entities to sue, they could, and should, have said so plainly (2004, 1179).

B. Hiasl (2007)

The chimpanzee Matthias 'Hiasl' Pan, who lived in Austria, has had a complicated life, passing through many hands and becoming the subject of numerous court cases to determine his legal status and his future. In 2006, when there was a risk that Hiasl would lose his home in an animal shelter in Vienna, a donor offered to support the costs of his maintenance by making a donation to the President of the *Verein gegen Tierfabriken* (Association Against Animal Factories, VGT) – a local animal rights association – on condition that a legal guardian was appointed for Hiasl. This resulted in a series of rulings concerning whether Hiasl could be treated as a person in the Austrian courts.

The President of VGT brought a case before the Mödling District Court in Lower Austria, arguing that Hiasl was a person under the Austrian Civil Code (1811) and that he should be appointed a legal guardian. The applicants supported their claim with expert evidence showing that both the sentience and genetics of Hiasl are similar to humans. It was reported that:

> Hiasl passed a mirror self-recognition test, he showed tool use and understanding, played with human caretakers, watched TV and drew pictures … This is supported by scientific findings on the cognitive abilities of chimpanzees in general. There is practically no quality or ability traditionally considered typically human that chimpanzees do not possess (Balluch and Theuer 2007: 338).

However, the District Court dismissed the case in 2007, finding that Hiasl did not fulfil the legal requirements for legal guardianship as he was neither mentally disabled nor under imminent threat. When attempting to appeal the decision, the applicants were turned down several times on the grounds that they lacked standing. The provincial court of Wiener Neustadt justified its dismissal of an appeal in 2007 with a catch-22 argument: only a legal guardian or the ward could appeal against the decision which refused to grant Hiasl a legal guardian and therefore the status of ward. As a result, the substantive question of personhood was not considered by the court. Two final appeals to the European Court of Human Rights (*Balluch v Austria* and *Stibbe v Austria* 2010) were both rejected, among other reasons because Hiasl did not legally qualify as a victim who is personally affected by a violation of a right protected by the European Convention on Human Rights.

C. Tilikum, Katina, Corky, Kasatka, and Ulises (2012)

Tilikum, Katina, Corky, Kasatka, and Ulises were five orcas who were kept in Sea World theme parks in Florida and California in conditions that – according to a legal action brought by the animal rights organisation PETA (People for the Ethical Treatment of Animals) – were unsuitable for wild animals. PETA filed its lawsuit as the orcas' 'Next Friends' – a procedural device that allows someone to bring a claim on someone else's behalf. PETA's argument was that the orcas were being kept in breach of the Thirteenth Amendment of the US Constitution, which was passed in 1865 after the American Civil War and prohibits slavery and involuntary servitude (see chapter eight).

The US District Court for the Southern District of California found in 2012 that only the Thirteenth Amendment itself could serve as a possible basis for standing for the five orcas, whom it recognised as the 'plaintiffs' in this case. It also held that PETA as Next Friends would only have standing if the orcas were covered by the Thirteenth Amendment. Hence, the Court needed (exceptionally) to deal with the substantive question as to whether an Amendment passed to prohibit human slavery and servitude could extend its protection to non-human animals.

The argument of the plaintiffs' Next Friends was that the word 'slavery' in the Thirteenth Amendment has, like many other constitutional words and principles, evolved over time and therefore could evolve – dynamically – to include animals. The Court resisted the argument, and dismissed the case, deciding that the words originally used were specifically meant to cover human slavery and therefore could not have an extended meaning:

> As 'slavery' and 'involuntary servitude' are uniquely human activities, as those terms have been historically and contemporaneously applied, there is simply no basis to construe the Thirteenth Amendment as applying to non-humans (US District Court, Southern District of California 2012, 1263).

D. Naruto (2016)

Naruto is a Macaque monkey living in a reserve in Indonesia who became well-known when he picked up nature photographer David Slater's camera and took pictures of himself – including the now-famous 'monkey selfies'. One question that immediately arose was: who owns the copyright of these selfies: Naruto? Slater? Or no one?

The website Wikimedia Commons took the third view. In 2011, it published the photos online, arguing that they were in the 'public domain' (ie not protected by copyright) because Naruto, as an animal, could not have the copyright, and that there was also no human owner in whom copyright could be placed.

PETA's 2015 lawsuit adopted the view that Naruto should be recognised as the owner of the photos and that Slater and his company – who had been selling the photos in a book – had infringed Naruto's copyright. As the holder of the copyright, PETA argued, Naruto, his family, and his community in the reserve should benefit from the proceeds of the photos (which would be distributed by PETA).

This lawsuit was unlike other animal rights cases insofar as it did not focus on saving an animal from captivity or protecting it from cruel treatment. Rather, the suit raised a different rights question: can animals have the right to property, in this case intellectual property? However, the case did have in common with many other animal rights cases that it turned – and failed – on the issue of legal standing.

In the ensuing hearing, PETA tried to appear as 'Next Friends' to bring a suit on Naruto's behalf (who was recognised as 'plaintiff'). In the first instance, the case was considered by the US District Court of the Northern District of California in 2016. The judge followed the arguments in *Cetacean Community*, according to which the relevant statutes could not be interpreted to grant standing to animals. It found that neither Naruto nor PETA had standing because US copyright law does not protect photographs produced by animals.

Upon appeal by PETA, the US Court of Appeals for the Ninth Circuit came to a similar conclusion in 2018. The Court first explored PETA's 'Next Friends' status and found that it failed to satisfy one of the criteria for being a Next Friend: it lacked 'some significant relationship with, and [being] truly dedicated to the best interests of, the petitioner [Naruto]' (US Court of Appeals, Ninth Circuit 2018: 7). Employing a cynical tone, the Court even went as far as to speculate in a footnote that 'PETA seems to employ Naruto as an unwitting pawn in its ideological goals' (2018: 8). The Court then confirmed the District Court's decision that Naruto lacks standing because US copyright law does not allow animals to file copyright suits.

Exercise 1: Legal Standing

1. If you could appeal on behalf of the animals in any of the cases described above, which case would you choose in order to have the greatest chances of success?
2. Is it a good strategy to pursue litigation requiring that animals are recognised as 'persons' with standing? What are the advantages and disadvantages of this approach?
3. 'Animals such as Tilikum are held in conditions of slavery and should therefore benefit from protection under the Thirteenth Amendment'. Write an essay of 500 words explaining whether you agree or disagree with this statement. You may find useful to reflect in your answer on the discussions in chapters two and eight.

III. Animals as Subjects of *Habeas Corpus*

As the previous section illustrates, standing rules have been a thorn in the side of animal rights lawyers. This is because the individuals directly affected – the animals – cannot bring legal actions themselves and the humans trying to act on their behalf have generally been unsuccessful in convincing courts that they have an interest in the matter.

In recent years, an alternative litigation strategy which tries to avoid the standing problem has emerged in numerous legal systems: the filing of petitions for so-called writs of *habeas corpus* (a Latin phrase meaning, roughly, 'deliver the body' (to court)). *Habeas corpus* has a long history, emerging in England in its recognisable form by the fifteenth century. Today, it is used predominantly in common law legal systems. However, as we will see, it is also available in some civil law legal systems.

In essence, *habeas corpus* makes it possible to bring to the attention of a court the unlawful imprisonment or captivity of another person, and to petition the court to bring that person before court to verify the legality of his or her detention – and to order release if the detention is unlawful. Standing requirements are naturally relaxed in *habeas corpus* cases because the relevant person is detained and therefore assumed to be restricted in their ability to petition a court. To make up for this, *habeas corpus* allows third parties to bring a petition on the detained person's behalf.

Traditionally, the detained 'person' under *habeas corpus* proceedings has been a human being. However, not all human beings were always included. For instance, slaves were notoriously excluded until the celebrated *Somerset v Stewart* decision in England in 1772 (see chapter eight). Steven Wise, an animal rights attorney from the US, has used this historic evolution (from some to all humans) to argue that the protection of *habeas corpus* should be extended further, to some captive animals. Although *habeas corpus* petitions on behalf of animals were filed as early as 1972 in Brazil, Wise's arguments and the litigation strategies of the Nonhuman Rights Project (NhRP) have been particularly influential in raising the profile of *habeas corpus* as a litigation strategy for animals. In tandem with independent efforts by lawyers in other countries, *habeas corpus* petitions have since been brought in Argentina, Brazil, Colombia, Ecuador, and the US, and are being planned in other countries.

A. Tommy and Kiko (2013)

The first animal for whom the NhRP filed a *habeas corpus* petition was the chimpanzee Tommy, who lives in a cage in New York and is owned by Patrick Lavery. There was no evidence that existing animal protection laws had been broken, so the conditions in which Tommy was kept were not challenged by the NhRP. Instead, in a petition which it brought in 2013 to the New York State Supreme Court in Fulton County (a first-instance court, despite its name), it demanded recognition that Tommy is a legal person with a fundamental right to bodily liberty and should be released from captivity. The question for the Court was whether a writ of *habeas corpus* could be issued for a chimpanzee or was only available to human beings.

Although the NhRP was granted a hearing to make its case for Tommy, the Court denied the *habeas corpus* petition in 2013, arguing that *habeas corpus* protection in New York does not extend to chimpanzees. The NhRP appealed this decision to the next court in the judicial hierarchy: the Appellate Division of the New York Supreme Court (Third Department). In 2014, that Court issued a ruling that, as we will see, would set an important precedent. They rejected the NhRP's appeal, thereby denying that Tommy can be a legal person entitled to the protections afforded by *habeas corpus*. To support its ruling, the Court emphasised that there is no precedent in state law or common law to support the view that an animal could be considered a 'person' for the purposes of *habeas corpus*: 'Not surprisingly, animals have never been considered persons for the purposes of habeas corpus relief, nor have they been explicitly considered as persons' (Appellate Division, New York Supreme Court 2014: 3). Although the Court acknowledged that the way *habeas corpus* has been interpreted has changed significantly over time, it argued that it would be erroneous to apply it to chimpanzees. The Court's reason was that

> the ascription of rights has historically been connected with the imposition of societal obligations and duties. Reciprocity between rights and responsibilities stems from principles of social contract ... Under this view, society extends rights in exchange for an express or implied agreement from its members to submit to social responsibilities (2014: 4).

In other words, the Court claimed that the right to bodily liberty which derives from *habeas corpus* can only be held by beings who can bear societal responsibilities (see also chapter three). On that view, there can be no rights without duties. Realising the potential difficulties this argument could create for certain human beings, such as infants or humans with severe mental disabilities, the Court hastened to add the following footnote:

> To be sure, some humans are less able to bear legal duties or responsibilities than others. These differences do not alter our analysis, as it is undeniable that, collectively, human beings possess the unique ability to bear legal responsibility. Accordingly, nothing in this decision should be read as limiting the rights of human beings in the context of habeas corpus proceedings or otherwise (2014: 5, footnote 3).

As we saw in chapter four, the argument that rights and duties are correlative has become a matter of scholarly controversy, with several legal scholars and recently also a consortium of seventeen philosophers (Andrews et al 2019) critiquing it.

The NhRP sought to appeal this decision as well as a similar decision that the Appellate Division of the New York Supreme Court (Fourth Department) had reached in the case of *Kiko* (2015) – another chimpanzee held in New York for whom the NhRP had also been pursuing a *habeas corpus* petition. Despite repeated attempts, the NhRP request was denied by the New York Court of Appeals (the state's highest court) in 2018 without further explanation. However, one of the judges – Judge Eugene Fahey – added an opinion to the decision in which he expressed considerable sympathy for the NhRP's lawsuits. Despite having to turn the case down on procedural grounds, Fahey emphasised that this does not mean that the NhRP's arguments are without merit. Specifically, he suggested that the Appellate Division's views about the correlativity of rights and duties are questionable:

> Even if it is correct, however, that nonhuman animals cannot bear duties, the same is true of human infants or comatose human adults, yet no one would suppose that it is improper to seek a writ of habeas corpus on behalf of one's infant child … The Appellate Division's conclusion that a chimpanzee cannot be considered a 'person' and is not entitled to habeas relief is in fact based on nothing more than the premise that a chimpanzee is not a member of the human species (New York Court of Appeals 2018: 3).

The judge also reflected on the inherent difficulty that animals and their legal advocates face because they are not considered 'persons' who can bring legal actions to remedy rights violations:

> The reliance on a paradigm that determines entitlement to a court decision based on whether the party is considered a 'person' or relegated to the category of a 'thing' amounts to a refusal to confront a manifest injustice (2018: 6).

For these reasons, Fahey noted, the Court has left open a question that

> will have to be addressed eventually. Can a non-human animal be entitled to release from confinement through the writ of habeas corpus? Should such a being be treated as a person or as property, in essence a thing? (2018: 2)

B. Hercules and Leo (2013)

Another early *habeas corpus* case brought by the NhRP was on behalf of Hercules and Leo – two chimpanzees who were kept at the State University of New York at Stony Brook. As in the *Tommy* and *Kiko* cases, the essence of the NhRP petition to the

New York State Supreme Court in Suffolk County (2013) was that Hercules and Leo should be recognised as legal persons for the purposes of *habeas corpus*.

To make its case, the NhRP submitted numerous affidavits from primatologists confirming that chimpanzees have, among other things,

> such complex cognitive abilities as autonomy, self-determination, self-consciousness, awareness of the past, anticipation of the future and the ability to make choices; display complex emotions such as empathy; and construct diverse cultures (Wise and Stein 2013: 2)

After the New York State Supreme Court in Suffolk County and the Supreme Court's Appellate Division dismissed the petition, the NhRP filed Hercules and Leo's case in the New York Supreme Court in New York County. In a world first, this Court ordered a hearing in 2015 to determine the lawfulness of the chimpanzees' captivity. A few months after the hearing, the judge – Judge Barbara Jaffe – issued a ruling that denied the petition on the ground that her Court was bound by the precedent of the Appellate Division of the New York Supreme Court (Third Department) in the *Tommy* case, which we discussed above. Nevertheless, Judge Jaffe showed openness to the idea of *habeas corpus* protection for animals.

For example, she offered a retort to the 'floodgates' argument that often arises in animal rights and personhood cases, according to which elevating animals' legal status could lead to a flood of litigation on behalf of other similarly placed animals. As the judge pointed out, if the law recognises a remedy then it has to be applied, regardless of the burdens this imposes. Judge Jaffe then ended her ruling on a hopeful note that reflected on the role of courts in bringing about legal change:

> The similarities between chimpanzees and humans inspire the empathy felt for a beloved pet. Efforts to extend legal rights to chimpanzees are thus understandable; some day they may even succeed. Courts, however, are slow to embrace change, and occasionally seem reluctant to engage in broader, more inclusive interpretations of the law, if only to the modest extent of affording them greater consideration (New York Supreme Court, New York County 2015: 32).

C. Cecilia (2016)

While the NhRP's lawsuits on behalf of chimpanzees have not been very fortunate in the US, the legal strategy of filing *habeas corpus* petitions for these animals was successfully employed in a different legal system: Argentina.

Despite being a civil law system, Argentina allows for *habeas corpus* actions, which have been pursued by Pablo Buompadre, the President of the *Asociación de Funcionarios y Abogados por los Derechos de los Animales* (Association of Officials and Lawyers for Animal Rights; AFADA) and the attorney Santiago Rauek. In 2015, Buompadre filed a petition which was heard by the Third Court of Guarantees in Mendoza (2016) on behalf of Cecilia, a chimpanzee kept at the local zoo who had lived in solitude ever since her two companions died. Arguing that Cecilia was practically treated as a slave and deprived of her freedom of movement, Buompadre petitioned the Court to recognise Cecilia as a legal person for the purpose of *habeas corpus* and to transfer her to the Chimpanzee Sanctuary of Sorocaba in Brazil.

In the Court's ground-breaking 2016 ruling, Judge María Alejandra Mauricio dismissed the state attorney's arguments that only humans can be entitled to *habeas corpus* and that Buompadre lacks standing. The first judge to ever do so, she granted AFADA's *habeas corpus* petition, declared that Cecilia is a 'non-human legal person', and ordered her transfer to the Sorocaba Sanctuary.

To support her decision, Judge Mauricio drew on a range of different arguments. One prominent rationale was her view that protecting Cecilia's interests is not simply a matter of individual rights, but also serves a collective good. Specifically, the Judge invoked the right to a healthy and balanced environment, which is enshrined in Article 41 of the Argentinian Constitution (1853) and has a collective component. As she argued, this right must be understood broadly to encompass the preservation of natural and cultural patrimony. Cecilia's interests are not only covered by this right, she suggested, but their protection is connected to the collective good more generally:

> the collective good and value is embodied in the wellbeing of Cecilia, a member of the 'community' of individuals of our zoo. This [is] because Cecilia is part of the natural patrimony … but also her relation with the human community – in my opinion – makes her part of the cultural patrimony of the community (Judicial Branch of Mendoza, Third Court of Guarantees 2016: 14).

Despite this constitutional obligation to protect Cecilia, the Judge found that her wellbeing had not been catered for sufficiently, and turned to what she called '*el gran interrogante*' (the great question) (2016: 22): Can a great ape like Cecilia be considered a non-human legal person and granted *habeas corpus* protection?

Drawing on sources ranging from expert evidence on animal sentience, Argentinian legal doctrine, the philosophies of Jeremy Bentham and Peter Singer, and deep ecology, Judge Mauricio presented a spirited argument in favour of declaring Cecilia a non-human legal person with certain fundamental legal rights such as the right to liberty as well as the 'right to be born, to live, grow and die in the proper environment for their species' (2016: 27).

Judge Mauricio also addressed how Cecilia's status as a non-human legal person could be regarded as compatible with Argentinian law, which – like all other legal systems – considers animals to be ownable things. The Judge was clear that 'classify[ing] animals as things is not a correct standard' (2016: 23) and pointed to different instances in which the law governing animals in Argentina already goes beyond treating them as simple property. One example she gives is that animals already benefit from anti-cruelty laws. The Judge did not spell out her conclusion explicitly, but suggested that Cecilia's non-human legal personhood is compatible with existing law. Her argument appeared to be either that animals' current status as (more than simple) property can be reconciled with some personhood rights, or that the law does not stand in the way of allowing some animals to shed their property status entirely.

Another point that is not entirely resolved in the judgment is whether 'non-human legal personhood' is different from human legal personhood. The ruling seems to suggest that it is, creating a special category of personhood, similar to what the animal rights scholar Saskia Stucki has called 'animal person' (*tierliche Person*) (Stucki 2016: 305; see also Pietrzykowski 2017). This is in line with the fact that Judge Mauricio stressed that granting legal personhood to Cecilia would not mean treating her like a human being:

> we are not stating that sentient beings – animals – are the same as human beings, and we are not raising to a human category all existent animals or flora and fauna, we are recognizing and confirming that primates are non-human legal persons and they possess fundamental rights that should be studied and listed by state authorities, a task that exceeds the jurisdictional scope (Judicial Branch of Mendoza, Third Court of Guarantees 2016: 26).

In 2017, a few months after the Court's order to grant *habeas corpus* had been issued, Cecilia was moved to the sanctuary in Sorocaba where she now lives. Her transfer to the sanctuary was, in fact, also supported by an agreement reached between AFADA and the zoo during one of the hearings. This contributed to the success of the case as it helped pre-empt a potential appeal against the ruling.

D. Chucho (2017)

Shortly after the Third Court of Guarantees in Mendoza had handed down its landmark decision in the *Cecilia* case, a similar judgment was issued in Colombia – which too is a civil law system – concerning the Andean bear Chucho. However, the judgment was overturned shortly thereafter. What happened?

In 2017, the lawyer and law professor Luis Domingo Gómez Maldonado petitioned the Superior Court of the Judicial District of Manizales, Civil Cassation Chamber, to issue a writ of *habeas corpus* for Chucho, who had been kept in the Barranquilla City Zoo. Invoking Judge Mauricio's decision, Gómez Maldonado argued that Chucho should be released from his captivity and moved to the La Planada Nature Reserve, where he was born. Located in the Andes, Gómez Maldonado argued, the Reserve provides a habitat that is more suited to Chucho's species needs than the hot and humid climate of coastal Barranquilla. When the Court rejected the petition in 2017 – among other reasons because it held that *habeas corpus* was not available to animals as they are not the subjects of rights – Gómez Maldonado appealed the decision to the Supreme Court, Civil Cassation Chamber.

This Court granted the appeal in 2017, ruling that Chucho has *habeas corpus* protection, and ordering that he should be moved to a more suitable habitat such as the Río Blanco Nature Reserve where he had lived before being transferred to the Barranquilla Zoo. After the *Cecilia* decision, this was the second decision to extend *habeas corpus* to an animal and therefore a historic success for animal rights litigants.

The reasoning presented by Judge Luis Armando Tolosa Villabona was no less striking than that in the *Cecilia* case. The judgment started with an exploration not only of the legal landscape relating to animals but also of the different philosophical traditions of thinking about humans and other animals. What emerged from this discussion was the Judge's view that the disregard of the interests of animals like Chucho must be seen in the broader context of an 'unwholesome' human-focused worldview that ought to be replaced with an 'ecocentric-anthropic' one: a way of seeing the world in which humans recognise that they are also 'living, animal beings' (Colombian Supreme

Court 2017: 4–6) who have the responsibility to guard rather than the right to exploit the environment on which they themselves depend for their survival.

The judge's legal approach was to effectively reverse the question, not asking 'Why?' it ought to grant *habeas corpus*, but 'Why not?':

> our current legal framework deems as subjects of rights the immense category of legal persons: commercial societies, associations, public collectives, entities that are acknowledged with a juridical personhood and procedural safeguards in virtue of their being inanimate realities. So what precludes us from acknowledging the other truly living sentient 'animated' realities with a juridical personhood, going beyond the traditional conception of nature as an object that humans have a duty to preserve? (2017: 6).

To develop the legal argument that animals can be legal persons, Judge Tolosa pointed to the fact that Article 655 of the Colombian Civil Code (1887) – which regulates movable property – had been amended through Law 1774 from 2016. Taking a similar step to dereifying animals other countries have done (see chapter one), Law 1774 changed animals' status from simple property to explicitly granting 'the quality of sentient beings to animals'. The Law also strengthened animal welfare protection in numerous other regards.

Interestingly, in contrast to other courts discussed in this chapter, the Judge did not invoke the capacity for autonomy as a prerequisite for granting *habeas corpus* protection. Instead, he suggested that sentience is sufficient:

> Since nonhuman animals are sentient beings capable of suffering, they must be holders of rights, and the law protects them. Therefore, nonhuman animals are entitled to freedom, to live a natural life, to prosper with the least possible pain and to lead a life with the standards that suit their status and condition, but essentially in a responsibly preserved habitat in the biotic chain (2017: 14).

Although Judge Tolosa did not mention the Appellate Division of the New York Supreme Court's *Tommy* jurisprudence by name, his judgment took aim at its argument that animals could only hold rights if they could also bear social responsibilities:

> we must relax the principle that holds that such a thing [a holder of rights] is reciprocally bound to comply with a set of duties; and we must accept from now on that nonhuman sentient subjects are subjects of rights despite not being reciprocally constrained by duties. Animals are right-holders that are free of duties, entities that cannot be burdened by obligations because they are sentient subjects of rights of whom we, precisely, are guardians, representatives and informal agents in charge of their care (2017: 8).

Like Judge Mauricio in the *Cecilia* case, Judge Tolosa also emphasised that granting rights to animals does not mean granting them the same rights as humans, but rather rights appropriate to their needs according to their species:

> The point is not to grant them rights in every respect analogous to those that human beings enjoy, and therefore think that bulls, parrots, dogs or trees, etc., will have their own courts, their own fairs and festivities, their own Olympic Games or colleges; nor that the other elements of nature must bear the same prerogatives or guarantees that human beings possess, but rather those which correspond to, or are fitting to or suit their species, rank and group (2017: 7).

In contrast to the *Cecilia* case, however, Chucho's *habeas corpus* writ became the subject of fatal legal challenges. In 2017, the Supreme Court of Justice, Labour Cassation Chamber, and the Criminal Court of the Superior Court of Justice granted a constitutional action by the Barranquilla Zoo which argued that its rights to due process and to defence had been violated by Judge Tolosa's decision. As a result, the *habeas corpus* writ for Chucho was declared null and void.

In a decision from 2020, the Colombian Constitutional Court confirmed the over-ruling of Chucho's *habeas corpus* writ. The Court's reasoning was that *habeas corpus* is 'linked to the defense of freedom of human beings' and is therefore an 'inappropriate mechanism' (Constitutional Court of Colombia 2020: 2) for the protection of non-human animals. The Court instead treated Chucho's case as an animal welfare matter and pointed to other legal actions that are available in Colombia to protect animals as part of the environment, rather than as individuals with their own interests.

However, two of the judges – Judges Diana Fajardo Rivera and Alberto Rojas Ríos – added dissenting opinions. Judge Fajardo Rivera held that Chucho has 'the right to animal freedom, to be understood as those conditions that allow him to express his vital patterns of behavior in [the] best way possible' (Constitutional Court of Colombia 2020: 4), adding that *habeas corpus* would have been appropriate in his case. Judge Rojas Ríos argued that legal personhood is not a biological concept but a legal fiction that is not limited to human beings, and could also be applied to sentient animals.

E. Beulah, Karen, and Minnie (2017)

Beulah, Karen, and Minnie were three elephants born in the wild but kept in the Commerford Zoo in the US state of Connecticut. In 2017, the NhRP applied for *habeas corpus* to enable Beulah, Karen, and Minnie to be moved to a sanctuary. To make its case, the NhRP again submitted numerous affidavits, including from pachyderm experts that gave evidence of the elephants' diverse abilities, including their capacity for autonomy.

The first Court to deal with the petition – the Connecticut Superior Court in Litchfield County – dismissed it in 2017. Interestingly, in contrast to the numerous other judges that had so far dealt with the NhRP's petitions, Judge James Bentivegna found that the NhRP *lacked* legal standing to bring its petition because it had failed to establish that it possesses a relationship with the elephants – an issue that also arose in the Naruto case, as we saw above. The judge went as far as to find that the petition was 'frivolous' (Superior Court, District of Litchfield 2017: 9) because there was no precedent or other authority showing that elephants could be legal persons.

In 2019, the Appellate Court of Connecticut dismissed the NhRP's appeal against Judge Bentivegna's decision, arguing that the elephants lacked standing because they are property under Connecticut law rather than legal persons. As it saw the elephants' legal standing to be tied with that of the NhRP, the Court also denied the NhRP standing. Putting another nail in the coffin, the Appellate Court went on to agree with the Appellate Division's ruling in the *Tommy* case, finding that 'it is inescapable that an elephant, or any nonhuman animal for that matter, is incapable of bearing duties and social responsibilities required by ... social compact' (Appellate Court of Connecticut 2019: 846).

The case continued – although only in respect of Minnie, as Beulah and Karen had since died. The Connecticut Supreme Court (the state's highest court) declined to hear the NhRP's appeal against the Appellate Court's decision in 2019, but that latter Court agreed to consider another filing by the NhRP – only to again deny *habeas corpus* relief to Minnie in 2020. After the Connecticut Supreme Court had refused to hear Minnie's case for a second time, the NhRP decided to discontinue its litigation efforts in Connecticut.

F. Happy (2018)

However, this was not the end of the NhRP's *habeas corpus* petitions on behalf of elephants. In 2018, it filed a petition for Happy, an elephant who lives in the Bronx Zoo in New York in a one-acre enclosure and, after the death of her companion Grumpy, without any other elephants for company.

Again, the Appellate Division's *Tommy* case would come to haunt the NhRP. After Happy's case unsuccessfully made its way through the lower courts, Judge Alison Tuitt of the New York State Supreme Court of Bronx County (2020) decided that 'regrettably' she was bound by the *Tommy* decision and could therefore not issue a writ of *habeas corpus*. Still, the judge showed considerable support, saying that

> This Court is extremely sympathetic to Happy's plight and the NhRP's mission on her behalf. It recognizes that Happy is an extraordinary animal with complex cognitive abilities ... akin to human beings ... The Court agrees that Happy is more than just a legal thing, or property. She is an intelligent autonomous being who should be treated with respect and dignity, and who may be entitled to liberty (New York State Supreme Court, Bronx County 2020: 16).

A further appeal to the Appellate Division of the Supreme Court of New York (First Department) was rejected (2020), with the Court reiterating its earlier point that 'decisions of whether and how to integrate other species into legal constructs designed for humans is a matter "better suited to the legislative process"' (Appellate Division, New York State Supreme Court 2020: 3).

The NhRP's appeal of that decision before the Court of Appeals – New York's highest court – was unsuccessful. In 2022, that Court ruled in a 5-2 decision that Happy is not a legal person and that the NhRP's *habeas corpus* petition on her behalf must therefore be dismissed. Largely ignoring the arguments that pro-animal rights amici curiae had presented in their briefs, Chief Judge Janet DiFiore's majority opinion followed well-trodden ground. It claimed that *habeas corpus* relief is meant to protect the liberty of human persons and therefore cannot apply to Happy; it noted that no other court in the country has extended *habeas corpus* to animals; it voiced concern about the 'odious comparison' (New York Court of Appeals 2022: 10) between animals and women, children, and enslaved persons; it argued that Happy would simply be moved 'from one confinement to another of slightly different form' (2022: 10); it contended that animals do not have 'the capacity to accept social responsibilities and legal duties' that are 'associated with legal personhood' (2022: 10–11); it invoked the slippery slope that granting *habeas corpus* to Happy 'would have an enormous destabilizing impact on modern society' (2022: 11); and it held that a decision with such an impact would have to be made by the legislature, not the courts.

The Court of Appeal's decision was accompanied by two powerful dissenting opinions by Judge Rowan Wilson and Judge Jenny Rivera. Judge Wilson began his 70-pages dissent by recounting the story of Ota Benga, a member of the Mbuti people who in the early twentieth century had also been put on display in the Bronx Zoo, and who had in common with Happy that 'both suffered greatly from confinement that, though not in violation of any statutory law, produced little or no social benefit' (New York Court of Appeals 2022: Wilson J, 3). Wilson carefully rebutted each of the majority's arguments, summarising his findings as follows:

> Even were Happy chattel – which she is not – the writ [of *habeas corpus*] may be used to address confinement of living beings deemed chattel. The fact that Happy is an animal does not prevent the law from granting rights to her. That positive law already provides Happy some rights does not restrain the writ. That positive law says the Zoo has control over Happy does not restrain the writ. That Happy cannot be released, but seeks transfer to a more suitable custodial situation, does not render the writ unavailable. That Happy would be the first animal able to test confinement by a writ of habeas corpus in our country does not render the writ unavailable. Allowing Happy to proceed by habeas corpus would not destabilize modern society; it would not even guarantee Happy's transfer, would not entitle any other elephant's release or transfer, and would not entitle any other type of animal to proceed by habeas corpus (2022: Wilson J, 69).

Regarding one of the majority's most central points – that Happy cannot bear social responsibilities – Judge Wilson noted that many animals, including dogs, dolphins, and elephants, are able to discharge social responsibilities. However, even if they were not, Wilson argued, it would not follow that they cannot benefit from *habeas corpus* protection. Correctly applying Wesley Hohfeld's theory (discussed in chapter four), Wilson held that rights can be (and have been) granted to animals without requiring them to reciprocate any duties. As he also noted, humans who lack the ability to reciprocate responsibilities nevertheless have rights. Hence, in line with Nussbaum (see chapter three) he pointed out that the majority 'confuses who can confer rights with who can hold rights' (2022: Wilson J, 12).

Judge Wilson furthermore developed a powerful rebuttal of the majority's arguments that the consequences of granting *habeas corpus* relief to Happy would have an 'enormously destabilising' impact on society, and that it is for the legislature to decide on questions of such significance. In response, Wilson pointed out that *habeas corpus* can by its nature only protect individual beings on whose behalf relief is sought; it cannot declare invalid legal rules, let alone legal institutions enabling oppression. Drawing on the famous *Somerset v Stewart* decision (discussed above and in chapter eight), Wilson observed that it did not destabilise society, nor lead to a flood of lawsuits. In fact, the year after that decision, 'only two enslaved persons received freedom during habeas corpus proceedings – and through settlement agreements, not through merits decisions' (2022: Wilson J, 66). What is more, because *habeas corpus* can only be granted to autonomous beings, the Judge maintained that it would not automatically free all other animals. Rather, courts would have to determine on a case-by-case basis which animals would qualify by balancing the different interests in play (see on balancing also chapter five). Dismissing the majority's argument that this does not fall within the purview of judges and would create a 'morass of confusing case-by-case inquiries' (2022: 14), he maintained: 'I do take issue with the idea that case-by-case determinations of competing rights and interests is a "morass" – it is the bread and butter of what courts do' (2022: Wilson J, 64).

Judge Rivera echoed many of Judge Wilson's arguments. Taking up the point about comparisons between humans and animals, she emphasised that

> As both Judge Wilson and I have made abundantly clear, no one is equating enslaved human beings or women or people with cognitive disabilities with elephants. Rather, we merely highlight a historical truth: Even when those classes of human beings have, by operation of law, been denied legal recognition of their humanity, the writ of habeas corpus was still available to them. The majority ignores this history, preferring instead the comforting incoherence of its circular logic: Humans have 'the right to liberty … because they are humans with certain fundamental liberty rights' (New York Court of Appeals 2022: Rivera J, 9–10).

'Day in and day out, Happy is anything but happy', Judge Rivera found, continuing: 'There lies the rub – Happy is an autonomous, if not physically free, being. The law has a mechanism to challenge this inherently harmful confinement, and Happy should not be denied the opportunity to pursue and obtain appropriate relief by writ of habeas corpus' (2022: Rivera J, 3).

Exercise 2: *Habeas Corpus* for Animals

1. In addition to relaxed standing requirements, what are the benefits of pursuing *habeas corpus*?
2. Looking at the judgments discussed in this section, what have proven to be barriers to successful *habeas corpus* claims on behalf of animals? Which of these barriers are more easily surmountable and which are less so?
3. What (if any) purpose does it serve if judges express regret at not being able to grant *habeas corpus* for an animal?
4. With fellow students or alone, imagine that you are animal rights lawyers who would like to file a *habeas corpus* petition to free a dolphin from a zoo in your country. Using the boxes below, indicate the order of the steps you would need to take before bringing the petition (filling in '1' for the first step, '2' for the second, etc).

You check whether *habeas corpus* is an available instrument in your legal system. ☐

You determine which zoo has dolphins in need of being freed. ☐

You investigate whether there is legislation in your legal system pertaining to *habeas corpus* for animals. ☐

You solicit expert statements from dolphin specialists. ☐

You check how courts in your legal system have decided other *habeas corpus* petitions (especially those relating to animals). ☐

You find out which judges might be most receptive to your petitions. ☐

You check whether there have been other decisions in other legal systems on *habeas corpus* for animals. ☐

IV. Fundamental Rights and Personhood Litigation Beyond *Habeas Corpus*

Seeking *habeas corpus* writs for animals has not been the only litigation strategy adopted to extend thick rights protection to non-human animals. In some countries, especially those where *habeas corpus* is not available, other legal actions have been brought to have animals recognised as holders of rights such as the right to life, to bodily and mental integrity, to liberty, and to food. In other cases, the focus was put on legal personhood or subjecthood for animals. And in some instances, courts discussed animals' thick rights or legal personhood even though they were dealing with more simple claims about violations of animal protection laws.

These cases are regarded as promising by some because they overcome some of the shortcomings thought to characterise the *habeas corpus* approach. For instance, *habeas corpus* litigation has been criticised (eg by Deckha 2018) for focusing on too narrow a group of animals – usually animals with mental capacities that look similar to those of human beings – and thereby risking making it more difficult for other animals to gain fundamental rights protection.

As we will see in the discussion below, courts are not always careful with the terminology or concepts they use when discussing animals' rights. Specifically, it is often unclear whether they use the term 'rights' to mean thin rights (corresponding to anti-cruelty or animal welfare duties imposed on humans) or thick rights (more similar to human rights) – a distinction we discussed in chapter four. For some, it is therefore important to exercise caution when reading judgments that may appear ground-breaking based on the language they employ, but are in reality run-of-the-mill animal welfare or cruelty cases. For others, judicial statements about animals' rights should be taken at face value, and can be accorded high significance.

Let us start by considering the key cases that have considered animals' rights to life, integrity, liberty, or food. We then address cases that focus more explicitly on legal personhood. The cases discussed here follow a thematic rather than chronological order.

A. Animal Welfare Board of India v Nagaraja (2014)

Already in 1997, the Bombay High Court had stated in *People for Animals v The State of Goa* (1997) that "[i]t cannot be disputed that all animals are born with an equal claim for life without any cruelty to them" (1997: 2). However, it was in the Indian Supreme Court's decision in *Animal Welfare Board of India v Nagaraja* from 2014 that animals' right to life figured most prominently.

This case dealt with the so-called *jallikattu* races, which we encountered in chapter one. As a reminder, these are events that involve the chasing and pulling down of bulls, and often result in harm or even death to the animals. Because of an action brought by the Animal Welfare Board of India – a public advisory body created pursuant to the Prevention of Cruelty to Animals Act 1960 – the Indian Supreme Court was asked to determine whether these races were in breach of that Act.

After considering the nature of bulls and the ways they are treated in *jallikattu* races, the Court found that these types of events violate the welfare and anti-cruelty norms enshrined in the Prevention of Cruelty to Animals Act (1960). Interestingly, however, the Court relied not only on that Act in its expansive argument but also invoked Article 21 of the Indian Constitution (1950), which states: 'No person shall be deprived of his life or personal liberty except according to procedure established by law'. The Court suggested that 'life' should be interpreted in a broad sense here and should not only include human life:

> Every species has a right to life and security, subject to the law of the land, which includes depriving its life, out of human necessity. Article 21 of the Constitution, while safeguarding the rights of humans, protects life and the word 'life' has been given an expanded definition and any disturbance from the basic environment which includes all forms of life, including animal life, which are necessary for human life, fall within the meaning of Article 21 of the Constitution. So far as animals are concerned, in our view, 'life' means something more than mere survival or existence or instrumental value for human-beings, but to lead a life with some intrinsic worth, honour and dignity (Indian Supreme Court 2014, para 62).

Importantly, however, the right to life that the Court attributes to animals appears different from – and weaker than – the fundamental right to life of humans. This is due, first, to the Court's qualification that animals can be deprived of their lives 'out of human necessity' and, second, to its comment that:

> When we look at the rights of animals from the national and international perspective, what emerges is that every species has an inherent right to live and shall be protected by law, subject to the exception provided out of necessity (2014, para 51).

As we saw in chapter four, many scholars think that animals currently have only 'thin' rights, if they have rights at all. In any event, and notwithstanding the striking language in this case, animals lack a right to life that is akin to humans' right to life. It remains to be seen whether the Indian Supreme Court will clarify its view on the nature of animals' right to life in future cases.

B. Kaavan (2020)

Another recent ruling that discussed the question of animals' right to life is *Islamabad Wildlife Management Board v Metropolitan Corporation Islamabad*, decided by the Islamabad High Court in Pakistan in 2020. The case concerned numerous animals who were reported to have been kept in poor conditions in the Marghazar Zoo in Islamabad. Among them was the elephant called Kaavan. An application was submitted to the Islamabad High Court for Kaavan and the other animals to be moved to sanctuaries. The Court's Chief Justice, Athar Minallah, based his decision on a specific question: 'Do animals have rights? Is there a duty on the part of the State and the human species to protect the wellbeing and welfare of the animal species?' (Islamabad High Court 2020: 30).

Perhaps partly due to the fact that Pakistan's Prevention of Cruelty to Animals Act – which dates from 1890 – is out of step with modern animal welfare laws in other countries, the Court drew on various sources of inspiration to answer the question: cases from other legal systems (including many discussed in this chapter), the non-binding Universal Declaration of Animal Rights (UDAR), as well as the injunctions of Islam and other religions:

> The emphasis and importance of 'life' and the protection of living beings cannot be over-stated in every religion and faith. Be it Islam, Judaism, Christianity, Buddhism, Hinduism or any other religion, there is no dispute that 'life' is the most precious and superior creation of the Creator. There is consensus amongst all religions of the world that animals are 'sentient beings' i.e. able to perceive and feel (2020: 47).

The Court noted that animals are not simple property and that, in the *Nagaraja* case discussed above, the Indian Supreme Court had extended the right to life under Article 21 of the Indian Constitution to animals. It also pointed out that

> animals also have natural rights which ought to be recognized. It is a right of each animal, a living being, to live in an environment that meets the latter's behavioral, social and physi-ological needs … It is also a natural right of every animal to be respected because it is a living being, possessing the precious gift of 'life' (2020: 60).

Despite this, the Court did not bring itself to explicitly recognise a right to life for animals. Perhaps to make up for this, it argued that the cruel treatment of animals violates the right to life of *humans*:

> The welfare, wellbeing and survival of the animal species is the foundational principle for the survival of the human race on this planet. Without the wildlife species there will be no human life on this planet. It is, therefore, obvious that neglect of the welfare and wellbeing of the animal species, or any treatment of an animal that subjects it to unnecessary pain or suffering, has implications for the right of life of humans guaranteed under Article 9 of the Constitution (2020: 56).

Nevertheless, the Court found that the answer to the question whether animals 'have legal rights' is 'without any hesitation … in the affirmative' (2020: 59), and it ordered that 'the pain and suffering of Kaavan must come to an end by relocating him to an appropriate elephant sanctuary, in or outside the country' (2020: 62). It also ordered the relocation of the other zoo animals. This result is interesting considering that the Court had stopped short of saying that animals have thick rights, and that no *habeas corpus* petition had been filed.

C. The Swiss Primate Rights Case (2019)

Not only a thick right to life but also thick rights to bodily and mental integrity were the subject of a 2020 decision by the Swiss Federal Supreme Court. The Supreme Court had received an appeal against a ruling by the Constitutional Court of the Canton (ie state) of Basel-Stadt from 2019. The Cantonal Court had validated a citizens' initiative (the so-called 'primate rights initiative') that demanded constitutional rights to life, bodily and mental integrity for all non-human primates. In a remarkable ruling, the Cantonal Court argued among other things that the cantons have the power to 'expand the circle of rights-holders beyond the anthropological barrier' (2019, para 3.7.3) and it proposed that fundamental rights for primates could be enforced by legal representatives.

The Swiss Federal Supreme Court was asked to decide whether the initiative was in compliance with federal Swiss law and should therefore be validated. In its decision, the Supreme Court agreed with the Cantonal Court that the initiative was valid, at least if its application was limited to public bodies rather than private individuals or corporations. The Court thereby gave the green light for a popular vote on the initiative in the Canton (discussed in chapter seven). Even though it did not directly have to rule on the question whether non-human primates should have fundamental rights – but instead on whether the people are allowed to vote on the initiative – its decision nevertheless yielded interesting insights for animal rights law.

For example, the Court did not even engage with the argument that animals cannot hold fundamental rights because they are not human, which, as we saw, other courts considered important. As we saw in chapter four, the Supreme Court specifically dismissed the view according to which animals cannot hold fundamental rights because they are not legal subjects of private law – that is, subjects capable of holding rights *and* bearing duties.

Nonetheless, the Court seemed to add a caveat, emphasising that one of the reasons why the initiative does not violate federal law is that it does not purport to extend human rights to animals, and therefore does not question 'the fundamental distinction between rights of animals and human rights' (Swiss Federal Supreme Court 2020, para 8.2).

D. Estrellita (2022)

Estrellita was a chorongo (woolly) monkey who had been living at the home of Ana Beatriz Burbano Proaño in the city of Ambato in Ecuador for over 18 years. After an anonymous complaint, the Ministry of Environment investigated the case and found that Ms Burbano Proaño kept Estrellita – who belonged to a species of wild fauna which is classified as endangered and vulnerable in Ecuador – without official permit.

In September 2019, the Ministry of Environment, together with other authorities, went to Ms Burbano Proaño's home and seized Estrellita. The authorities then placed Estrellita in the San Martín Eco Zoo for medical observation where, only one month later, she died of cardiac arrest. Not having been informed about Estrellita's death, Ms Burbano Proaño, in December 2019, filed a petition of *habeas corpus*, arguing that Estrellita is suffering in the Zoo and should be moved back to her house.

In February 2020, the Multicompetent Judicial Unit of Baños dismissed Ms Burbano Proaño's petition. Her appeal before the Specialized Criminal, Military Criminal, Police Criminal and Traffic Court of the Provincial Court of Justice of Tungurahua was denied by that Court in June 2020. In July 2020, Ms Burbano Proaño filed a special action, which the Constitutional Court of Ecuador selected for its docket in December 2020. In January 2022, that Court rendered its decision, which declared Estrellita a subject of rights with the rights to life and to bodily and mental integrity, among other rights.

Because Estrellita had already passed away, the Court held that the *habeas corpus* petition was inadmissible. Despite this, the Court's majority – to the protestations of the dissenting Judge Carmen Corral Ponce – dealt with the case from a substantive point of view, taking it as an opportunity to elaborate on whether other living beings can be subjects of rights.

The Court's majority opinion started by drawing attention to the fact that the Ecuadorian Constitution rejects the anthropocentric approach of other constitutions and instead adopts 'sociobiocentrism' (Constitutional Court of Ecuador 2022: 56). To explain this, the judges referred to the Constitution's preamble, which 'celebrat[es] nature, the Pacha Mama (Mother Earth), of which we are a part and which is vital to our existence' and proclaims the will to build 'A new form of public coexistence, in diversity and in harmony with nature, to achieve the good way of living, the sumak kawsay'. The Court also invoked another unique provision, Article 83:

Article 83 – Constitution of Ecuador (2008)

Ecuadorians have the following duties and obligations, without detriment to others provided for by the Constitution or by law: …

(6) To respect the rights of nature, preserve a healthy environment and use natural resources rationally, sustainably and durably …

As the judges note, the Constitution recognises not only human beings as subjects of law and rights: nature, too is seen as 'a subject of rights with an intrinsic value, which implies that it is an end in itself and not only a means to achieve the ends of others' (2022: 57). However, the rights of nature do not only protect nature as a collectivity, but also the entities and elements that make up nature. To put it another way, the Court bridged the gap that we saw in chapter three between conservationists and animal rights proponents, that is, between the protection of species and biological communities on the one hand and individuals on the other. It did so by interpreting the protection of rights of nature as protecting *both* species *and* individuals. This interpretation is what allowed the Court in previous cases to extend 'the quality of rights holders to ecosystems such as mangroves, rivers and forests' (2022: 70).

The novel question the Court answered in the Estrellita case was whether also *individual* animals, such as Estrellita, are *right-holders* under the constitutional protection of rights of nature. It answered that question in the affirmative: 'Within the levels of ecological organization, an animal is a basic unit of ecological organization, and being an element of Nature, it is protected by the rights of Nature and enjoys an inherent individual value' (2022: 73). According to the Court, among the specific rights that wild animals like Estrellita have are the right to life, the right to bodily and mental integrity, the right to food, the 'right to the free development of their animal behavior' (2022: 112), as well as 'right not to be hunted, fished, captured, collected, extracted, kept, retained, trafficked, traded or exchanged' (2022: 112). Although the majority opinion is ambiguous on the question as to whether the rights it recognised for wild animals also extend to other animals, some commentators (see Montes and Stilt 2022) have suggested that certain rights would indeed apply to all animals.

What the Court made clearer is that the rights of animals have a procedural dimension:

> Article 71 of the Constitution recognizes the right of any individual or legal entity, collectivity or human group to exercise legal actions and resort to public authorities, in the name of Nature, to demand the protection and reparation of its integrity or that of its elements, which includes animals (Constitutional Court of Ecuador 2022: 161).

Like courts in other countries, the Court took pains to emphasise that these findings do not equate animals with human beings. Rather, it held that one has to recognise that 'each species has its own protection needs that stand out for their own characteristics and qualities' (2022: 89). As a result, the legal protection and rights afforded to each species will be different – an approach that resembles the Species Membership Approach, which we discussed in chapter five.

How far-reaching are animals' rights, and how can animals' rights be made compatible with human rights? The court proposed two interesting principles to deal with these questions: the 'interspecies principle' and the 'principle of 'ecological interpretation' (2022: 97).

According to the *interspecies principle*, rights protection of animals must be attuned to the specific 'characteristics, processes, life cycles, structures, functions and evolutionary processes that differentiate each species' (2022: 98). For example, the Court notes that: 'the right to respect and conserve the areas of distribution and migratory routes, is a right that can only be protected in those species of animals with migratory behaviors' (2022: 99).

According to the *principle of ecological interpretation*, one must respect existing interactions within a species and between different species – including antagonistic ones such as predation. This principle is key because it allows the Court to qualify the rights to life, bodily and mental integrity, and other rights in ways that would not normally be possible for thick rights. For instance, the Court argues that when a predator follows their natural instinct and kills a prey animal on whom their survival depends, then the prey's right to life is not violated. Because, as the Court argues, also 'human beings are predators' (2022: 103), their right to eat animals cannot constitute a violation of animals' right to life either. Effectively limiting the implications of its finding that animals can be right-holders, the Court emphasises that many current human uses of domesticated animals – such as for food, transport, work, clothing, recreation, and to control pests – are all protected under Article 74 of the Constitution, pursuant to which '[p]ersons, communities, peoples, and nations shall have the right to benefit from the environment and the natural wealth enabling them to enjoy the good way of living'.

Focusing on Estrellita in particular, the Court noted that Estrellita's right to life and to bodily and mental integrity had been violated. This occurred both through her being kept by Ms Burbano Proaño in conditions that were unsuited to the needs of woolly monkeys as well as through her seizure by the authorities. The Court found that the seizure was carried out with insufficient consideration being given to Estrellita's needs, and ordered the Ministry of Environment to develop a protocol on the confiscation of animals that takes into account the animals' particular circumstances.

Finally, the Court ordered that the Ombudsman's Office ought to 'prepare within a period of up to six months a bill on animal rights' (2022: 183) spelling out the minimum conditions of how wild animals ought to be kept and treated by both private persons and public authorities. Going even further – and arguably against the idea of separation of powers – the Court ordered '[t]hat the National Assembly [i.e. parliament], within a term of up to two years, debate and approve a law on animal rights' (2022: 183).

E. People for Animals v Md Mohazzim (2015)

As the Estrellita case illustrates, there are courts that have taken steps toward recognising a right to liberty for certain animals. This happened first with the 2015 ruling *People for Animals v Md Mohazzim* of the Delhi High Court in India. A legal action had been brought by People for Animals, an animal welfare organisation, which challenged a person in New Delhi for keeping a large number of birds in small cages in violation of India's Prevention of Cruelty (Capture of Animals) Rules (1979).

Pointing to the case *Animal Welfare Board of India v A Nagaraja* (2014), which we discussed above, the judge on the Delhi High Court – Judge Manmohan Singh – argued that the Supreme Court had recognised, among other rights, animals' fundamental right 'to live with dignity' (Delhi High Court 2015: 1). The Judge then went on to state that trading with birds violates the rights of these animals. As he noted, 'all the birds have fundamental rights to fly in the sky and all human beings have no right to keep them in small cages for the purposes of their business or otherwise'. The Judge then ordered that the birds be 'set free in the sky' (2015: 2).

In 2011, the Gujarat High Court had already reached a similar conclusion in *Abdulkadar v State*, which involved a similar set of facts:

[E]very bird / animal has a right to move freely and it cannot be disputed that so far as the birds are concerned, they have right [*sic*] to move freely in the open sky / air and they cannot be kept in cages at all and that too with such a brutality. To keep the birds in the cages would be illegal confinement of such birds against their wish which would be against the fundamental right of the birds to move freely (2011, para 8.11).

An appeal against the Gujarat High Court decision is currently pending before the Indian Supreme Court.

F. Stray Dogs (2021)

Another animal right that was recently recognised by a court is the right to food. In June 2021, the Delhi High Court was faced with a complaint against a person who had been feeding stray dogs near the entrance of a residence – an issue the parties were later able to resolve in a settlement. Nonetheless, Justice JR Midha saw the case as an opportunity to take on the matter of feeding stray dogs.

In his ruling, Justice Midha invoked Article 21 of the Indian Constitution, which, following the case law discussed above, he held 'protects life of all species' (Delhi High Court 2021: 110). He also relied heavily on Article 51A(g) of the Constitution, which – as we saw in chapter one – imposes a duty on citizens 'to protect and improve the natural environment including forests, lakes, rivers and wild life, and to have compassion for living creatures'. As the Justice reasoned, this provision must be read in conjunction with Sections 3 and 11 of the Prevention of Cruelty to Animals Act (1960). Section 11 is a general anti-cruelty provision, listing several cruel acts that are prohibited, while Section 3 imposes a duty of care, similar to what can be found in other animal welfare acts:

Section 3 – Prevention of Cruelty to Animals Act (1960)

Duties of persons having charge of animals: It shall be the duty of every person having the care or charge of any animal to take all reasonable measures to ensure the well-being of such animal and to prevent the infliction upon such animal of unnecessary pain or suffering.

According to Justice Midha, both these sections read in conjunction with Article 51A(g) of the Constitution guarantee that a 'right to live in a healthy and clean atmosphere and right to get protection from human beings against inflicting unnecessary pain or suffering is a right to the animals' (2021: 116). The Justice also noted that '[a]nimals have a right under law to be treated with compassion, respect and dignity' (2021: 124), and held that animals 'require food, water, shelter, normal behaviour, medical care, self-determination' to flourish (2021: 125).

Building on this, Justice Midha went on to declare that stray dogs have a right to food:

Community dogs (stray/street dogs) have the right to food and citizens have the right to feed community dogs but in exercising this right, care and caution should be taken to ensure that it does not impinge upon the rights of others or cause any harm, hinderance, harassment and nuisance to other individuals or members of the society (2021: 126).

Interestingly, as this shows, the Justice qualified the dogs' right to food by emphasising that this right would have to be balanced against countervailing human rights. Although the idea of balancing animal rights against human rights would not be incompatible with viewing the right to food as a thick right, the judgment also contained observations that seemed to suggest that the Justice may potentially view that right as a thin right. For instance, the Justice reasoned that '[n]o person can restrict the other from feeding of dogs, until and unless it is causing harm or harassment to that other person' (2021: 132). It is arguable that, in the case of human beings, a right to food could not be limited by the fact that this would cause 'harassment' to another person.

Regardless of whether it is a thin or thick right, the Justice went on to clarify its implications: the Animal Welfare Board of India, in consultation with Resident Welfare Associations, must designate suitable areas for feeding. Also, every Resident Welfare Association or – where such Associations are not available – the Municipal Corporation has a duty 'to ensure that every community dog in every area has access to food and water in the absence of caregivers or community dog feeders in the said area' (2021: 129), as well as to ensure that stray dogs are sterilised.

G. Karnail Singh v State of Haryana (2019)

Even though the concept of legal personhood has appeared in some of the other judgments discussed in this chapter, there have been cases in which legal personhood (or legal subjecthood) has played the lead role – and fundamental rights only a supporting one. One example is the Indian case *Karnail Singh v State of Haryana* (2019). This case involved a legal action brought by the authorities against a group of persons after they had been apprehended in the state of Uttar Pradesh with two trucks that were transporting nearly 30 cows – apparently destined for slaughter – in violation of the state of Punjab's Prohibition of Cow Slaughter Act (1955), the national Prevention of Cruelty to Animals Act 1960, and laws pertaining to the transport of animals.

The judge in this case – Justice Rajiv Sharma from the High Court of Punjab and Haryana – gave a detailed judgment, carrying out a broad review of Indian case law on animal welfare protection, legal personhood, and standing; religious traditions that demand compassion for animals; environmental destruction; as well as recent scholarly accounts of animals' natures and their personhood and rights.

Even though the ruling's actual orders were more mundane – essentially requiring that the existing animal welfare laws are upheld – Justice Sharma concluded by suggesting that animals are legal entities with a distinct form of personhood:

> The entire animal kingdom including avian and aquatic are declared as legal entities having a distinct persona with corresponding rights, duties and liabilities of a living person. All the citizens throughout the State of Haryana are hereby declared persons in loco parentis as the human face for the welfare/protection of animals (High Court of Punjab and Haryana 2019: 104).

H. Sandra (2014)

Another example for a legal personhood-focused case is the *Sandra* case from Argentina. The AFADA, whom we encountered earlier with *Cecilia*, already filed a *habeas corpus* petition as early as 2014 on behalf of Sandra, an orangutan, to have her moved from the Buenos Aires Zoo to a sanctuary. Sandra's complex litigation spanned numerous court decisions.

The *habeas corpus* petition was denied (and the denial later affirmed on appeal) primarily on the basis that a 'person' in Argentinian law must have characteristic signs of humanity (National Chamber of Criminal and Correctional Appeals 2014: 1).

Sandra's case then reached the Federal Criminal Court of Appeals. In its 2014 ruling, the failure of the *habeas corpus* suit was not in question – but animals' legal status more generally was. The majority of the judges stated that a 'dynamic' inter-pretation of the law must be employed, and that animals ought to be recognised as legal subjects because they hold rights (Federal Criminal Court of Appeals 2014, para 2).

AFADA then pursued a so-called *amparo* action: a type of injunction often used in Spanish-speaking legal systems to protect individual rights. The first *amparo* hearing, before the Judicial Branch of the Autonomous City of Buenos Aires in 2015, affirmed animals' status as rights-holding non-human persons (or 'subjects of law' and 'subjects of rights': 2015, para II). The judge, Elena Liberatori, found that there is 'no legal impediment' (2015, para II) to seeing Sandra as a non-human subject of rights. Three points can be noted about her reasoning.

First, she made reference to Article 1 of Argentina's Law on Abuse and Acts of Cruelty Toward Animals (1954), which provides that animals can be 'victims' who are owed duties by humans, as well as Article 10 of the Civil and Commercial Code (2014), according to which 'law does not protect the abusive exercise of rights'. This general limitation on ownership rights and the anti-cruelty norms implied that animals have legally protected entitlements, which the Judge also characterised as rights.

Second, the judge pointed to the example of dereification of animals in France (another civil law system), to show that animals could be conceived as sentient property – or things with rights – within civil law systems that have codified the person/thing binary. As a consequence, the judge argued, animals' newfound legal status would not upset Argentina's own codification of this binary.

Third, the judge elaborated on the 'dynamic' approach of the previous court, reasoning that classifications of legal status are not biologically or objectively deter-mined, but are 'social constructions':

> Every way to classify and categorize the world is a social construction. And these types of classification match a particular way of appropriating reality … Therefore, far from being 'natural', uniform and static, the categories are 'inherently' dynamic, heterogeneous and changing according to the social context that produced them (2015, para IV).

Instead of ordering the transfer of Sandra to a sanctuary, however, Judge Liberatori ordered three experts to decide Sandra's fate. This was one of the reasons why AFADA appealed the decision to the Judicial Branch of the Autonomous City of Buenos Aires, arguing that Liberatori had all the necessary information to determine where to trans-fer Sandra. However, that Court (2016) reinterpreted the case as not being about an individual animal's rights, but about humans' collective right to have their common heritage (in particular, endangered species) protected. Consequently, the Court revoked Judge Liberatori's holding that animals are legal subjects, while upholding the less contentious aspect of the prior decision, namely that the Government of Buenos Aires must ensure living conditions adequate to protect Sandra's wellbeing. Sandra was later voluntarily moved to the Center for Great Apes in Florida.

Exercise 3: Fundamental Rights Beyond *Habeas Corpus*

1. Take a close look at the quotations and case summaries provided in this section. Using the distinction drawn in chapter four section three between thin and thick rights, try to determine whether the relevant passages were actually about thin or thick rights protection for animals.
2. Are there any provisions or principles in the constitution of your own country that could be used in animal rights litigation? If so, how would you build a strong case on that basis?
3. 'Animals have fundamental legal rights today'. Do you agree or disagree with this statement? Why? Consider how case law affects theory when answering.

V. Conclusion

This chapter has reviewed three main categories of animal rights cases: cases on standing, cases on *habeas corpus*, and cases discussing fundamental rights or legal personhood beyond *habeas corpus*. As we have seen, many of these have involved creative legal strategies aimed at moving legal boundaries, and extending to animals some of the same or similar protections that humans enjoy under existing laws.

Despite a recent trend of courts being increasingly willing to consider granting fundamental rights and/or legal personhood to animals, we have seen that legal success for animal rights litigants has so far been limited. This is especially so if we take into account the sometimes-flowery prose that courts have used in rulings whose actual outcomes may not always have lived up to their language. Nevertheless, even to the limited degree that animals have already been granted fundamental rights or legal personhood, this represents a ground-breaking legal development. What is more, even when cases were unsuccessful in the courts, they could often still garner significant media attention and raise awareness of animal rights.

There are more cases – past and ongoing – that we could not mention in this chapter. On our companion website, you will not only find links to the above-discussed cases, but can also find information about additional cases, and can stay up to date on the latest legal developments.

Of course, litigation is not the only possible avenue to pursue animal rights. The route preferred by some – and advised by some of the courts discussed in this chapter – is to push for animal rights legislation. The next chapter looks at existing legislative efforts taken in different countries and discusses what future laws could look like.

Exercise 4: Animal Rights in Litigation

1. Consider the different types of animals in the left-hand column and try to identify which kind of litigation approach (if any) could be pursued for these animals.

	Animal welfare litigation	*Habeas corpus* litigation	Other fundamental rights litigation
Zoo bonobos	☐	☐	☐
Wild bonobos	☐	☐	☐
Pet dogs	☐	☐	☐
Laboratory mice	☐	☐	☐
Farmed chickens	☐	☐	☐
Cod in the sea	☐	☐	☐

2. What approach to securing legal animal rights through litigation would be most likely to succeed in your legal system? Why?
3. What do you consider to be the most significant animal rights case described in this chapter? What were the crucial factors that led the court to reach its decision in that case?
4. In a group or alone, reflect on the different litigation strategies. Which is the best, and which is the worst overall? Judge this against an important goal of your choosing, like achieving fundamental rights, or abolishing institutionalised exploitation.
5. 'Creative animal rights litigation is unlikely to produce legal change that is either sustainable in the long term or beneficial in practice to the majority of animals that would benefit most from increased protection. In fact, it is likely to be counterproductive'. Discuss this statement.

Useful References

Animal Legal and Historical Center, available at www.animallaw.info/.
Colb, SF (2020) 'Should Animals Be Allowed to Sue?' *Verdict*, available at verdict.justia.com/2020/01/29/should-animals-be-allowed-to-sue.

Ewasiuk, C (2017) 'Escape Routes: The Possibility of Habeas Corpus Protection for Animals under Modern Social Contract Theory' 48 *Columbia Human Rights Law Review* 69.

Jardine, A (2018) 'The Pedagogic Value of Science Fiction: Teaching about Personhood and Nonhuman Rights with Planet of the Apes' 20 *The University of Notre Dame Australia Law Review* 6, 1.

Kansal, V (2016) 'The Curious Case of Nagaraja in India: Are Animals Still Regarded as "Property" With No Claim Rights?' 19 *Journal of International Wildlife Law & Policy* 3, 256.

Montes Franceschini, M (2021) 'Animal Personhood: The Quest for Recognition' 17 *Animal and Natural Resource Law Review* 93.

Staker, A (2017) 'Should Chimpanzees Have Standing? The Case for Pursuing Legal Personhood for Non-Human Animals' 6 *Transnational Environmental Law* 485.

7

Animal Rights in Legislation

I. Introduction

The previous chapter looked at court cases brought around the world to progress animal rights by way of litigation. Considering the attention some of these cases have received in both the media and scholarly debates, one could be forgiven for thinking that animal rights improvements are only sought in court. However, this would be to overlook another important domain for animal rights change: legislation. This chapter focuses on proposals to introduce national and international animal rights legislation.

We use the term 'legislation' in a wide sense to encompass international treaties, declarations, as well as national constitutional laws and statutes. As in previous chapters, our focus will be on thick legal rights for animals: complex rights that protect animals' fundamental interests in a way that is dynamic, privately enforceable, and not easily infringeable. As we will see, there is currently no animal rights legislation in this sense (future editions of this book may tell a different story). However, there are a wide variety of proposals – some of which more advanced than others – for national and international animal rights legislation. These proposals form the focus of this chapter.

The chapter starts by canvassing the animal rights laws that have been proposed on the domestic (ie constitutional and statutory) level. We then turn to proposals for animal rights on the international level (ie international treaties and declarations). To give structure to all these proposals, we will focus on four themes: *scope* (which animals the proposals cover); *legal status* (what legal categorisation of animals they propose or presuppose, in particular whether or not animals are legal persons); *procedural rights* (how they propose that animals can enforce their rights in court); and *substantive rights* (which substantive protections they propose). Lastly, the chapter discusses issues to consider for those drafting future animal rights legislation.

Central Issues

1. Animal rights change is not only sought in courts but also through legislation. Legislative reform can occur by way of international declarations, treaties, domestic constitutional law, or domestic statutory law. Despite numerous proposals that have been put forward, there is currently no binding animal rights legislation.

2. Domestic proposals for animal rights have been advanced in several countries. Two of the most prominent proposals are the Swiss primate rights initiative in the Canton of Basel-Stadt and the Finnish proposal for a new animal rights chapter of the Finnish Constitution. While both proposals aim at constitutional change, their scope and the breadth of substantive rights they demand are remarkably different.

3. Animal rights proposals on the international level have focused on (non-binding) declarations rather than (binding) international treaties. This has to do with the current difficulty of creating an international treaty in this area. The Universal Declaration of Animal Rights and the Declaration of Rights for Cetaceans are two leading examples of international declarations.

4. Given the novelty of the field and the current lack of binding animal rights legislation that could serve as a model, drafters of animal rights laws have to consider a range of issues, including the mechanics of law reform as well as questions of scope, legal status, procedural and substantive rights.

II. Domestic Proposals for Animal Rights Laws

Proposals for domestic animal rights legislation for primates have been presented in numerous countries, including in Germany (Giordano Bruno Stiftung 2014) and Spain (Glendinning 2008). Some proposals are of a largely declaratory nature, that is, without any pretension to become legally binding. Others are phrased in a way that would at least in principle allow them to become binding law. In this section, we focus on two of the most important recent proposals that follow the latter approach: the Swiss primate rights initiative and the Finnish Animal Rights Lawyers Society's proposal for a new animal rights chapter of the Finnish Constitution.

A. The Swiss Primate Rights Initiative

In 2016, the Swiss animal rights NGO Sentience Politics launched what would become thus-far the most advanced proposal for constitutional animal rights reform.

The proposal came in the form of a popular initiative – a direct democratic tool allowing citizens to propose and vote on constitutional amendments – to change the Constitution of the Canton of Basel-Stadt. The initiative proposed to grant all non-human primates the right to life and to bodily and mental integrity. Because the Constitution already guarantees these rights for human primates, the initiative thus effectively proposed to extend these rights to all primate species. Concretely, the initiative wanted to add a new provision to the Constitution's Article 11(2), which contains additional human rights protections that go beyond the basic rights guaranteed in Article 11(1):

Article 11 – Constitution of the Canton of Basel-Stadt (2006)

Guarantees of fundamental rights

… (2) This Constitution also protects: …

c. [proposed] the right of non-human primates to life and bodily and mental integrity.

The *scope* of the initiative is evident from its title: it proposed to extend legal rights to all non-human primates: a biological order containing over 300 species, including chimpanzees, orangutans, gorillas, mandrills, spider monkeys, gibbons, and other species.

The *substantive rights* demanded by the initiative – a right to life and a right to bodily and mental integrity – are limited compared to the broad range of rights that humans possess. The drafters' motivation behind limiting the list of rights was two-fold: first, the rights to life and bodily and mental integrity would protect primates' vital interests in remaining alive and in avoiding both physical and psychological suffering. Because these are core interests, they would not only make a significant difference to the animals' lives, but could also potentially serve as the grounds on which future rights could be built. Second, demanding additional rights was seen as reducing the initiative's chances of success. Given the popularity of the local Basel Zoo, the drafters in particular regarded it as tactically preferable not to demand a right to liberty.

While the initiative's proposed text does not explicitly mention the *legal status* that primates would have, the litigation that ensued as a result of the cantonal authorities' resistance to the initiative (discussed in chapter six) made it clear that the courts assumed that the primates would become legal subjects. As we saw in chapter six, the Swiss Federal Supreme Court took the view that, although existing constitutional rights are focused on protecting humans, there is nothing that prevents turning non-humans into legal subjects of public law.

Although the initiative did not discuss *procedural rights* and other questions of enforcement, this issue too was taken up by the courts. As the Constitutional Court of the Canton of Basel-Stadt noted, the primates would require legal representation to enforce their legal rights. Unprompted by the legal parties, the Court went on to consider how such implementation could be carried out:

A member of the veterinary office or the KESB [Child and Adult Protection Authority], an ombudswoman or an independent primate advocate could for example be envisaged. Also envisaged could be an association's right to appeal or other forms of fiduciary legal protection and even whether (as seems unlikely) agency without specific authorisation [*Geschäftsführung ohne Auftrag*] would be applicable (Constitutional Court of the Canton of Basel-Stadt, 2019, para 4.3, our translation).

After the Federal Supreme Court declared the primate rights initiative to be legally valid, it was put to a vote by the citizens of Basel-Stadt in February 2022. While 25.3 per cent voted to approve the proposed amendment, 74.7 per cent rejected it, thus putting an end to the initiative.

B. The Finnish Rights Proposal

Having been discussed and voted on by citizens – and become the subject of litigation going all the way to the Supreme Court – the Swiss primate rights initiative is institutionally the most advanced animal rights proposal to date. However, considering its limited scope and its short list of substantive rights, it has not been the most exhaustive proposal. A more comprehensive proposal was developed in 2019 in Finland. There, the Finnish Animal Rights Lawyers Society put forward what is effectively a proposal for an animal bill of rights, drafted as a new chapter to the Constitution of Finland. This new Chapter 2A 'on the fundamental rights of animals' (2020) would complement the Constitution's existing Chapter 2, which lists the basic rights and liberties guaranteed for all humans.

The proposal's *scope* extends to all sentient animals, with a precautionary principle aimed at solving the problem that the sentience of certain species is uncertain and scientific views about it ever-evolving:

[Proposed] Chapter 2A, Section 1 – Constitution of Finland (1999)

(1) Sentient animals are individuals whose fundamental rights and welfare requirements must be fully respected by humans. All animals shall be presumed to be sentient unless otherwise can be determined …

The wording of the proposal makes no explicit reference to the exact *legal status* of animals. However, the drafters' accompanying explanatory notes make clear that they do not rule out that an animal can be owned but still possess the rights protected in the proposed chapter. For instance, the notes state that '[t]he individuality of an animal must also be taken into account in ownership disputes' (2020).

In contrast to the Swiss primate rights initiative, the Finnish rights proposal explicitly regulates *procedural rights*. In Section 1(3), it provides:

[Proposed] Chapter 2A, Section 1 – Constitution of Finland (1999)

(3) Animals have legal standing. Animals' right to be heard shall be exercised by their legal representative. The legal representation of animals is further specified by law …

As the explanatory notes make clear, an animal's representative would not only have the right to be heard in cases that affect the animal's interests, but could also file documents and appeal against decisions. Who would act as a representative? According to the drafters, this could be 'a person specifically approved and appointed for this task by the authorities and who fulfils the prescribed qualification requirements' (2020), with animal protection authorities and associations having a right to nominate suitably skilled and experienced persons. In addition, the drafters state that registered associations could be given a right to represent animals. Even an animal's owner would be allowed to represent the animal provided that 'the interests of the animal and the owner do not conflict' (2020).

These provisions are well thought-through, but where the Finnish rights proposal really shines is with regard to its wide-ranging list of *substantive rights.* The proposal deals with the rights of wild animals (Section 3), the rights of animals dependent on human care (Section 4), and contains further provisions regarding the prohibition of breeding animals in ways that cause harm (Section 5).

On the rights of wild animals, for instance, the proposal states:

[Proposed] Chapter 2A, Section 3 – Constitution of Finland (1999)

(1)   A wild animal has the right to life and the right to live in freedom, in the animal's natural habitat.

(2)   A wild animal has the right to receive help if sick, injured or otherwise incapacitated. If an animal is in a condition such that keeping the animal alive is obviously cruel, the animal has the right to be euthanized. Animals must be in such cases killed as laid down by law.

The substantive rights for wild animals are – with the exceptions listed in Subsection 2 – limited to negative rights (ie rights not to be interfered with, as discussed in chapter three). By contrast, the rights for animals who are dependent on human care contain numerous positive rights (ie rights to be provided with certain care), as illustrated in Subsections 1, 3, 4, and 5 of Section 4:

[Proposed] Chapter 2A, Section 4 – Constitution of Finland (1999)

(1)   An animal has the right to life as well as the right to express natural behaviours and have the animal's basic needs fulfilled.

(2)   An animal has the right to experience and express positive emotions, and the right to be protected against and free from fear, pain, distress and suffering caused by humans.

(3)   An animal has the right to food and drink that is suitable for maintaining the animal's welfare and health. An animal has the right to decide when to eat and drink.

(4)   An animal has the right to a suitable living environment, including shelter and a resting area.

(5)   An animal has the right to receive appropriate treatment without delay. If an animal is in a condition such that keeping the animal alive is obviously cruel, the animal has the right to be euthanized. Animals must be in such cases killed as laid down by law respecting the animal as an individual, sentient being.

Even in the more 'negatively' phrased second part of Subsection 2, Section 4 builds on expansive concepts to ensure that animals' living conditions are such that they can flourish. Hence, it draws for example on the concept of the Five Freedoms, which we looked at in chapter one.

Finally, and going beyond other proposals, the Finnish rights proposal also contains a provision (Section 2) discussing how animals' rights would have to be safeguarded practically:

[Proposed] Chapter 2A, Section 2 – Constitution of Finland (1999)

(1)   Public authorities must safeguard the realisation of fundamental animal rights and develop society in a way, which guarantees the fundamental rights of animals. Companies must respect fundamental animal rights in their activities.

(2)   Fundamental animal rights may only be limited if it is necessary for safeguarding the fundamental rights of human beings or animals. Limitations have to be as minor as possible with regard to the pursued aim. The enactment of a limitation must respect the central content of said rights. The limitations have to be regulated by law.

Subsection 2 is of particular interest, because it connects with a topic we discussed in chapter five: resolving rights conflicts by means of the proportionality test. As we saw there, potential conflicts between human and animal rights could be addressed with the aid of the proportionality test, which involves balancing animal rights against other rights or the public interest. That the Finnish proposal seems to endorse this approach can be deduced from the fact that it sees animal rights as qualified or relative, which can therefore justifiably be 'limited' as long as limitations are necessary to protect others' rights and do not violate the core of the right. This holds even for the right to life, which the proposal also treats as a qualified right.

C. Evaluating the Proposals

As will have become obvious, the Swiss and Finnish proposals are different in their approaches: the Swiss rights initiative is narrow and focused, both with regard to its scope and its proposed substantive rights. The Finnish rights proposal, by contrast, is wide in its scope and the procedural and substantive rights it demands.

To compare the two approaches in some more detail, consider one area of difference: *scope*. In the Swiss primate rights initiative, the scope covers only non-human primates. The Finnish rights proposal, by contrast, extends to all sentient animals. Which approach is better? Without more empirical evidence, this question is difficult to answer and will likely depend on the circumstances of the given societies and legal systems, as well as tactical questions about which might be more likely to get public support. A proposal more comprehensive in scope, like the Finnish proposal, would in principle seem preferable. However, we can speculate that this advantage is at the same time also a weakness: so far, the Finnish proposal exists only on paper and has not yet been formally introduced to the Finnish Parliament. At the time of writing, the Finnish Animal Rights Lawyers Society is planning an online petition that – if signed by 50,000 citizens – would require Parliament to consider the proposal.

Regardless of which approach is found to be more suitable for a given society, both proposals show that anyone proposing new animal rights legislation will have to answer important questions that can determine the outcome of their proposal. We will return to these questions in section IV below.

III. International Proposals for Animal Rights Laws

In this section, we turn from domestic law to international law. International animal rights proposals can be roughly divided into proposals for international treaties, that is, conventions between states (which are legally binding), and international declarations (which are not legally binding). We first explore the reasons that speak in favour of and against adopting an international treaty on animal rights. We then turn to two of the most important international declarations on animal rights that activists have developed: the Universal Declaration of Animal Rights (UDAR), and the Declaration of Rights for Cetaceans. We then discuss these proposals using the four themes identified earlier. You can find links to other declarations not discussed here – such as the Universal Charter of Rights of Other Species, the Declaration of Animal Rights, and the World Declaration on Great Apes – at the end of the chapter.

A. An International Treaty on Animal Rights?

Although it is a matter of domestic law whether an international treaty is directly binding in any given state, treaties generally enfold important legal effects. Perhaps just as importantly, they bring together countries interested in reform, and reflect consensus at some level among participating countries about new legal norms. As such, they can set a common framework for signatory countries, establishing agreed principles for national legislation and sometimes even providing templates for national legislation.

As the international law scholar Anne Peters has pointed out, many aspects of human-animal interactions – such as food production and animal experimentation – are not merely domestic phenomena but happen partially between states, on a global level. For this reason, she proposes that an international treaty would be required to truly achieve change in animal rights law, rather than risk problems being outsourced to countries with weaker animal rights regimes. Peters has coined the term 'Global Animal Law' (2016a) to refer to a system that operates on the international level but is complemented by regional and domestic laws. As Peters points out, '[a]n international benchmark would allow [animal welfare and rights activists] to devote their scarce resources on implementation of that acknowledged standard' (2016a: 19).

Even if it was largely aspirational, an international treaty on animal rights would still reflect a level of consensus among participating countries – a joint intention to introduce new domestic legislation and provide a common framework for that legislation. This framework could then facilitate the creation of new norms and provide momentum for other countries to join, reducing the risk of free-riders. However, exactly because international treaties operate on an inter-country level, they also tend to be hard to achieve and slow to develop.

Considering that no state has so far passed any domestic animal rights legislation, it is hardly surprising that no international treaty on animal rights exists. In fact, there has not even been a proposal for such a treaty yet. International treaties have thus far only been proposed (but not yet adopted) in the domain of animal welfare law (see eg Favre 2012).

What is more, even if a treaty on animal rights could be created in the near future, the development of such a treaty could risk bringing protections down to the lowest common denominator, meaning that consensus would be achieved at the expense of the strength of protections. This aspect is reflected in Favre's proposal for an International Treaty for Animal Welfare: its welfare protections are relatively basic compared to those found in more advanced domestic animal welfare laws (although he provides for the possibility of accompanying protocols for states that want to go further in a specific area).

B. Universal Declaration of Animal Rights

The Universal Declaration of Animal Rights (UDAR) was written by George Heuse, a member of the Secretariat of the Director General of UNESCO. Its first version was proclaimed in 1978 at the headquarters of the United Nations Educational, Scientific and Cultural Organization (UNESCO) in Paris, and its revised version was submitted to the Director General of UNESCO in 1990.

Starting with UDAR's *scope*, its first article makes clear that, with its extension to all animals, it has the broadest ambit of all proposals considered so far. Unlike other proposals, it does not distinguish between sentient or non-sentient animals, and does not reserve rights for specific species or groups of species:

Article 1 – Universal Declaration of Animal Rights (UDAR; 1990)

All animals have equal rights to exist within the context of biological equilibrium ...

The fact that UDAR does not take sentience as its founding principle becomes obvious from its Article 3(3):

Article 3 – Universal Declaration of Animal Rights (UDAR; 1990)

(3)   A dead animal must be treated with decency.

UDAR addresses the *legal status* of animals and their *procedural rights*. However, the provision it devotes to these issues remains rather vague:

Article 9 – Universal Declaration of Animal Rights (UDAR; 1990)

(1)   The specific legal status of animals and their rights must be recognised by law.
(2)   The protection and safety of animals must be represented at the level of Governmental organizations.

By contrast, it lists a considerable number of *substantive rights*. Some of these rights, such as the 'right to be respected' (Article 2), apply to all animals. Others focus on animals used for specific purposes. Specifically, UDAR distinguishes between wild animals, animals dependent on humans, animals used in entertainment, and animals used in experimentation. In its first version, it also contained provisions on working animals and animals in the food industry. Regarding working animals, for instance, its Article 7 stated:

Article 7 – Universal Declaration of Animal Rights (UDAR; 1978)

All working animals are entitled to a reasonable limitation of the duration and intensity of their work, to the necessary nourishment, and to rest.

Interestingly, UDAR also goes on to outline the criminal consequences of violating some of its substantive rights. For the mass killing of wild animals and other forms of interferences that threaten wild species' survival, it introduces the crime of 'genocide':

Article 8 – Universal Declaration of Animal Rights (UDAR; 1990)

(1)   Any act compromising the survival of a wild species and any decision leading to such an act are tantamount to genocide, that is to say, a crime against the species.
(2)   The massacre of wild animals, and the pollution and destruction of biotopes are acts of genocide.

Generally, the systematic killing of animals is commonly referred to as 'speciecide' (see Bunge 1973: 291), not genocide.

C. Declaration of Rights for Cetaceans

As we saw, UDAR adopts a truly universal approach not only in being an international declaration, but also in applying to all animals. The Declaration of Rights for Cetaceans: Whales and Dolphins takes a different approach. Adopted in 2010 at a conference in Helsinki under the leadership of Paola Cavalieri, the Declaration of Rights for Cetaceans focuses – as its name suggests – on cetaceans, and on whales and dolphins in particular. Its *scope* is thus considerably narrower than UDAR's and it adopts something akin to the Species Membership Approach (SMA; discussed in chapter five) to select the species which it aims to protect.

In contrast to other documents, the Declaration of Rights for Cetaceans explicitly (albeit briefly) addresses the question of cetaceans' *legal status*. As it provides in Article 4:

Article 4 – Declaration of Rights for Cetaceans: Whales and Dolphins (2010)

No cetacean is the property of any State, corporation, human group or individual.

While the Declaration does not contain any *procedural rights* as such, it does have several articles that deal with its implementation in the broader sense. For example, Articles 7 and 8 address how the international and domestic legal systems have to be structured to facilitate the protection of cetaceans' rights:

Article 7 – Declaration of Rights for Cetaceans: Whales and Dolphins (2010)

The rights, freedoms and norms set forth in this Declaration should be protected under international and domestic law.

Article 8 – Declaration of Rights for Cetaceans: Whales and Dolphins (2010)

Cetaceans are entitled to an international order in which these rights, freedoms and norms can be fully realized.

Which *substantive rights* have to be protected in international and domestic law? As the Declaration's preamble affirms, its beating heart is its commitment to 'the right to life, liberty and wellbeing', which all cetaceans have in virtue of being 'persons'. The Declaration backs this up by invoking in its preamble the 'scientific research giv[ing] us deeper insights into the complexities of cetacean minds, societies and cultures'. The Declaration fleshes out the three above-mentioned rights as follows.

The right to life is protected in Article 1, and the right to liberty is protected in Articles 2 and 3:

Article 1 – Declaration of Rights for Cetaceans: Whales and Dolphins (2010)

Every individual cetacean has the right to life.

Article 2 – Declaration of Rights for Cetaceans: Whales and Dolphins (2010)

No cetacean should be held in captivity or servitude; be subject to cruel treatment; or be removed from their natural environment.

Article 3 – Declaration of Rights for Cetaceans: Whales and Dolphins (2010)

All cetaceans have the right to freedom of movement and residence within their natural environment.

The right to wellbeing is not protected in any one provision, but is mirrored in Article 2's protection against cruelty as in Articles 5 and 6:

Article 5 – Declaration of Rights for Cetaceans: Whales and Dolphins (2010)

Cetaceans have the right to the protection of their natural environment.

Article 6 – Declaration of Rights for Cetaceans: Whales and Dolphins (2010)

Cetaceans have the right not to be subject to the disruption of their cultures.

The Declaration is bookended by a provision that addresses the problem with international documents that we discussed in Subsection A above: that such documents are often relatively limited in content because they represent a lowest common denominator. To remedy this issue, the Declaration makes clear that it consists only of a set of minimum standards that domestic legal systems are welcome to go beyond:

Article 10 – Declaration of Rights for Cetaceans: Whales and Dolphins (2010)

Nothing in this Declaration shall prevent a State from enacting stricter provisions for the protection of cetacean rights.

D. Evaluating the Proposals

The two above-discussed proposals contain several interesting substantive rights, of which we will focus on three for discussion: the right to respect; the right to protection of culture; and the right to a protected habitat.

Regarding the *right to respect*, UDAR's Article 3(3) provides that all animals (even dead ones) have an entitlement to be respected; and Article 5(4) – which deals with animals used in entertainment – provides that '[e]xhibitions, shows and films involving animals must also respect their dignity and must not include any violence whatsoever'. It is no coincidence that UDAR focuses on the themes of respect and dignity, considering that these are also considered to be the lynchpins of modern human rights law. The Preamble to the Universal Declaration of Human Rights (UDHR), on which UDAR was modelled, justifies the rights that follow with the statement that 'recognition of the inherent dignity and of the equal and inalienable rights of all members of the human family is the foundation of freedom, justice and peace in the world'. In a similar vein, the Constitution of South Africa (1996) for example refers to the foundational value of human dignity in Section 1:

Section 1 – Constitution of the Republic of South Africa (1996)

The Republic of South Africa is one, sovereign, democratic state founded on the following values:

a.   Human dignity, the achievement of equality and the advancement of human rights and freedoms …

By including dignity and respect, the drafters of UDAR followed this tradition, recognising that respect and dignity for animals can have a significant symbolic importance.

In addition, its inclusion serves to establish at least an indirect connection between human rights and animal rights. As such, UDAR can be seen as acknowledging that language closely connected with one group can also apply to another and potentially serve to reset the basis of the relationship between humans and animals from one of superiority and inferiority to one of equality. As the first sentence of the Preamble of the Declaration of Rights for Cetaceans emphasises: it is '[b]ased on the principle of the equal treatment of all persons'.

Second, an unusual right, the *right to protection of their cultures*, is guaranteed in the Declaration of Rights for Cetaceans. As noted above, this right builds on increased scientific understanding of the rich social lives of cetaceans that warrant the term 'culture'. For instance, as a recent study (Fox et al 2017) has shown, cetaceans not only hunt cooperatively, but also teach each other how to hunt and use tools. They have been found to have dialects that differ from region to region, which include sounds that identify individuals (thereby 'naming' them); and they have developed practices to look after each other's children.

Finally, the Declaration of Rights for Cetaceans also grants cetaceans a right to protection of their natural environment, that is, *protection of their habitat*. As we saw in previous section, a similar right is protected in Section 3 (on wild animals) of the Finnish rights proposal. While it is not uncommon for proposals to include rights for wild animals, there is still considerable theoretical disagreement about how extensive rights for animals in the wild should be. For instance, as we saw in chapter three, Sue Donaldson and Will Kymlicka argue that wild animals should be conceived as sovereign communities with largely negative rights not to be interfered with. As Kymlicka puts it with regard to wolves, 'our obligation would largely be to leave them alone, to live freely on their own habitat' (2017: 134). By contrast, cosmopolitan political philosophers like Alasdair Cochrane argue that wild animals should essentially have the same rights as other animals, including both positive and negative rights. As he submits, 'recognizing wild animals as equal members within mixed human–animal communities – not as separate sovereign communities – is the best means of granting them equal concern and protecting their rights' (2018: 79, emphasis removed).

Exercise 1: International Proposals for Animal Rights Laws

1. You (and your fellow students) are the representatives of an expert commission tasked with proposing a draft animal rights declaration to protect elephants in the wild. Draft the provisions, and explain the choices you made in developing the declaration.
2. You are asked to review a law reform proposal to give rights to wild animals. It refers to the need for 'respect' from humans. Advise what difference that makes to the overall reform.

IV. Drafting Animal Rights Laws

The previous sections have looked at some of the existing proposals for animal rights legislation in both national and international law. In this section, we change perspectives and turn from readers of animal rights legislation to drafters. We ask what some of the mechanics of law reform are that drafters of animal rights laws need to be aware of, and then turn to how drafters can approach the themes of scope, legal status, procedural rights, and substantive rights. This exercise can help us get a sense of how rights might develop in the future and what some of the issues are that will need to be addressed. Our focus is primarily on the drafting of national law – where, as we saw above, animal rights proposals are more advanced than on the international level – but many insights of our discussion can also be applied to the drafting of international laws.

A. The Mechanics of Law Reform

Drafting laws is a craft, and like any craftsperson, those drafting animal rights legislation have to deal with the mechanics of their trade. In the case of animal rights these are the mechanics of law reform. There are two important and interrelated questions that drafters have to think about when working on reform proposals: first, should reform occur on the statutory or constitutional level? Second, should the drafting be narrow or broad? Depending on how drafters answer these questions this may have an impact on their proposal's chance of success and on its ease of implementation.

Starting with the first question, drafters need to decide on whether the animal rights laws they want to put forward should become part of (national or state) *constitutions or be drafted as a statute*. Constitutionally embedded rights are at the top of the legal hierarchy and thus have an important legal role to play because they can render invalid countervailing statutes. Beyond their legal role, constitutional provisions can also have great symbolic importance as they represent the foundational norms of a given community. As we saw in chapter one, only a few states have enshrined animal protection in their constitutions. However, so far, no state has included any explicit safeguards of animal *rights* in their constitution. As we saw, the more common approach is to include state objectives, which are primarily aspirational. Given the high legal and social status of constitutional norms, they are difficult to create and usually require a qualified majority in parliament and/or a referendum to be adopted.

By contrast, statutes generally face lower legislative hurdles than changes to constitutions because they are placed below the constitution and are meant to concretise and give effect to constitutional provisions. For this reason, statutory provisions tend to be more focused and more detailed in their wording than constitutional provisions. In contrast to constitutions, legislation normally also includes more detailed mechanisms for enforcement that make compliance more likely. Because statutes are easier to pass than changes to the constitution, they may present a more obvious choice for animal rights drafters. However, given that statutes are generally not allowed to violate constitutional norms, such a statutory approach can become problematic. This is because animal rights laws are sometimes seen as being in tension with foundational principles such as the right to property, which tend to be enshrined in constitutions.

Second, and related, drafters need to decide on whether to phrase rights provisions using *broad or detailed language*. Using broad language has the advantage of making the rights provision cover a wide range of potential circumstances. Broadly phrased norms can also appear more powerful because they are not as limited in their scope as more narrowly phrased norms. On the other side of the coin, broadly phrased provisions can risk being stretched so thinly that they have limited purchase. Take, for example, the EU Directive 2010/63/EU on the protection of animals used for scientific purposes:

Preambular paragraph 12 – Directive 2010/63/EU of 22 September 2010 on the protection of animals used for scientific purposes

Animals have an intrinsic value which must be respected …

The idea that animals have intrinsic value can be a powerful one, as is the obligation ('must') to respect it. In principle, this could give animals a status in society not so different from humans. However, there are two ways in which such broad language can be undermined. First, broad and aspirational language can be watered down if it is embedded in a legal document containing detailed regulations that – like the above-mentioned Directive – permits infringing animals' vital interests and therefore makes the statement about 'intrinsic value' largely devoid of content. Second, there is the danger that law-interpreting bodies like courts can undermine broad statutory language by interpreting it in narrow ways.

By contrast, detailed wording can help progress an issue because it focuses people's attention on particular matters. Consider another example from the EU, the Council Directive 2008/120/EC on laying down minimum standards for the protection of pigs.

Article 3 – Council Directive 2008/120/EC of 18 December 2008 on laying down minimum standards for the protection of pigs

(1) …

(b) the total unobstructed floor area available to each gilt after service and to each sow when gilts and/or sows are kept in groups must be at least 1,64 m2 and 2,25 m2 respectively. When these animals are kept in groups of fewer than six individuals the unobstructed floor area must be increased by 10 %. When these animals are kept in groups of 40 or more individuals the unobstructed floor area may be decreased by 10 %.

Given its level of detail and measurability, a provision of this type makes it easier to determine whether it is being complied with or breached. However, given its narrow wording, it does not have the same potential as more broadly phrased provisions. Although the example given here is not one about rights, it illustrates the kinds of choices that drafters of animal rights laws will have to make.

Among the other choices that drafters will have to make are the scope of animals protected, their legal status, their substantive rights, and procedural rights that help them enforce those rights.

B. Scope

Starting with the issue of scope, there are three questions in particular that drafters need to consider: should rights be granted to all animals, or only some animals? Should animals be selected for rights due to species or individual characteristics? And – if they are chosen based on their species – what species should drafters focus on?

Starting with the question as to *whether all or only some animals should be granted rights*, it is worth noting that neither the Swiss primate rights initiative nor the Finnish rights proposal extend rights beyond animals who belong to species whose members are normally sentient. The same is true for the numerous international animal rights declarations, only two of which (the UDAR and the Toulon Declaration) apply to all animals. Granting rights to all animals (even those who lack sentience) could be said to be simpler as it avoids the issue of determining who is sentient and of explaining why sentience matters more than, say, being alive. It would also avoid the problem – highlighted by ecofeminist scholars – that giving rights to sentient but not non-sentient animals amounts to a mere redrawing of lines that reproduces rather than abolishes problematic binary thinking. Indeed, as we saw in chapter six, some countries, such as Ecuador, even extend the scope of rights to nature more generally.

However, extending the scope of a piece of legislation beyond sentience would go against the widespread acceptance in many legal systems that animal sentience is a useful marker for the scope of animal protection laws. It would also be in tension with the position many philosophers take that beings that are not sentient do not need protection for their own sake. For these reasons, at this stage of the law reform process, it would seem sensible for drafters to operate with sentience as a necessary (albeit perhaps not sufficient) condition for animal rights. As the Finnish rights proposal shows, a precautionary principle can then be used to 'soften the edges' by ensuring that potentially sentient animals are not excluded.

Should animals be selected for rights due to species or individual characteristics? As we saw in chapter five, there are, broadly, two alternative principles of selection for rights-holders: the Species Membership Approach (SMA), which holds that eligible animals should be selected on the basis of their *species* membership or similar group-based categories, and what Fasel calls the Meritocratic approach, according to which rights are distributed to deserving individuals on the basis of their *individual* characteristics. The Swiss primate rights initiative broadly followed the SMA because its scope was determined not by an individual's characteristics, but by the biological order of primates, which includes all primate species. By contrast, according to its Section 1, the Finnish rights proposal makes the possession of rights dependent on an individual animals' sentience. Hence, in principle, courts would have to assess the sentience of individual animals before they could determine whether these animals are entitled to any rights (although, as noted above, the presumption in favour of sentience makes it easier to meet this condition).

Finally, if drafters opt to focus on specific species, then the question becomes *how to select them*. The Swiss primate rights initiative followed what we can call the *elite species approach*. This approach tries to secure rights for charismatic animals who have both public appeal and limited economic and cultural impact. The idea behind the approach is that the public appeal of these animals will make it easier for people to take an interest in them, and their limited economic and cultural impact means that granting rights to such species will not significantly interfere with people's lives and livelihoods. In the case of Switzerland – and many other countries – primates have both public appeal and granting them rights would have little impact on existing cultural traditions or the national economy. This is why primates were seen as promising candidates for animal rights in this instance. However, other species too could come to benefit from the elite species approach. For instance, rights for whales could receive considerable public support: in most countries, only a few people would be directly affected from such a measure and only a small industrial sector would be damaged by the loss of catching and killing whales.

The elite species approach is not without its problems, however. For instance, it can only save a small number of animals and not the ones kept on factory farms who are seen as needing rights most urgently. Some may also question whether the elite species approach can ever lead the way for all animals. This is because it is not yet clear whether rights for elite species would break the mould and enable other, less charismatic species to follow. While approaches that focus on non-elite species do not have that problem, they run into their own, inverse problem: non-elite animals – eg animals used in food production such as chickens – would benefit more from the rights because their interests are arguably more severely violated and because more of them have their interests violated than primates. However, if chickens were put forward as candidates for thick rights this would challenge vested economic interests, as well as the personal preferences of people who eat chickens, which is why a proposal to extend rights to chickens would appear to be less likely to succeed, at least in the near term.

C. Legal Status

Another important question for drafters involved in law reform is whether to be silent on the issue of legal status, or whether to discuss it explicitly, such as by stating that animals are legal persons. As we saw earlier in the chapter, the silent approach was adopted in the Swiss primate rights initiative and the Finnish rights proposal. Neither of these explicitly state what the legal status of animals would be – although, as we saw, inferences can be drawn from other provisions, such as those granting rights or legal standing or providing that animals can remain property. The second, explicit approach was followed in the Toulon Declaration, which French jurists proclaimed in Toulon in 2019 and which is modelled after the Cambridge Declaration on Consciousness (2012). The Toulon Declaration states that 'animals must be universally considered as persons and not things' and that 'animals must be recognized as persons in the legal sense of the term'.

Although we saw in chapter four that the relevance of legal personhood in animal rights law is debated by scholars, we also saw in chapter six that legal personhood still plays an important role because many courts see it as a precondition for holding thick rights, such as the right to bodily liberty protected by *habeas corpus*. It is therefore not surprising that the Toulon Declaration explicitly declares animals to be legal persons. Another way at arriving at the same result would be to amend the definition of 'person' in existing legislation to include animals. This latter approach, however, could have unintended consequences because – depending on the legislation at stake – a 'person' may not only benefit from certain rights, but also carry responsibilities that may be inappropriate for animals.

While being silent on the issue of legal status avoids this problem, it runs into a different issue: the question of legal status cannot remain unresolved forever and leaving it open in legislation means leaving it up to courts to determine it. As we saw in chapter six, the Swiss courts found that animals could be considered legal persons in public law – but that finding was not a foregone conclusion.

One potential solution for drafters could be to explicitly mention animals' status as legal persons *and* to ensure that animals' personhood is sufficiently tailored to their needs so as to avoid the inappropriate imposition of responsibilities or unsuitable rights. This could be achieved for instance by following the approach the Swiss Civil Code adopts for artificial legal entities (such as corporations). Pursuant to its Article 53, '[l]egal entities have all the rights and duties *other than those which presuppose intrinsically human attributes*, such as gender, age or kinship' (emphasis added).

D. The Procedural Rights of Animals

For animals' rights to be effective in practice, drafters would have to put in place mechanisms that allow animals' interests to be properly considered by the relevant authorities. For instance, drafters could try to do so by *requiring decision-makers to take into account animals' interests* in all decisions that have an impact on their lives. A principle along those lines was suggested by the legal theorist Tomasz Pietrzykowski, as part of his proposal that animals should be recognised as 'non-personal subjects of law' (2017: 58). As he argues, this status would give animals 'the right to be taken into account, or – speaking more precisely – to have one's own individual interests considered as relevant in all decisions that may affect their realisation' (2017: 59). He proposes that 'at least the most vital interests' (2017: 59) of an animal should be considered by all persons. His view is that this would help transform the way animals are perceived, and enable their interests to be balanced with the competing human good.

A potential problem with this approach is that the notion of 'vital interests' is relatively vague, making it uncertain what the threshold is when decision-makers need to take them into account. What is more, the requirement may not be sufficient to protect animals' interests if these animals are unable to bring their cases (through representatives) to the decision-makers.

For this reason, Pietrzykowski believes that *granting legal standing* to animals is necessary, too. As we saw in chapter six, animals do not usually qualify for legal standing in court. In cases such as *Tilikum, Katina, Corky, Kasatka, and Ulises* (2012), the courts refused to hear the plaintiffs' arguments because it did not consider the orcas to have legal standing. From a drafting point of view, as the court noted in *Cetacean Community* (2003), the legislature could simply authorise animals to sue. If drafters were to adopt this more expansive approach, not only would animals need to be declared as having legal standing, but detailed procedural rules on how animals can exercise their standing would likely have to be put in place. Specifically, the question of how to choose suitable representatives would have to be addressed. As we saw in

Section 2, the Cantonal Constitutional Court of Basel-Stadt already carried out an initial assessment of possible ways of operationalising legal standing, and drafters could usefully draw on this.

E. The Substantive Rights of Animals

Finally, drafters will have to decide on which substantive rights they want to grant animals. Throughout this chapter, we have come across various substantive rights, including the right to life, to bodily integrity, to protection of one's habitat, and to liberty. Many other rights have been proposed in other documents and in scholarship. These include, for example, the right to be rescued from situations of distress and exploitation (Article 5 in Rose's Law); the right to reproduce, live with their offspring, families, tribes or communities (Article 5 of the Declaration of Rights); and the right to recognition of social membership (Kymlicka 2017). In this subsection, we focus on one substantive right that has so far only rarely been included in animal rights proposals, and that drafters may want to include more often in the future: *labour rights*.

Labour rights for animals may initially seem less intuitive than some more commonly invoked rights like the right to bodily integrity, and have been less widely recognised. However, the idea of protecting working animals already exists in some legal systems in the form of explicit human duties. For instance, Article 14(2)(2) of the Polish Animal Protection Act (1997) provides that it is forbidden to 'use animals sick or undernourished for work' and that '[a] person using animals for work is obligated to ensure them during each twenty four hour period, rest appropriate for a given species, to recuperate their strength' (Article 14(3)). What is more, as we saw with UDAR (1978)'s Article 7, the idea of protecting working animals' access to food, rest, and to limited work hours and intensity as an entitlement of the animals – rather than simply a human duty – is not new either. In recent years, the idea of labour *rights* for animals specifically has gained significant traction, and may well soon again be on the agenda of drafters.

Animals play key roles in societies around the world, from serving in the police and army, to guiding persons with visual impairments, to working in fields and transporting goods. Some of the work that animals perform is skilled and – at least for some animals – enjoyable. However, the vast majority of animal work is hard and dangerous, and emblematic of the ways that animals are instrumentalised and exploited. This raises a fundamental question for drafters: should they provide for labour rights protections, or simply ban problematic practices outright?

Abolitionist drafters would pursue the second path as they hold that humans simply do not have the right to use animals. The first path would be adopted by drafters following recent voices in scholarship who hold that co-operation of humans and some species of animals does not have to be exploitative and may be beneficial for both parties. For example, as Charlotte Blattner, Kendra Coulter, and Will Kymlicka argue, if we can regulate animal work then it 'could serve as a potentially valuable site of social membership, personal meaning, and material security, and an exemplary case of how to secure both rights and relationships with animals' (2019: 4).

Assuming drafters were to follow this second approach, what labour rights could they create? First, it is worth noting that even those taking the more co-operative approach hold that the 'work' of most farmed animals would have to be banned because it often involves the suffering and always involves the death of the animals, and can therefore not be beneficial to them. In other domains where work need not necessarily be exploitative, authors like Donaldson and Kymlicka have argued that animals are entitled to a right to labour. They also explore what amounts to exploitation:

> It is exploitation if animals are coerced (or manipulated) to do activities they don't want to do, or if those activities are inappropriate or dangerous, or if there is a lack of balance between work and other dimensions of life, or if their contribution is ignored or trivialized. But the mere fact that animals might engage in activities that are useful, or that make forms of contribution to the sanctuary community, is not inherently exploitative (2011: 62).

Regulating labour rights first involves making sure that the conditions are in place that ensure that work is enjoyable. According to some authors, this requires that 'labour is properly regulated, with provisions for fair wages, workplace safety, rest and leisure, retirement pensions, and rights to workplace participation' (Blattner et al 2019: 12). Regulations of this sort already exist in the case of human work. While adapting them for animals may not always be straightforward, it is not impossible. Once such conditions are in place, labour can potentially also serve as a site for social inclusion. As Kymlicka puts it, animals could turn from 'property or equipment' to being seen as 'colleagues and co-workers' (2017: 148).

In addition to thinking about how humans and animals can share the workplace and society more generally, there is also a need to focus on the nature of animal work itself in order to achieve what Cochrane calls 'good work' (2019). To bring about the conditions necessary for good work, he identifies a non-exhaustive list of five key labour rights that animals should have: 'The right to representation by a labour union, the right to a decent standard of remuneration, the right to healthy and safe working conditions, the right to rest and leisure and the right to a decent retirement' (2016: 27). Cochrane also noted one more characteristic of good work, which is valuable both in itself and because of the benefits it brings: *esteem*. As he points out, 'we can reasonably assume that if animals *are* held in esteem by the communities in which they labour, they are more likely to receive better treatment, and not be regarded as mere tools or instruments for human ends' (2019: 60).

Exercise 2: Drafting Animal Rights Laws

1. Take the animal protection act of your jurisdiction or a jurisdiction of your choosing. Identify which provisions use broad language, and which more detailed language. What advantages lie in the detailed provisions as opposed to broad ones, and in broad provisions as opposed to detailed ones?

2.   You and your fellow students have been asked to prepare a set of guide-lines for a police authority and their working police dogs. In drafting your guidelines, try to include and expand on what 'good work' means for police dogs.

V. Conclusion

This chapter explored various proposals for both domestic and international animal rights legislation. The proposals we considered vary in style and content, and we analysed them using four themes: scope, legal status, procedural rights, and substantive rights. As we saw, some proposals opt for a wide scope, including all animals or all sentient animals, while others focused on narrow groups of species. Regarding legal status, some proposals do not address the question at all, leaving it to judges and other interpreters to determine. How animals would be able to enforce their rights procedurally is also a question that is left open by many proposals, although some gesture in the direction of how this could be operationalised. Finally, all proposals contain a range of different substantive rights for animals. Most of these rights are closely modelled on existing human rights.

Perhaps most strikingly, none of the proposals we considered in this chapter has been enacted into law yet. For this reason, the chapter ended with a consideration of some of the questions that drafters of future animal rights legislation have to consider when creating what may one day become binding animal rights laws.

Exercise 3: Model Animal Rights Laws

1.   Should animal rights primarily be advanced on the international or the national level?
2.   Prepare a statement explaining what the Swiss primate rights initiative would have meant for Swiss society had it been adopted. Include in the statement a consideration of the implications the proposal might have had for other species.
3.   Explain the difference between the Species Membership Approach and an individual characteristics-based approach to determining the scope of a proposed animal rights law.

4.   You have been asked to select animals that would come to benefit from a bill of rights for animals. Consider the following criteria that you can use to select suitable species. Use the arrows below to indicate how important these criteria would be in your selection.

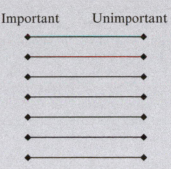

	Important	Unimportant
Evidence of high levels of sentience	◆———————	———◆
Similarity of DNA to humans	◆———————	———◆
Public perception of intelligence	◆———————	———◆
Large public affection	◆———————	———◆
Human-like attributes	◆———————	———◆
Economic relevance to society	◆———————	———◆
Cultural relevance to society	◆———————	———◆

Useful References

Animal Rights Proposals

Animal Bill of Rights (Rose's Law), available at www.roseslaw.org.

Declaration of Rights for Cetaceans: Whales and Dolphins, available at www.cetaceanrights.org.

Declaration on Animal Rights, available at www.declarationofar.org/textSign.php#.

Finnish Animal Rights Lawyers Society's Chapter of the Finnish Constitution, available at www.elaintenvuoro.fi/english/.

Swiss Primate Rights Initiative, available at www.primaten-initiative.ch/en/initiative/.

Toulon Declaration, available at www.univ-tln.fr/spip.php?page=imprimer&id_article=2794.

Universal Charter of the Rights of Other Species, available at www.all-creatures.org/articles/ar-universal-charter-rights-species.html.

Universal Declaration of Animal Rights, available at constitutii.files.wordpress.com/2016/06/file-id-607.pdf.

World Declaration of the Great Apes, available at www.projetogap.org.br/en/world-declaration-on-great-primates/?_ga=2.109202115.796902056.1651156167–1712649113.1651156167.

Literature

Cochrane, A (2019) 'Good Work for Animals' in CE Blattner, K Coulter and W Kymlicka (eds), *Animal Labour: A New Frontier of Interspecies Justice?* (Oxford, Oxford University Press).

Donaldson, S and Kymlicka, W (2015) 'Farmed Animal Sanctuaries: The Heart of the Movement?' 1 *Politics and Animals* 50.

Fasel, R et al (2016) 'Fundamental Rights for Primates', Policy Paper by Sentience 1, 1–16, available at www.ea-foundation.org/files/Fundamental-Rights-for-Primates.pdf.

Stone, CD (1972) *Should Trees Have Standing? Law, Morality, and the Environment* (Oxford, Oxford University Press).

Neumann, JM (2012) 'The Universal Declaration of Animal Rights or the Creation of a New Equilibrium Between Species' 19 *Animal Law* 91.

8

Animal Rights as a Social Justice Movement

I. Introduction

Social justice concerns the distribution of privileges, wealth, and opportunities on the level of society. Social justice *movements* seek to address existing imbalances in this distribution and bring about more fairness by changing people's attitudes and behaviours. The #MeToo and Black Lives Matter movements are only some of the latest and most prominent examples of social justice movements. Most social justice movements focus on human needs. They champion the interests of humans who are oppressed – socially, politically, culturally – and are aimed at politicians, lawmakers, and the general public, to change laws and the way people behave.

The animal rights movement has long been seen as a movement whose supporters seek to change how humans treat animals. As such, it has parallels to the environmental protection movement, which aims to change our impact on nature more generally. In recent decades, the animal rights movement has increasingly also been cast as a social justice movement in the tradition of other large movements such as the feminist or the abolitionist movement. As we saw in chapter three, many animal rights thinkers argue that animals should be subjects of justice under the law. Some, like the philosopher Robert Jones have built on these thinkers to explicitly argue that 'animal rights is a social justice issue' (2015: 469). According to authors like Jones, the issues traditionally challenged by other social justice movements can be readily seen to apply also to animals: domination, oppression (both institutional and individual), violence, and powerlessness. Because of this link between the animal rights and other movements, the legal scholar and activist Jay Shooster has proposed that '[i]t is only a matter of time before animal rights is accepted as an integral part of a comprehensive social justice agenda' (2015: 44).

This chapter explores this perspective by discussing the commonalities as well as differences between human-focused social justice movements and the animal rights movement. We begin by considering the links between animal rights and the (human) abolitionist movement, and discuss the Abolitionist perspective on animal rights.

We then look at the common ground with other social justice movements as well as some differences, focusing in particular on the feminist movement. Finally, we consider what animal rights proponents can learn from the tactics adopted by other movements.

Central Issues

1. The animal rights movement is today often cast as a social justice movement, with many drawing links to other social justice movements such as the feminist movement or the abolitionist movement.
2. The Abolitionist movement in animal rights is directly inspired by the human abolitionist movements of the eighteenth and nineteenth centuries in Europe and the US. Abolitionism in animal rights is based on the view that animals should have a right not to be property – a principle that also underlay human abolitionism.
3. Despite some differences, there is considerable overlap between the issues facing animal rights and those facing social justice movements such as the feminist movement. All are dealing with oppression, the use of violence, and unequal treatment.
4. Lessons that animal rights proponents can learn from other movements include the importance of direct action, consciousness-raising, and the opportunities provided by social media. Among the challenges facing the animal rights movement are the necessity of political compromise.

II. The Animal Rights Movement as Abolitionist

In this section, we give an overview of the original human abolitionist movement which advocated for the abolition of human slavery. We then consider the origins and implications of abolitionism in the animal rights movement, with a particular focus on what chapter two has referred to as Abolitionism: the view popularised by Gary Francione and his followers that animals should have a right not to be property.

A. Human Abolitionism

The human abolitionist movement developed in the late eighteenth century and challenged the trade in forcibly taking Africans to work as slaves on plantations in the Caribbean and North America. In England, the Court of King's Bench in *Somerset v Stewart* (1772) (mentioned in chapter six) played an important role in setting in motion the later prohibition of slavery. The case, decided by Lord Mansfield, involved a *habeas corpus* petition filed by the abolitionist Granville Sharp on the behalf of James Somerset, who was a slave aboard a ship lying in the river Thames and was destined to be sold in Jamaica. Despite containing strong language condemning the institution of slavery, Lord Mansfield's decision – constrained by the nature of *habeas corpus* petitions to the protection of individual persons – was limited to setting free Somerset. Nevertheless, it helped spark broader legal change.

At first, however, slave trade continued from English ports such as Liverpool and Bristol, as well as from other ports in Europe such as Nantes, Lisbon, and Barcelona. Transporting slaves from Africa to the Caribbean and bringing back sugar and other commodities was a profitable part of Europe's overseas trade. Equally significant, slavery and the slave trade were widely accepted not only as legal but also as proper: the Church of England, for example, was an investor in both plantations and slave ships.

The abolitionist movement was particularly prominent in Britain, and was led by well-known abolitionists such as William Wilberforce, Hannah More, Olaudah Equiano, Thomas Clarkson, as well as Granville Sharp. Like the abolitionist movements in other countries, its proponents were opposed to the idea that people could be owned and treated as things. The type of slavery they took aim at is often referred to as 'chattel slavery', because the slaves were treated as *chattels*, that is, pieces of property of their owners. The abolitionist movement was arguing, among other things, for a change in slaves' legal status and for fundamental legal equality. The movement also encouraged people to make personal changes such as not eating slave-produced sugar. Eventually, the movement was successful in changing the law. In the UK, the Parliament passed the Slave Trade Act 1807, which banned the slave trade; and in 1833 it passed the Slavery Abolition Act, which banned the purchasing and owning of slaves throughout most of the British Empire.

The moral convictions of the abolitionists, as well as the scale of their success and the consequential powerful aversion to slavery around the world, made them an obvious group to emulate. However, it bears noting that despite the abolitionists' success in formally abolishing chattel slavery, other types of slavery continue to this day in many parts of the world. Modern slavery encompasses for instance forced labour, forced marriages, the recruitment of child soldiers, and organ trafficking. According to the latest Global Slavery Index (2018), more than 40 million people were the victims of modern slavery in 2016.

B. The Origins of Abolitionism in Animal Rights

In chapter two, we considered Abolitionism – the view promoted by Gary Francione and others as an alternative to Welfarism. According to Abolitionism, all sentient animals should have a right not to be treated as property, that is, a right to personhood. What are the origins of this Abolitionist approach to animal rights?

Although, as we saw in chapter one, concern for animals is a global phenomenon going back thousands of years, the roots of animal rights can be traced back to the eighteenth century. This is when, in Europe, consideration for animals as having moral worth became prominent and some, such as the French Enlightenment thinker Jean-Claude Delamétherie proposed that sentient animals should have the rights to life, health, and 'enjoyments' (Fasel 2019: 59). In the nineteenth century, the animal advocate Henry Salt explicitly adopted ideas from human abolitionism. According to him, there are common threads between the oppression of human slaves and the oppression of most animals, which he thought were both 'founded on a lack of imaginative sympathy' (Salt 1894: 21). However, momentum faltered in the twentieth century and the period up to the mid-1960s has been described as 'a barren period in the evolution of the animal rights ethic' (Ryder 1989: 143).

As we saw in chapter one, the mid-1960s onwards witnessed a revival of interest in the moral status of animals, with books such as Ruth Harrison's *Animal Machines* (1964) and the UK government's Brambell Report (1965) on farmed animals having an impact far beyond the UK. In the US, there was a similar increased interest in animal rights. For example, Helen Jones's National Catholic Society for Animal Welfare changed its name in 1972 to the Society for Animal Rights (now the International Society for Animal Rights, ISAR). In the UK, animal rights regained prominence in the early 1970s at the University of Oxford with the emergence of a group later known as the 'Oxford Group', whose members included, among others, Richard Ryder, Ruth Harrison, Andrew Linzey, John Harris, and Roslind and Stanley Godlovitch.

During this revival, the views of these animal rights advocates had some closeness to the animal welfare movement. For example, members of the Oxford Group encouraged people to eat meat from animals who had better lives than those raised on factory farms. This was seen as a stepping stone to giving up meat altogether. At the same time, we can find in the Oxford Group the roots of what would become the paradigm of Abolitionism under Francione. For example, the Godlovitchs and Harris proposed an Abolitionist approach to animal rights in their edited volume *Animals, Man and Morals* (1971) – albeit without using the term. As they noted in the introduction of that book: 'We have not assembled this book to provide the reader with yet another manual on how to make brutalities less brutal'. Instead, they were calling for a 'cessation' of cruel treatment and the killing of animals (1971: 7). Members of the Oxford Group believed that removing the property status of animals was a natural fit for a movement that demanded moral equality for humans and animals. Hence, similar to the original abolitionists who made changes to avoid products associated with slavery, these animal rights proponents advocated a switch to veganism. Equally importantly, their advocacy was based on a rejection of speciesism, a concept we discussed in chapter three.

These initial explorations of a proto-Abolitionism later became a movement in its own right. The author and activist Billy Ray Boyd first used the term Abolitionism in the title of his book *The New Abolitionists: Animal Rights and Human Liberation* (1987). However, it was not until the legal scholar Francione developed Abolitionism into a powerful theoretical position that it gained the prominence it has today.

Francione made two main points about the connection between Abolitionism and human abolitionism. First, he argued that animals will never get fair treatment as long as they have the status of property. As with human slavery, he pointed out that animals cannot receive the consideration they are due as sentient beings because their property status makes their wellbeing dependent on their owners' whim, rather than protecting it as a matter of right. Second, Francione noted that human slavery and animal ownership are 'structurally identical' (2004: 122) and therefore that the positions of human abolitionists and Abolitionists are aligned. As he points out:

> Slave welfare laws failed for precisely the same reason that animal welfare laws fail to establish any meaningful limit on our use of animal property. The owner's property interest in the slave always trumped any interest of the slave who was ostensibly protected under the law. The interests of slaves were observed only when it provided an economic benefit for the owners or served their whim (2004: 123).

Due to Francione's influence, the Abolitionist movement grew quickly, particularly in the US, so that in 2011 an observer could note that there were two broad categories working within animal advocacy in the US:

> In one category are those seeking to end the property status of animals, grant them basic rights and/or protections, and thereby abolish institutionalized exploitation ([A]bolitionists or liberationists). In the other category are those seeking to reform current practices to reduce animal suffering (welfarists or reformists) (Kim 2011: 315).

C. The Implications of Abolitionism in Animal Rights

There are various implications in the adoption of an Abolitionist approach to animal rights. Later in the chapter we are going to look at the implications on the potential for compromise. For the purposes of this subsection, we can focus on a legal case that was based directly on Abolitionist ideas and that helps illustrate the implications of the Abolitionist approach.

The case – which chapter six explored from a legal perspective – was brought by the People for the Ethical Treatment of Animals (PETA) in 2012 on behalf of the orcas Tilikum, Katina, Corky, Kasatka, and Ulises – five orcas kept at Sea World Orlando and San Diego. In its lawsuit, PETA argued that the orcas were kept in breach of the Thirteenth Amendment of the US Constitution:

Thirteenth Amendment, Section 1 – United States Constitution (1789; 1865)

Neither slavery nor involuntary servitude, except as a punishment for crime whereof the party shall have been duly convicted, shall exist within the United States, or any place subject to their jurisdiction.

In invoking this provision, PETA argued that the orcas were slaves. It held in particular that the orcas were:

(1) held physically and psychologically captive; (2) without the means of escape; (3) separated from their homes and families; (4) unable to engage in natural behaviours and determine their own course of action or way of life; (5) subjugated to the will and desires of Sea World; (6) confined in unnatural, stressful and inadequate conditions; and (7) subject to artificial insemination or sperm collection for the purposes of involuntary breeding. (2012, 1261)

The Court considered PETA's argument from various perspectives (including President Abraham Lincoln's Emancipation Declaration), and came to the conclusion that the concept of slavery only applied to human persons, noting that slavery was a uniquely human activity that could not apply to orcas.

It is arguable that one of the strong suits of the Abolitionist animal rights move-ment is its clear and simple approach to demanding rights for animals. Just as human abolitionists rejected the legal distinction of people into some who are free and others who are objects of property, so the animal Abolitionists reject the legal position that separates some animals (ie humans) into legal persons and others (ie non-humans) into property. As such, the Abolitionist movement was an important counterbalance to the thinking at the time which was still primarily welfare-focused, thus revitalising the animal rights movement.

On the other hand, as we saw in chapter two, the Abolitionist approach is seen by some as simplistic, if not problematic. Boiled down to its essence, it is based on the assumption that once animals are no longer property – and everyone adopts veganism – the problems with animal cruelty and exploitation will disappear. However, looking at slavery in the human context and the problems that remain to this day with modern forms of slavery and structural racism, it appears that some Abolitionists have been too optimistic in this respect. Being property is not a neces-sary condition for cruelty. Hence, just as domestic violence continues even though its human victims are not property, ending property rights over animals will not in itself end cruelty and oppression.

III. Animal Rights and Connections with Other Rights Movements

Many scholars and activists find common ground between the animal rights move-ment and the anti-racist, anti-ableist, and feminist movements: all these movements are fighting oppression by the powerful; oppose the use of violence and force to perpetuate the *status quo*; and reject justifications of unfair entitlements based on tradition, socio-cultural, or religious values.

In this section, we focus on three areas where links have been established between the animal rights movement and other social justice movements. First, we look at analogies that animal rights advocates have made with other social justice issues and discuss their often-critical reception by other social justice movements. We then focus on the links between animal rights and feminism, before considering whether what some see as a systemic failure of the law reform process for social justice movements also applies to animal rights law reform.

A. Analogies with Other Movements to Support Animal Rights

Some in the animal rights movement have proposed that the treatment of animals is analogous to that of certain groups of humans. To illustrate, let us focus on two concrete campaigns where comparison has been made with animal rights: slavery and the Holocaust. Both campaigns were by PETA, but ran nearly twenty years ago and as such do not necessarily represent the organisation's current campaigns.

Starting with the first campaign, in 2005 PETA held an exhibition called 'The Animal Liberation Project: We Are All Animals'. In this campaign, various images of animals and slaves were juxtaposed. For example, a shackled human leg was shown next to a chained elephant. In response to criticism, PETA argued that the exhibition did not use the association of animals and black people to denigrate the latter, but rather to uplift animals. Nonetheless, it was widely criticised and subsequently withdrawn. The second campaign, called 'Holocaust on your Plate', followed in 2006. In it, PETA compared how animals are treated in factory farms and how Jews were treated in the Holocaust. It showed photographs of factory farms and slaughterhouses side-by-side with photos from Nazi death camps.

Both campaigns generated roughly three types of response: first, that the comparisons are unjustifiable; second, that they may be justifiable, given the challenges the animal rights movement has to face; and, third, that what is important is not whether but how comparisons are made.

Many have taken the first approach and rejected the use of such comparisons altogether. For example, the critical legal scholar Angela Harris condemned the comparison between animals and slaves on the ground that it 'implicitly constructs a gaze under which slaves and animals appear alike … [but which] ignores the dynamic relationship between people of color and animals given their historic linkage in the white western mind' (2009: 27). She also points out that the animal rights movement is perceived by some African Americans as 'a white thing' (2009: 15), which may compound the problem of making comparisons. Reflecting on the issue of comparisons more broadly, the political scientist Claire Jean Kim (2011) notes that although those who, like PETA, are making analogies may at first glance seem to be connecting different movements, they are at risk of instrumentalising other causes by treating them as a mere means to their own ends.

Kim's analysis explains why some stakeholders supported the second response to PETA's campaigns: that they are justifiable in light of the obstacles the animal rights movement needs to overcome. She identifies two considerations in particular that would seem to support the campaigns. First, there is the moral urgency created by industrial animal farming where suffering is so extreme that it justifies campaigns that may otherwise not be permissible. Second, there is the issue that the animal rights movement faces an enormous challenge:

> the singular dilemma PETA faces as an above-ground abolitionist group: that it needs to do nothing less than destabilize the sacrosanct human/animal divide in order to achieve its aim of convincing people that nonhuman animals have the intrinsic moral right not to be treated as the means to human ends (Kim 2011: 318).

She continues by observing that, to make matters worse,

> to illuminate the hidden violence and suffering farm animals endure, PETA's exhibits face the challenge of reaching a public that has been conditioned through many cultural products – including children's books and movies and the pointed advertising of the milk, egg, and meat industries – to not know (2011: 319).

The third response – which urges us to focus not on what comparisons are made but how they are made – is encapsulated in a contribution by the ethicist David Sztybel.

Focusing on industrial animal production and the Holocaust, Sztybel carries out a detailed comparison, concluding that it is not factually inaccurate to say that the two can be compared. The real question, he argues, is thus not whether animal suffering and human suffering in the Holocaust can be compared, but 'whether we should dare to make the comparison' (2006: 99). Sztybel makes three mains points which are relevant not only to Holocaust comparisons but to analogies in support of a cause more generally. First, he points out that liberal debate requires toleration and respect:

> A certain amount of upset with those who disagree is part of a liberal culture of toleration and respect of differences, and cannot be used as a grounds to silence any given side of an honest debate. I ... do not deny that there are, indeed, offensive ways of comparing animal treatment to the Holocaust, although perhaps all of these can be avoided (2006: 121–22).

Second, he claims that it is not an 'insult' to object to an oppressive practice, and what liberationists seek to do is to overthrow all oppression. According to Sztybel, animal rights proponents do not intend to insult with their comparisons, but rather intend to protect vulnerable beings from both physical and more subtle insults. Third and finally, he argues that while there are numerous differences between the way animals are treated in modern societies and Jews were treated in the Holocaust, there are also some similarities:

> The point is that none of them [the differences] erase the prominent similarities which give point to the comparison in the first place. No analogy is perfect. It is remarkable how harsh and systematic discrimination can have chillingly comparable form, even when the victims are of different species (2006: 125–26).

For these reasons, Sztybel concludes that comparisons between the treatment of animals and the Holocaust not only can be made but that such comparisons can be 'potentially useful and illuminating, and may help to underline the gravity of our oppression of nonhuman animals' (2006: 130).

Other scholars have taken similar views and proposed recognising the value (or at least the absence of harm) in *some* comparisons while also being cautious about *how* those comparisons are made. In an analysis of PETA campaigns that used sexual imagery, Maneesha Deckha argues that while 'it is difficult to criticize the conviction that animates PETA's campaigns' (2008: 48) and while some of its campaigns are understandable given the need to get the public's attention,

> animal [rights] advocates must take care that their use of the female form does not re-enact problematic tropes of commodification and its concomitant objectification as well as other hegemonic modes of exploitation (2008: 66).

In a similar vein, according to Kim (2011), the animal rights movement must, first, be careful to avoid both stereotypes and denigration. Second, and more practically, if the animal rights movement wants to be a social justice movement, it needs to avoid alienating other movements from being allies. According to the writer and activist Syl Ko, the way the animal rights movement should do this is by de-centring whiteness, which 'requires taking seriously non-white art, literature, music, systems of belief, and other rituals as a way of reimagining the world outside of the constraints developed by white supremacy' (2017: 43). According to Ko, this need for de-centring whiteness stems from the fact that it is white supremacy – and not so much speciesism – which discriminates against animals and black people.

B. Links with Feminism and Interlocking Oppression

As we saw in chapter three, many feminist writers recognise links between feminism and the treatment of animals, and some scholars and activists have argued for a recognition of the interlocking structures of domination – thus connecting the feminist and animal rights movements.

In her pioneering book *The Sexual Politics of Meat* (1990), the activist and writer Carol Adams identified a connection between feminism and vegetarianism, meat-eating, and masculinity. In later works, she developed the concept of the 'interlocking oppression' (Adams 2010: 304) – a term that was coined in the Combahee River Collective Statement (1977) – focusing on the oppression of women and animals through the use of language and of sexual imagery. Adams and Josephine Donovan put the idea of interconnectedness plainly when stating:

> We believe that all oppressions are interconnected: no one creature will be free until all are free-from abuse, degradation, exploitation, pollution, and commercialization. Women and animals have shared these oppressions historically, and until the mentality of domination is ended in all its forms, these afflictions will continue (1995: 3).

More recently, an increasing number of scholars and activists have argued for the need to include animal oppression as a matter of intersectionality. The critical race theorist Kimberlé Crenshaw coined the term 'intersectionality' (1989: 140) to describe the ways in which race, class, gender, disability, and other ideas intersect and overlap to become more than the sum of their parts. The focus of intersectionality theorists like Crenshaw is not on any individual's single identity, but on the intersecting nature of different structures of harm, with multiple systems of oppression intersecting to concentrate cumulative power in the hands of an elite. According to intersectionality thinkers, the project of challenging this power dynamic is what binds different social justice movements together.

For intersectionalists, there is not only common ground between different social justice movements, but also a common *cause*. According to them, racism, sexism, classism, and speciesism *intersect* because they are all the product of the same structures of patriarchy, domination, violence, and imperialism. Take modern industrialised agriculture, which for Jones 'provides a clear case of the intersection between speciesism, racism, classism, and environmental justice' (2015: 478). This type of agriculture is seen as reflecting speciesism in the use and killing of animals for food; racism in its exploitation of migrant workers; classism in its promotion of products like fur as class markers; and environmental justice in the water and other environmental pollution its factories create.

The sociologist Corey Lee Wrenn too emphasises the commonalities between the human and non-human abolitionist movements, and the need to recognise intersectionality between different forms of inequality. For her, these commonalities also offer opportunities for Abolitionists to adopt some of the tactics used by the human abolitionists due to the considerable overlap, 'specifically in the need to simultaneously address property status and oppressive ideology' (2014: 177). Because of these intersections between women and animals (and other oppressed groups), ecofeminist scholars such as Adams and Donovan have cautioned against feminism failing to include support for animal issues:

> The presumption that these efforts are opposed to each other arises from the dualistic premise that humans' and animals' needs are in conflict. It also implies that human needs are paramount, reinforcing a status hierarchy that has favored neither women nor other animals. It is a haunting repetition of the traditional trivializing of women's issues (1995: 3).

As the ecofeminist writer Greta Gaard points out, feminists would contradict the philosophical commitments of their own position if they did not extend moral concern to animals: '[e]xcluding or omitting the oppression of animals from feminist and ecofeminist analyses ... is inconsistent with the activist and philosophical foundations of both feminism (as a "movement to end all forms of oppression") and ecofeminism' (2002: 130).

C. A Failure in the System?

As we saw in chapter three, some ecofeminist authors have suggested that the animal rights movement is built on flawed foundations. They believe that animal rights (and other rights movements) are based on a problematic liberal and male view of atomistic and disembodied individuals. But that is not their only worry. Among the other issues identified by some ecofeminist scholars are: first, the idea that humans have the right to grant rights; second, that extending rights to other species simply moves the boundary between those with and without rights; and, third, that the movement is trying to operate within legal systems that have already failed animals. These are theoretical worries that are relevant for activists: if the system as such is flawed, why work within it rather than try to topple it?

Starting with the first issue, some have emphasised that the very discussion of granting rights to animals emphasises the *power of humans to grant such rights*. According to Kappeler, the idea that humans have a right to grant rights is absurd:

> Even the most radical animal rights position, which would grant rights to all species of animals, is no different in theory from that which denies such rights ... The very project of granting and extending rights is fundamentally speciesist, exempting the human agent and judge into the category of subject ruling over an object world ... The question is, rather, why such an abuse of power and such a will to dominance – constituted in white, male, Western, adult, expert supremacy, but exercised in the name of humanity – continues to be seen and defined as a *right*. (1995: 334–35)

Ecofeminist theorists like Donovan are sceptical of the idea of extending rights to animals because they view it as simply redrawing the lines between those who are included and those who are excluded, thus *maintaining binary thinking*. This is the second issue, which we encountered in chapter three. The idea here is that when animal rights advocates discuss the criteria for rights-holding (eg sentience), they are challenging the content of the categories (can only humans or also sentient non-humans have rights?), but they are not challenging the categories themselves (why focus on rights at all?). As Kappeler puts it, the 'idea of the ladder of categories – of the "objective" classification of given, "natural" species – remains unquestioned and unchallenged, in the interest of those who see the chance of being adopted into the top class' (1995: 331).

Philosopher Lori Gruen and legal scholar Justin Marceau (2022) recognise the risks of using the existing system:

> [S]ocial justice activists, including animal activists, and cause lawyers, including those who work to elevate the status of animals, have often worked within the logic of the law and legal system to try to gain more expansive and inclusive results ... there is a risk that litigation efforts aimed at celebrating the potential of the legal system to serve as a check on itself will legitimize and confirm the very hierarchies and problematic systems in question (2022: 316).

Gruen and Marceau here voice the third issue: that there is a tension in animal rights proponents' belief in legal change considering that legal systems around the world have so far *failed to bring about meaningful change* for many animals. However, one can take the view that legal systems have served to systematically discriminate against animals, and still believe that law has the potential to become more protective of animals' interests. Along these lines, thinkers such as Deckha have argued in favour of changing the legal system from within by using legal tools and rethinking legal concepts to tear down rather than uphold animals' status as property. As we noted in chapter four, she proposes to 'replace the exploitative property classification for animals' that exists in all legal systems 'with a new, transformative legal status or subjectivity, which I [Deckha] term "beingness"' (2020: 6).

Exercise 1: Animal Rights and Other Rights Movements

1. An activist group would like to launch an animal rights campaign in which women without clothes are placed in cages to draw attention to the plight of captive animals. You are asked to consult the group on the issues to be considered with this campaign.
2. Imagine that you are trying to convince your friends – who are ardent supporters of #MeToo and Black Lives Matter – that they should see animal rights as a social justice matter. What arguments would you use to convince them? What counterarguments could your friends make? You can do this exercise in groups or on your own.
3. Prepare a short (3 minutes) presentation on what scholars and activists see as the systematic issues that the animal rights movement faces. Try to address each of these issues.

IV. Learning Lessons

If, as many now believe, the animal rights movement is a social justice movement, then animal rights advocates can potentially learn from the tactics and strategies that other rights movements have employed to advance their causes. Much ink has been spilled on the strategies of other movements. In the disability rights movement, for example, there are studies on the importance of grass-roots organisations (eg Oliver 1997), the use of direct action such as demonstrations and sit-ins (eg Shakespeare 1993), and working with political elites (eg Pettinicchio 2019). In the women's rights movement, scholars have researched autonomous organisations that are independent of political parties (eg Weldon and Htun 2013), consciousness raising (eg Banaszak and Ondercin 2016), and the use of social media (eg Brunner and Partlow-Lefevre 2020). And the changing of hearts and minds has been studied in various social movements (eg Crutchfield 2018).

In this section, we focus on two areas where the animal rights movement can learn lessons from other movements: first, in the adoption of a range of awareness-raising activities common among social justice movements (direct action, consciousness raising, and the use of social media); and second, in the need for compromise.

A. Direct Action, Consciousness-Raising, the Use of Social Media, and New Directions

Through *direct action*, social justice activists in numerous movements have been able to increase awareness of their struggles by causing disruption. Direct action can be violent or non-violent, and can range from strikes and boycotts, to coordinated protests or marches taking place nationwide and or even worldwide, to acting in defiance of laws such as measures to limit the right to hold peaceful public protests. The animal rights movement has a history of both non-violent and violent direct-action campaigns. Though a causal link between direct action and law reform is difficult to establish, the political scientist Berenice Carroll (1989) has suggested that direct action has played a major role in all successful feminist movements, and Wrenn (2014) has identified non-violent direct action as a successful tactic used by the abolitionists of human slavery.

Consciousness-raising is another tactic used by many social justice movements. For instance, it was a central tool in feminist organising in the US in the 1970s. The feminist legal scholar Catherine MacKinnon describes it as a technique of analysis and political practice to uncover 'the impact of male dominance' (1989: 8), both individually and within society. One objective of the feminist movement at the time (and still today) was to encourage women to be aware of their own oppression, and develop a collective understanding of sexist structures. This idea of consciousness-raising can also be relevant for animal rights because of the importance of raising people's awareness of animal oppression and their own (direct or indirect) involvement in its continuation.

Finally, the use of *social media* has become a distinct tool in modern day organising, one that overlaps with consciousness-raising. Historically, movements have used traditional types of media, such as magazines and pamphlets, to spread their message. Today, the mainstream use of social media has opened up a new front for communication and engagement. The 2017 #MeToo movement is just one example of a movement taking place primarily on Twitter, but which led to widespread discussions of sexual harassment, to powerful men losing their jobs, and to improvements in workplace protections for women. Similarly, in 2020, the Black Lives Matter movement attracted significant support on social media, which catalysed worldwide protests against police brutality towards African Americans as well as structural racism. While the path from social media campaigning to actual legal change is full of bends, the use of such campaigns appears to be an increasingly important tool for any social justice movement.

B. Compromise

It is a commonplace that all social justice movements need to compromise to progress and to turn ideology into practical effective change. Sometimes, compromise is necessary because agendas change when a movement's goals are achieved or because public opinion has shifted. And sometimes it is necessary simply to make any progress.

In the case of the animal rights movement, there appears to be a need for compromise both within the movement itself, as well as between it and the animal welfare movement. As we saw in chapter two, one of the challenges to compromise is that those within the animal rights movement who adopt an Abolitionist position risk creating a schism with both Classic and New Welfarists. The Abolitionist Francione noted this himself when stating:

> The problem is that the welfarist and rights positions are in fundamental and irreconcilable tension both as a theoretical and a practical matter. The welfarist approach – however it is packaged or presented – regards the lives of animals as having less moral value than the lives of humans. The defining features of the rights position as I defend it involves a rejection of the notion that animal life has a lesser value than human life (Francione and Garner 2010: 5).

Francione's Abolitionist position makes it virtually impossible for defenders of rights to endorse animal welfare improvements, so that the two approaches appear to be at odds. However, as we saw in chapter two, Francione's position on animal rights is not the only one. Rather, there is a plethora of animal rights theories which – although they also promote the abolition of animal exploitation – differ from Francione's position in for example allowing animals to remain property or by permitting the use of animals under certain circumstances. We called these theories 'abolitionist' to distinguish them from Francione's position, which we called 'Abolitionist'.

The steady growth of (small-a) abolitionist theories shows that there is not only evolution within the animal rights movement, but also the possibility and willingness to compromise. At the same time, the emergence of such theories also reflects disagreements about what the concept of animal rights itself entails. We have looked at these questions in previous chapters, which is why it will be sufficient to simply recapitulate some of the conceptual questions and strategic compromises that animal rights proponents are currently debating:

- Do animals need legal personhood status similar to humans? Or should they be accorded a lesser status – for example a type of *sui generis* personhood, or some other equivalent status – in order to become holders of rights?

- Must animals cease to be property? Or can they continue to be property, or be some more nuanced form of property, such as living property?

- Do animals require legal standing to be able to appear in court (through a representative)? Or is it sufficient that their interests are protected indirectly through animal welfare agencies?

- Do all animals need to have rights, or only certain species?

- Do animals need broad rights, or more narrow rights to protect the most important aspects of their lives?

- Will animals be prohibited from working for or with humans? Or do they have a right to certain types of labour?

- Should wild animals have exclusive or non-exclusive rights over their habitats?

V. Conclusion

We started this chapter considering whether animal rights is a social justice issue. Most social justice movements address injustice for humans. We have seen that there are numerous points of similarity between the animal rights movement and many human-focused social justice movements. Despite the existence of differences, we have seen that there are also many areas of overlap and evidence of mutual support. For these reasons, many scholars have taken the view that animal rights is a social justice movement. What is more, according to intersectional theorists, the animal rights movement and other social justice movements should be seen as fighting an interconnected struggle against intersecting forms of oppression. For them, there can never be complete success on one social justice matter as long as other forms of oppression remain.

To be sure, despite this now increasingly common view in scholarship, it is possible that animal rights will only be fully recognised as a social justice issue once there is widespread recognition among the public that animals suffer from systematic oppression similar to marginalised human groups. Other social justice movements had to start by generating public understanding and support. Human abolitionism had first to overcome the hurdle of the widespread view that slavery is not a problem. Feminism had to deal with a similar problem, which is why consciousness-raising was one of the first areas its advocates addressed. It is possible that animal rights too will only become a full-blown social justice movement once all animals start to be accepted as part of society, and not outside it.

Exercise 2: Animal Rights as a Social Justice Movement

1. What role should Abolitionism play in the current animal rights movement? Do you think it remains a useful doctrine? Was it at least a useful doctrine at the time?

2. You have been asked to prepare a campaign to encourage awareness of animal rights. Consider the following elements and think about how important they could be to increase the campaign's likelihood of success. Use the arrows below to indicate how inclined you are to use or not use these elements in your campaign.

	Would Use	Would Not Use
Compare the treatment of animals and slaves	◆———————————◆	
Compare the treatment of animals and women	◆———————————◆	
Describe the cruelty that is done to animals	◆———————————◆	
Emphasise the weakness of welfare laws	◆———————————◆	
Emphasise interconnection of oppressions	◆———————————◆	

3. Analyse a campaign to address consciousness-raising conducted by anti-racism, feminism, or disability rights movements, and consider how this campaign may be relevant for the animal rights movement. To identify such campaigns, you may find it helpful to browse the websites of NGOs working in these areas.

4. Is animal rights a social justice movement?

Useful References

Chiesa, E (2016) 'Animal Rights Unravelled: Why Abolitionism Collapses Into Welfarism and What it Means for Animal Ethics' 28 *Georgetown Environmental Law Review* 4, 557.

Cohen, M (2017) 'Animal Colonialism: The Case of Milk' 111 *AJIL Unbound* 267.

Cordeiro-Rodrigues, L (2017) 'Animal Abolitionism and "Racism without Racists"' (2017) 30 *Journal of Agricultural & Environmental Ethics* 6, 745.

Brunner, E and Partlow-Lefevre, S (2020) '#MeToo as networking collective: examining consciousness-raising on wild public networks' 17 *Communication and Critical/Cultural Studies* 2, 166.

MacKinnon, CA (2004) 'Of Mice and Men: A Feminist Fragment on Animal Rights' in C Sunstein and MC Nussbaum (eds), *Animal Rights: Current Debates and New Directions* (Oxford, Oxford University Press).

Singer, J (ed) (2021) *Antiracism in Animal Advocacy: Igniting Cultural Transformation* (Brooklyn, Lantern Publishing).

Trigg, R (2021) 'Intersectionality: An Alternative to Redrawing the Line in the Pursuit of Animal Rights' 26 *Ethics & the Environment* 73.

Conclusion

We began this textbook with Roscoe Pound's finding that law must walk a tightrope between being stable and adapting to changing circumstances. The ensuing chapters explored how legal systems around the world have responded to the growing trend for animal rights laws, which we mapped from the perspectives of comparative law, philosophy, legal theory, human rights, case law, legislative reform, and social movements. The book has aimed to provide readers with an understanding of the key issues, giving them the tools to critically engage with the developments we are currently seeing in scholarship and law.

In chapter one, we introduced the legal status quo of animals by drawing on examples from legal systems around the world. The picture that emerged from this sketch of global animal law is one in which 79 per cent of UN Member States have some form of animal protection law, with around half protecting not only cruelty against animals but also providing more 'positive' welfare protections. However, we saw that even states that possess such laws do not come near where animal rights proponents would like them to be. This is due to the fact that these legal systems still largely subject animals to the rules governing property that allow infringements of their basic interests; they provide for exceptions and exemptions to existing protections; and they can often fail to enforce these protections.

To draw this out, chapter two focused on the debate between Abolitionists who argue that all use and killing of animals should end and that animals should cease to be property, and Welfarists who argue that humans can continue to own, use, and kill animals, as long as they ensure protections of their welfare in the process. Starting with the New Welfarists – according to whom welfare improvements now do not stand in the way of granting rights to animals in the future – the floor was then opened to a consideration of more recent alternative approaches to animal rights that go beyond the Welfarism/Abolitionism dichotomy.

To better understand the breadth of animal rights approaches, chapter three shed light on some of the central ethical theories for and against animal rights. Peter Singer's utilitarian approach, Tom Regan's deontological theory, Martha Nussbaum's capabilities approach, and Sue Donaldson and Will Kymlicka's political theory were presented as the main pro-animal rights theories. These were then contrasted with critiques from ecofeminists, conservationists, and contractualist philosophers. It is worth reiterating, however, that the lines we drew are not sharp and that there are thinkers from these three latter traditions who support animal rights.

Building on these philosophical foundations, chapter four explored key questions in the theory of animal rights law. Taking as our starting point the view of some sceptics that animal rights is simply 'loose talk' by animal lovers, we discussed three questions that animal rights lawyers need to be able to answer: first, whether animals can have rights, second, whether they already do have rights and, third, whether – to have rights – animals would need to become legal persons and cease to be property.

We discovered that a lot depends on whether one understands animal rights as thin or thick rights – an insight that helped us in chapter five when examining the relationship between human rights and animal rights, which in this context are often understood as thick rights. The chapter explored arguments invoked by those who believe that only humans should have thick rights and brought them into conversation with animal rights proponents' views that animal rights and human rights are conceptually alike and mutually supportive in practice. Because conflicts are likely inevitable even on such more harmonious views, we then discussed some of the instruments the law provides to resolve them.

In chapters six and seven, we provided an overview of the leading global efforts to bring about animal rights through litigation and legislative reform, respectively. In chapter six, we encountered the issue of animals' general lack of legal standing and discussed how *habeas corpus* petitions are used to circumvent this problem and have individual animals recognised as legal persons with a right to bodily liberty. Because not all litigation is about *habeas corpus*, we then cast light on other cases where, among others, animals' rights to life, bodily and mental integrity, food, as well as legal personhood, were at stake.

In chapter seven, we studied proposals pursuing similar animal rights change through a different strategy: changing domestic or international legislation. In contrast to litigation efforts – some of which have been successful – no proposal for animal rights legislation has so far been enacted into law. For this reason, after discussing illustrative proposals on both the domestic and international level, the chapter asked what considerations those drafting future animal rights laws should take into account.

Finally, chapter eight gave more context to the previous chapters by exploring whether animal rights is a social justice issue along the lines of other large social justice movements such as feminism or abolitionism. The chapter first analysed the human abolitionist movement and discussed in more detail the animal rights Abolitionist movement, which claims to build on the former. We then focused on overlaps between animal rights and the feminist movement and discussed the issue of drawing comparisons with other social justice causes more generally. This helped us identify a number of lessons that animal rights proponents can learn from other movements.

As you will have noticed when reading these chapters, animal rights law is still a young field, despite its richness and dynamism. As a result, we expect that subsequent editions of this textbook will be able to both provide more answers on existing questions, as well as raise new questions that no one is asking yet. Although neither of us can foretell the future, we can nevertheless try to highlight some developments that may become more prominent in the years to come. Let us focus on three.

First, we can expect to see continuing creativity in the use of existing legal tools. As chapter six has shown, animal rights lawyers are developing increasingly sophisticated legal strategies using legal instruments and protections which – though created in a human context – could lend themselves to being interpreted more inclusively. Petitions of *habeas corpus* are only the most prominent example. Another was recently pursued in the US State of Oregon in the case of *Justice v Gwendolyn Vercher*. In this case, the Animal Legal Defense Fund (ALDF) – a US-based legal advocacy organisation for animals – tried to secure animal personhood for the horse Justice through the novel route of arguing that Justice is a victim of the tort of 'negligence per se'. Justice's case is based on Vercher's neglect of him, in contravention of the state's anti-cruelty law. In Oregon, for a negligence per se action to succeed, the plaintiff must demonstrate that the defendant violated a statute, which caused the plaintiff to suffer an injury the statute was designed to prevent, and, crucially, that they are a 'person' the statute was intended to protect. The Washington County Circuit Court rejected the case in 2018, but the ALDF has since appealed it to the Oregon Court of Appeals.

Second, deeper engagement with existing animal protection laws and their transformative potential as well as their limits is likely to occupy animal rights thinkers in the near future. As we saw in chapters two and four, animal rights law has only recently begun waking up from what we might call the 'dogmatic slumber' induced by the debate between Abolitionists and Welfarists. Emerging theories that go beyond Abolition and Welfare are often based on a more nuanced understanding of the workings of welfare laws, and the meaning of concepts like personhood and rights. As a result, we are seeing legal theorists who engage in more sophisticated ways with animal welfare laws and the fact that they may not be as problematic as Abolitionists make them out to be. At the same time, insights from critical legal scholars may help fill the gap in our understanding as to how animals' status as an excluded and commodified 'other' reflects an anthropocentric paradigm that makes significant leaps in welfare difficult if not impossible.

Finally, the intersection of animal rights and rights of nature promises to grow in relevance. The Estrellita case (2022), discussed in chapter six, has brought out the connection between rights of nature and the rights of individual animals particularly vividly due to the Ecuadorian Constitution's emphasis on living in harmony with nature and its explicit embracement of rights of nature. However, also other cases, such as the cases of Cecilia (2016) and Kaavan (2019), highlighted the importance of environmental concerns and the need to strive for a more sustainable relationship between humans and nature. With the rising urgency of the climate crisis, of deforestation, the extinction of species, and zoonotic diseases, it is likely that there will also be increased awareness and understanding of the links between animal rights and rights of nature. This may be both the result of a recognition of the inherent value of animals and potentially other forms of life, as well as due to more instrumental human concerns. To use Jeff Sebo's term, '[s]aving animals, saving ourselves' (2022), may become a rallying cry of future animal rights lawyers.

In the introduction of this textbook, we remarked that we are currently witnessing the dawn of animal rights law. While far from guaranteed, it is at least possible that with the help of these and other future developments, we will be moving from animal rights law's dawn to its day, as it becomes an ever-more established area of law.

Bibliography

Abstimmungserläuterungen (2021), 21 December, available at www.staatskanzlei.bs.ch/politische-rechte/wahlen-abstimmungen/resultate-archiv.html.

Adams, CJ and Donovan, J (eds) (1995) *Animals and Women* (Durham NC, Duke University Press).

Adams, CJ (1990) *The Sexual Politics of Meat* (New York, Continuum).

—— (1991) 'Ecofeminism and the Eating of Animals' 6 *Hypatia* 1, 125.

—— (1994) *Neither Man Nor Beast: Feminism and the Defense of Animals* (London, Bloomsbury).

—— (2010) 'Why Feminist-Vegan Now?' 20 *Feminism & Psychology* 3, 302.

Alexy, R (2010) *A Theory of Constitutional Rights* (Oxford, Oxford University Press).

Andrews, K, Comstock, GL, Crozier, GDK, Donaldson, S, Fenton, A, John, TM, Johnson, SM, Jones, RC, Kymlicka, W, Meynell, L, Nobis, N, Pena-Guzman, D, and Sebo, J (2019) *Chimpanzee Rights: The Philosophers Brief* (Abingdon, Routledge).

Balluch, M and Theuer, E (2007) 'Trial on Personhood for Chimp "Hiasl"' 24 *ALTEX* 4, 335.

Banaszak, LA and Ondercin, HL (2016) 'Public Opinion as a Movement Outcome: The Case of the U.S. Women's Movement' 21 *Mobilization* 3, 361.

Barak, A (2012) 'Proportionality' in M Rosenfeld and A Sajó (eds), *The Oxford Handbook of Comparative Constitutional Law* (Oxford, Oxford University Press).

Beitz, CR (2009) *The Idea of Human Rights* (Oxford, Oxford University Press).

Bentham, J (1789) *An Introduction to the Principles of Morals and Legislation* (London, Mews Gate).

—— (2012, first published 1843) 'Anarchical Fallacies, Being an Examination of the Declarations of Rights Issued During the French Revolution' in P Schofield, C Pease-Watkin, and C Blamires (eds), *The Collected Works of Jeremy Bentham: Rights, Representation, and Reform: Nonsense upon Stilts and Other Writings on the French Revolution* (Oxford, Oxford University Press).

Best, S (2014) *The Politics of Total Liberation* (London, Palgrave Macmillan).

Bilchitz, D (2016) 'Animal Interests and South African Law: The Elephant in the Room?' in D Cao and S White (eds), *Animal Law and Welfare: International Perspectives* (New York, Springer).

Birch, J (2017) 'Animal Sentience and the Precautionary Principle' 16 *Animal Sentience* 1, 1.

Blattner, CE (2019a), *Protecting Animals Within and Across Borders: Extraterritorial Jurisdiction and the Challenges of Globalization* (Oxford, Oxford University Press).

—— (2019b) 'Animal Labour: Toward a Prohibition of Forced Labour and a Right to Freely Choose One's Work' in CE Blattner, K Coulter, and W Kymlicka (eds), *Animal Labour: A New Frontier of Interspecies Justice?* (Oxford, Oxford University Press).

Blattner, CE, Coulter, K, and Kymlicka, W (2019) 'Introduction' in CE Blattner, K Coulter and W Kymlicka (eds), *Animal Labour: A New Frontier of Interspecies Justice?* (Oxford, Oxford University Press).

Boyd, BR (1987) *The New Abolitionists: Animal Rights and Human Liberation* (San Francisco, Taterhill Press).

Buchanan, A (2006) 'Taking the Human out of Human Rights' in R Martin and DA Reidy (eds), *Rawls's Law of Peoples: A Realistic Utopia?* (Oxford, Blackwell).

Bunge, WW (1973) 'The Geography of Human Survival' 63 *Annals of the Association of American Geographers* 3, 275.

Brunner, E and Partlow-Lefevre S (2020) '#MeToo as Networked Collective: Examining Consciousness-raising on Wild Public Networks' 17 *Communication and Critical/Cultural Studies* 2, 166.

Callicott, JB (1980) 'Animal Liberation: A Triangular Affair' 2 *Environmental Ethics* 4, 311.

Cambridge Declaration on Consciousness (2012), 7 July, available at fcmconference.org/img/Cambridge DeclarationOnConsciousness.pdf.

Cao, D (2015) *Animals in China: Law and Society* (London, Palgrave Macmillan).

Carroll, B (1989) '"Women Take Action!" Women's Direct Action and Social Change' 12 *Women's Studies International Forum* 1, 3.

Carruthers, P (1992) *The Animals Issue* (Cambridge, Cambridge University Press).

Cassuto, DN and Eckhardt, C (2016) 'Don't Be Cruel (Anymore): A Look at the Animal Cruelty Regimes of the United States and Brazil with a Call for a New Animal Welfare Agency' 43 *Revista Juris Poiesis* 1, 1.

Cavalieri, P (2001) *The Animal Question: Why Nonhuman Animals Deserve Human Rights* (Oxford, Oxford University Press).

Cavalieri, P and Singer, P (1993) *The Great Ape Project: Equality Beyond Humanity* (New York, St. Martin's Press).

Chiesa, LE (2016) 'Animal Rights Unraveled: Why Abolitionism Collapses into Welfarism and what it Means for Animal Ethics' 28 *Georgetown Environmental Law Review* 4, 557.

Cochrane, A (2009) 'Ownership and Justice for Animals' 21 *Utilitas* 4, 424.

—— (2010) *An Introduction to Animals and Political Theory* (London, Palgrave Macmillan).

—— (2012) *Animal Rights Without Liberation: Applied Ethics and Human Obligations* (New York, Columbia University Press).

—— (2013a) 'Cosmozoopolis: The Case Against Group-Differentiated Animal Rights' 1 *Law, Ethics and Philosophy*, 127.

—— (2013b) 'From Human Rights to Sentient Rights' 16 *Critical Review of International Social and Political Philosophy* 5, 655.

—— (2016) 'Labour Rights for Animals' in R Garner and S O'Sullivan (eds), *The Political Turn in Animal Ethics* (Lanham, Rowan & Littlefield).

—— (2018) *Sentientist Politics: A Theory of Global Inter-Species Justice* (Oxford, Oxford University Press).

Cochrane, A and Cooke, S (2016) '"Humane Intervention": The International Protection of Animal Rights' 12 *Journal of Global Ethics* 1, 106.

Colb, S and Dorf, M (2016) *Beating Hearts: Abortion and Animal Rights* (New York, Columbia University Press).

Colb, SF (2018) 'Are Animal Rights and Human Rights in Tension?' 12 March, Verdict, available at verdict. justia.com/2018/03/12/animal-rights-human-rights-tension.

Crenshaw, K (1989) 'Demarginalizing the Intersection of Race and Sex: A Black Feminist Critique of Antidiscrimination Doctrine, Feminist Theory and Antiracist Politics' 1 *University of Chicago Legal Forum* 8, 139.

Crimston, CR, Bain PG, Hornsey, MJ and Brock, B (2016) 'Moral Expansiveness: Examining Variability in the Extension of the Moral World' 111 *Journal of Personality and Social Psychology* 4, 636.

Crutchfield, LR (2018) *How Change Happens: Why Some Social Movements Succeed While Others Don't* (Hoboken, Wiley).

Cupp, RL (2012) 'Children, Chimps, and Rights Arguments from "Marginal" Cases' 45 *Arizona State Law Journal* 1, 1.

—— (2016) 'Letter-brief of Amicus Curiae Richard L. Cupp Jr. in Opposition to Petitioner-Appellant's Appeal of Denial of Petition for Writ of Habeas Corpus and Order to Show Cause', 14 November, available at www.nonhumanrights.org/content/uploads/CuppAmicus.pdf.

—— (2017) 'Cognitively Impaired Humans, Intelligent Animals, and Legal Personhood' 69 *Florida Law Review* 465.

—— (2022) 'Brief of Amicus Curiae Richard L. Cupp Jr. in Support of Respondents-Respondents', 7 April, available at www.nonhumanrights.org/content/uploads/Richard-Cupp-Amicus-in-Opposition-to-Happy.pdf.

de Lazari-Radek, K and Singer, P (2014) *The Point of View of the Universe: Sidgwick and Contemporary Ethics* (Oxford, Oxford University Press).

Deckha, M (2008) 'Disturbing Images: PETA and the Feminist Ethics of Animal Advocacy' 13 *Ethics and the Environment* 2, 35.

—— (2018) 'Humanizing the Nonhuman: A Legitimate Way for Animals to Escape Juridical Property Status?' in A Matsuoka and J Sorenson (eds), *Critical Animal Studies: Towards Trans-species Social Justice* (Lanham, Rowman & Littlefield).

—— (2020) *Animals as Legal Beings: Contesting Anthropocentric Legal Orders* (Toronto, University of Toronto Press).

Department for Environment, Food & Rural Affairs (2021) 'Review of the Welfare of Animals at the Time of Killing (England) Regulations 2015: Post Implementation Review', available at www.gov.uk/government/publications/welfare-of-animals-at-the-time-of-killing-england-regulations-2015-post-implementation-review.

Dhont, K et al (2014) 'Social Dominance Orientation Connects Prejudicial Human–Human and Human–Animal Relations' 61–62 *Personality and Individual Preferences* 105.

Donaldson, S and Kymlicka, W (2011) *Zoopolis: A Political Theory of Animal Rights* (Oxford, Oxford University Press).

Donovan, J and Adams, C (eds) (2007), *The Feminist Care Tradition in Animal* Ethics (New York, Columbia University Press).

Donovan, J (1990) 'Animal Rights and Feminist Theory' 15 *Signs* 2, 350.

Dundes Renteln, A (2004), *The Cultural Defense* (Oxford, Oxford University Press).

Dworkin, R (1997) *Taking Rights Seriously* (London, Bloomsbury).

Etinson, A (2018) 'Introduction' in A Etinson (ed), *Human Rights: Moral or Political?* (Oxford, Oxford University Press).

Fasel, RN and Butler, SC (2020) 'The Dawn of European Animal Rights Law' 8 *Global Journal of Animal Law* 1.

Fasel, RN (2018) 'Simply in Virtue of Being Human? A Critical Appraisal of a Human Rights Commonplace' 9 *Jurisprudence* 3, 461.

—— (2019), *More Equal Than Others: Animals in the Age of the Human Rights Aristocracy* (PhD in Law Thesis, University of Cambridge).

Favre, D (2010) 'Living Property: A New Status for Animals Within the Legal System' 93 *Marquette Law Review* 3, 1021.

—— (2012) 'An International Treaty for Animal Welfare' 18 *Animal Law* 237.

Foreman, E (2014) 'Brain-Damaged Babies and Brain-Damaged Kittens: A Reexamination of the Argument from Marginal Cases' 4 *Journal of Animal Ethics* 1, 58.

Fox, KCR, Muthukrishna, M and Shultz, S (2017) 'The social and cultural roots of whale and dolphin brains' 1 *Nature Ecology & Evolution* 1699.

Francione, GL and Garner R (2010) *The Animal Rights Debate: Abolition or Regulation?* (New York, Columbia University Press).

Francione, GL (1995) *Animals, Property, and the Law* (Philadelphia, Temple University Press).

—— (1996) 'Animal Rights and Animal Welfare' 48 *Rutgers Law Review* 2, 397.

—— (2004) 'Animals – Property or Persons?' in CR Sunstein and MC Nussbaum (eds), *Animal Rights: Current Debates and New Directions* (Oxford, Oxford University Press).

—— (2021) *Why Veganism Matters* (New York, Columbia University Press).

Gaard, G (2002) 'Vegetarian Ecofeminism: A Review Essay' 23 *Frontiers: A Journal of Women's Studies* 3, 117.

Garner, R (2005) *The Political Theory of Animal Rights* (Manchester, Manchester University).

—— (2008) 'The Politics of Animal Rights' 3 *British Politics* 1, 110.

George, KP (1994) 'Discrimination and Bias in the Vegan Ideal' 7 *Journal of Agricultural and Environmental Ethics* 1, 19.

Gewirth, A (1996) *The Community of Rights* (Chicago, University of Chicago Press).

Gilligan, C (1982) *In A Different Voice* (Boston, Harvard University Press).

Giordano Bruno Stiftung (2014) 'Verfassungsziel Speziesismus', 2 June, available at www.giordano-bruno-stiftung.de/meldung/verfassungsziel-speziesismus.

Glendinning, L (2008) 'Spanish parliament approves 'human rights' for apes', 26 June, *The Guardian*, available at www.theguardian.com/world/2008/jun/26/humanrights.animalwelfare.

Global Animal Law (2021), Animal Law Courses Globally, available at www.google.com/maps/d/viewer?mid=1Hdgt9cZy_JxSsv0QnAmJ_xAKQbU.

Global Slavery Index (2018), Global Findings, available at www.globalslaveryindex.org/2018/findings/global-findings/.

Godlovitch, S, Godlovitch, R and and Harris, J (1971) *Animals, Men and Morals: An Enquiry into the Maltreatment of Non-humans* (London, Victor Gollancz).

Griffin, J (2008) *On Human Rights* (Oxford, Oxford University Press).

Gruen, L and Marceau, J (eds) (2022) *Carceral Logics: Human Incarceration and Animal Captivity* (Cambridge, Cambridge University Press).

Harris, AP (2009) 'Should People Of Colour Support Animal Rights?' 5 *Journal of Animal Law* 15.

Harrison, R (2013, first published 1964) *Animal Machines* (Wallingford, CABI Publishing).

Hart, HLA (1955) 'Are There Any Natural Rights?' 64 *The Philosophical Review* 2, 175.

—— (1982), *Essays on Bentham: Studies in Jurisprudence and Political* Theory (Oxford, Oxford University Press).

Haslam, N (2006) 'Dehumanization: An Integrative Review' 10 *Personality and Social Psychology Review* 3, 252.

Hohfeld, WN (1913) 'Some Fundamental Legal Conceptions as Applied in Judicial Reasoning' 23 *Yale Law Journal* 1, 16.

Honoré, AM (1961) 'Ownership', in AG Guest (ed), *Oxford Essays in Jurisprudence* (Oxford, Oxford University Press).

Huffman, T (1993) 'Animals, Mental Defectives, and the Social Contract' 9 *Between the Species* 1, 20.

Jones, R (2015) 'Animal Rights is a Social Justice Issue' 18 *Contemporary Justice Review* 4, 467.

Joy, M (2011) 'Our Voices Our Movement: How Vegans Can Move Beyond the "Welfare-Abolition Debate"', One Green Planet, available at www.onegreenplanet.org/animalsandnature/our-voices-our-movement-how-vegans-can-move-beyond-the-welfare-abolition-debate/.

Kant, I (1997, first published 1784) 'Moral Philosophy: Collin's Lecture Notes' in P Heath and JB Schneewind (eds), *Lectures on Ethics* (Cambridge, Cambridge University Press).

—— (1998, first published 1785), *Groundwork of the Metaphysics of Morals* (Cambridge, Cambridge University Press).

Kappeler, S (1995) 'Speciesism, Racism, Nationalism … or the Power of Scientific Subjectivity' in CJ Adams and J Donovan (eds), *Animals and Women* (Durham NC, Duke University Press).

Kateb, G (2014) *Human Dignity* (Boston, Harvard University Press).

Kelch, TG (2012) 'A Short History of (Mostly) Western Animal Law: Part I' 19 *Animal Law* 23.

Kim, C (2011) 'Moral Extensionism or Racist Exploitation? The Use of Holocaust and Slavery Analogies in the Animal Liberation Movement' 33 *New Political Science* 3, 311.

—— (2015), *Dangerous Crossings: Race, Species, and Nature in a Multicultural Age* (Cambridge, Cambridge University Press).

Kniess, J (2019) 'Bentham on Animal Welfare' 27 *British Journal for the History of Philosophy* 3, 556.

Ko A and Ko S (2017), *Aphro-ism: Essays on Pop Culture, Feminism, and Black Veganism from Two Sisters* (Brooklyn, Lantern Books).

Kramer, MH (1998) 'Rights Without Trimmings' in MH Kramer, NE Simmonds, and S Hillel (eds), *A Debate Over Rights: Philosophical Enquiries* (Oxford, Oxford University Press).

—— (2001) 'Do Animals and Dead People Have Legal Rights?' 14 *Canadian Journal of Law & Jurisprudence* 1, 29.

Kurki, VAJ (2019) *A Theory of Legal Personhood* (Oxford, Oxford University Press).

—— (2021) 'Legal Personhood and Animal Rights' 11 *Journal of Animal Ethics* 1, 47.

Kymlicka, W (2017) 'Social Membership: Animal Law Beyond the Property/Personhood Impasse' 40 *Dalhousie Law Journal* 1, 123.

—— (2018) 'Human Rights Without Human Supremacism' 48 *Canadian Journal of Philosophy* 5, 763.

Leopold, A (1949) *A Sand County Almanac and Sketches Here and There* (Oxford, Oxford University Press).

Liao, SM (2010) 'The Basis of Human Moral Status' 7 *Journal of Moral Philosophy* 2, 159.

MacDonald, M (1984) 'Natural Rights' in J Waldron (ed), *Theories of Rights* (Oxford, Oxford University Press).

MacKinnon, C (1989) *Toward a Feminist Theory of the State* (Boston, Harvard University Press).

Marris, E (2018) 'When Conservationists Kill Lots (and Lots) of Animals', 26 September, *The Atlantic*, available at www.theatlantic.com/science/archive/2018/09/is-wildlife-conservation-too-cruel/569719/.

McCausland, C (2014) 'The Five Freedoms of Animal Welfare as Rights' 27 *Journal of Agricultural and Environmental Ethics* 649.

Meijer, E (2019) *When Animals Speak: Toward an Interspecies Democracy* (New York, New York University Press).

Miller, D (2012) 'Grounding Human Rights' 15 *Critical Review of Social and Political Philosophy* 5, 407.

Montes, M and Stilt, K (2022) 'Historic Milestone in Ecuador: Constitutional Court Recognizes Individual Animals as Subjects of Rights Protected by the Rights of Nature', 8 May, World Lawyers' Pledge on Climate Action, available at lawyersclimatepledge.org/historic-milestone-in-ecuador-constitutional-court-recognizes-individual-animals-as-subjects-of-rights-protected-by-the-rights-of-nature/.

Naffine, N (2009) *Law's Meaning of Life: Philosophy, Religion, Darwin, and the Legal Person* (Oxford, Hart).

Noddings, N (1982) *Caring: A Feminine Approach to Ethics and Moral Education* (California, University of California Press).

Nussbaum, MC (2006) *Frontiers of Justice: Disability, Nationality, Species Membership* (Boston, Harvard University Press).

Oliver, M (1997) 'The Disability Movement is a New Social Movement!' 32 *Community Development Journal* 3, 244.

Organ, TW (1970) *The Hindu Quest for the Perfection of Man* (Ohio, Ohio University Press).

Peters, A (2016a) 'Global Animal Law: What It Is and Why We Need It' 5 *Transnational Environmental Law* 1, 9.

—— (2016b) 'Liberté, Égalité, Animalité: Human-Animal Comparisons in Law' 5 *Transnational Environmental Law* 1, 25.

—— (2018) 'Rights of Human and Non-Human Animals: Complementing the Universal Declaration of Human Rights' 112 *AJIL Unbound* 355.

—— (2021) *Animals in International Law* (Leiden, Brill).

Pettinicchio, D (2019) *Politics of Empowerment: Disability Rights and the Cycle of American Policy Reform* (Boston, Stanford University Press).

Phillips, A (2015), *The Politics of the Human* (Cambridge, Cambridge University Press).

Pietrzykowski, T (2017) 'The Idea of Non-Personal Subjects of Law' in V Kurki and T Pietrzykowski (eds), *Legal Personhood: Animals, Artificial Intelligence and the Unborn* (New York, Springer).

Plumwood, V (1993) *Feminism and the Mastery of Nature* (Abingdon, Routledge).

—— (2002), *Environmental Culture: The Ecological Crisis of Reason* (Abingdon, Routledge).

Pound, R (1923) *Interpretations of Legal History* (London, Macmillan).

Porat, I (2021) 'The Starting at Home Principle: On Ritual Animal Slaughter, Male Circumcision and Proportionality' 41 *Oxford Journal of Legal Studies* 1, 30.

Porphyry, 'On Abstinence from Animal Food' in Kerry S. Walters and Lisa Portmess (eds), *Ethical Vegetarianism: From Pythagoras to Peter Singer* (New York, SUNY Press, 1999).

Proposed Brief by Amici Curiae Philosophers in Support of the Petitioner-Appellant (2018), Nonhuman Rights Project (Tommy) v Lavery, 23 February, Index Nos 162358/15 150149/16.

Rawls, J (1971) *A Theory of Justice* (Boston, Harvard University Press).

—— (1999) *Law of the Peoples* (Boston, Harvard University Press).

Raz, (1984) 'On the Nature of Rights' 93 *Mind*, 191.

Regan, T (1983) *The Case for Animal Rights* (California, University of California Press).

—— (1987) 'The Case for Animal Rights' in MW Fox and LD Mickley (eds), *Advances in Animal Welfare Science* (New York, Springer).

Riffkin, R (2015) 'In U.S., More Say Animals Should Have Same Rights as People', 18 May, *Gallup*, available at news.gallup.com/poll/183275/say-animals-rights-people.aspx.

Robinson, F (2003) 'Human Rights and the Global Politics of Resistance: Feminist Perspectives' 29 *Review of International Studies* 161.

Rolston III, H (2008) 'Human Uniqueness and Human Dignity: Persons in Nature and the Nature of Persons' in *Essays Commissioned by the President's Council on Bioethics* (Washington DC, President's Printing Office).

Ryder, R (1989) *Animal Revolution: Changing Attitudes Towards Speciesism* (Oxford: Basil Blackwell).

—— (2004) 'Speciesism Revisited' 2 *Think* 6, 83.

Salt, HS (1980, first published 1894), *Animals' Rights: Considered in Relation to Social Progress* (Clarks Summit PA, Society for Animal Rights); electronic version available at www.animal-rights-library.com/texts-c/salt01.htm.

Sebo, J (2022) *Saving Animals, Saving Ourselves: Why Animals Matter for Pandemics, Climate Change, and Other Catastrophes* (New York, Oxford University Press).

Sen, A (1980) 'Equality of What?' in S McMurrin (ed), *The Tanner Lectures on Human Values* (Cambridge, Cambridge University Press).

Shakespeare, T (1993) 'Disabled People's Self-organisation: A New Social Movement?' 8 *Disability, Handicap & Society* 3, 249.

Shooster, J (2015) 'Justice for All: Including Animal Rights in Social Justice Activism' 40 *NYU Review of Law & Social Change* 39.

Simmonds, NE (2016) 'Constitutional Rights and the Rule of Law' *Analisi e diritto* 251.

Singer, P (1987) 'Animal Liberation or Animal Rights?' 70 *The Monist* 1, 3.

—— (1990) 'Ethics and animals' 13 *Behavioral and Brain Sciences* 1, 45.

—— (2002, first published 1975) *Animal Liberation* (New York, Harper Collins).

—— (2020) *Why Vegan?* (London, Penguin).

Slicer, D (1991) 'Your Daughter or Your Dog? A Feminist Assessment of the Animal Research Issue' 6 *Hypatia* 1, 108.

Soulé, ME (1985) 'What is Conservation Biology?' 35 *BioScience* 11, 727.

Steiner, H (1998) 'Working Rights' in MH Kramer, NE Simmonds, and S Hillel (eds), *A Debate Over Rights: Philosophical Enquiries* (Oxford, Oxford University Press).

Stucki, S (2016) *Grundrechte für Tiere: Eine Kritik des geltenden Tierschutzrechts und rechtstheoretische Grundlegung von Tierrechten im Rahmen einer Neupositionierung des Tieres als Rechtssubjekt* (Baden-Baden, Nomos) [in German].

—— (2020) 'Towards a Theory of Legal Animal Rights: Simple and Fundamental Rights' 40 *Oxford Journal of Legal Studies* 3, 533.

—— (2022) *One Rights: Human and Animal Rights in the Anthropocene* (New York, Springer).

Sunstein, CR (2003) 'The Rights of Animals' 70 *University of Chicago Law Review* 387.

Sztybel, D (2006) 'Can the Treatment of Animals Be Compared to the Holocaust?' 11 *Ethics and the Environment* 1, 97.

Talbott, WJ (2010) *Human Rights and Human Well-Being* (Oxford, Oxford University Press).

Tasioulas, J (2015) 'On the Foundations of Human Rights,' in R Cruft, SM Liao, and M Renzo (eds), *Philosophical Foundations of Human Rights* (Oxford, Oxford University Press).

Taylor, N (1999) 'Whither Rights? Animal Rights and the Rise of New Welfarism' 3 *Animal Issues* 1, 27.

Taylor, S (2017) *Beasts of Burden: Animal and Disability Liberation* (New York, The New Press).

Combahee River Collective Statement (first published 1977), available at collectiveliberation.org/wp-content/uploads/2013/01/Combahee_River_Collective_Statement.pdf.

Tier im Recht (2021) 'Schweizer Tierschutzstrafpraxis 2020' available at www.tierimrecht.org/documents/4174/Analyse_Schweizer_Tierschutzstrafpraxis_2020_Gutachten.pdf.

Tonsor, GT and Olynk, NJ (2011) 'Impacts of Animal-Wellbeing and Welfare Media on Meat Demand' 62 *Journal of Agricultural Economics* 1, 59.

Turner, B (2006) *Vulnerability and Human Rights* (University Park PA, Penn State Press).

UCL, Transcribe Bentham, JB/072/214/001, available at transcribe-bentham.ucl.ac.uk/td/JB/072/214/001.

UCL, Transcribe Bentham, JB/072/214/004; available at transcribe-bentham.ucl.ac.uk/td/JB/072/214/004.

Vink, J (2020), *The Open Society and Its Animals* (London, Palgrave Macmillan).

Wallach, AD, Bekoff, M, Batavia, C, Nelson, MP and Ramp, D (2018) 'Summoning Compassion to Address the Challenges of Conservation' 32 *Conservation Biology* 6, 1255.

Wagman, A, Waisman, SS and Frasch, PD (2019) *Animal Law: Cases and Materials* (6th edn Durham NC, Carolina Academic Press).

Weldon, SL and Htun, M (2013) 'Feminist Mobilisation and Progressive Policy Change: Why Governments Take Action to Combat Violence Against Women' 21 *Gender and Development* 2, 231.

Wills, J (2020) 'Animal Rights, Legal Personhood and Cognitive Capacity: Addressing 'Levelling-Down' Concerns' 11 *Journal of Human Rights and the Environment* 2, 199.

Wise, S and Stein, E, Esq (2013) Verified Petition, In the Matter of The Nonhuman Rights Project (Hercules and Leo) v Stanley, 2 December.

Wise, S (2010) 'Legal Personhood and the Nonhuman Rights Project' 17 *Animal Law Review* 1.

—— (2013) 'Nonhuman Rights to Personhood' 30 *Pace Environmental Law Review* 3, 1278.

Wolfson, DJ and Sullivan, M (2004) 'Foxes in the Hen House: Animals, Agribusiness, and the Law: A Modern American Fable' in CR Sunstein and MC Nussbaum (eds), *Animal Rights: Current Debates and New Directions* (Oxford, Oxford University Press).

World Organisation for Animal Health, Website (as of 1 June 2022) available at www.woah.org/en/who-we-are/mission/.

Wrenn, CL and Johnson, R (2013) 'A Critique of Single-issue Campaigning and the Importance of Comprehensive Abolitionist Vegan Advocacy' 16 *Food, Culture & Society* 4, 651.

Wrenn, CL (2014) 'Abolition Then and Now: Tactical Comparisons Between the Human Rights Movement and the Modern Nonhuman Animal Rights Movement in the United States' 27 *Journal of Agric Environ Ethics* 177.

—— (2016) *A Rational Approach to Animal Rights: Extensions in Abolitionist Theory* (London, Palgrave Macmillan).

Glossary

3Rs: a framework of principles, non-binding in many states, to encourage those conducting experiments on animals to use alternative ways of doing research where possible ('replace'), reduce the number of animals used in experiments ('reduce'), and minimise the suffering of animals used ('refine').

Abolitionism: an approach to **animal rights**, popularised by the legal scholar Gary Francione, according to which the **property** status and all types of use and killing of animals should be abolished. Abolitionism is generally seen as conflicting with **Welfarism**. We use the term 'abolitionist' with a small 'a' to describe other animal rights theories that also want to abolish animal exploitation but do not endorse all aspects of Abolitionism with a capital 'A', such as its commitment to abolishing animals' property status.

Absolute rights: a term describing rights that cannot be limited or restricted under any circumstances (eg freedom from torture). Absolute rights are contrasted with **relative (or qualified) rights**.

Administrative law: a branch of law that is part of **public law** and that is concerned with how public authorities exercise their powers. In animal law, administrative law describes measures (eg granting licences or issuing prohibitions on the keeping of animals) that state agencies can adopt to govern humans and animals.

Affidavit: a statement that is sworn to be true by the person making it and that is used as evidence.

Amicus curiae: Latin for 'friend of the court', this term describes the offering of information or advice to a court by an individual or group with relevant expertise who is not a party to the legal case. An 'amicus brief' is a written submission to the court by an amicus curiae.

Animal protection laws: a term that we use to describe a general category of laws that comprise **anti-cruelty** and **animal welfare laws**.

Animal rights law: the emerging field of law concerned with the legal rights and status of animals.

Animal rights: a term describing the rights that animals do or should have. The term is usually used in contrast to **animal welfare**. For different meanings of the term, see **thin rights** and **thick rights**.

Animal welfare laws: laws that seek to promote animals' wellbeing in positive ways. As such, animal welfare laws are seen as going further than **anti-cruelty laws**, which are limited to negatively prohibiting certain cruel treatments against animals. Some welfare laws refer to the **Five Freedoms** to improve the quality of life of animals. Enforcement of such laws usually involves both **criminal law** and **administrative law** mechanisms.

Animal welfare: a term describing the welfare protections that animals do or should have. The term is usually used in contrast to **animal rights**.

Anti-cruelty laws: laws that prohibit treating animals in particular ways that are seen as cruel, for instance because they inflict suffering on the animal. Breach of these laws is primarily enforced through **criminal law** sanctions.

Anti-foundationalism: a philosophical approach to rights that avoids explaining rights by reference to their holders' empirical properties (eg the ability to reason). Instead, anti-foundationalists explain rights by referring to political practices and/or decisions. Anti-foundationalism is contrasted with **foundationalism**.

Balancing: an important stage of the **proportionality test**, in which competing interests are weighed against each other to help determine whether the limitation of a right is justified (see **relative (or qualified) rights**).

Capabilities approach: a philosophical approach developed by philosopher Martha Nussbaum which holds that all sentient beings have capabilities typical for their species (see **species norm**) which should be promoted by political institutions so that these beings can flourish and live with dignity.

Choice-based approach to rights: sometimes also called will theory of rights, an approach to the function of rights according to which rights serve to express and protect the choices made by autonomous individuals. This approach is usually contrasted with the **interest-based approach to rights**.

Civil law: a category of legal systems (including eg Italy, China, and Russia) that are based on the tradition of Roman Law. This category is distinguished from **common law** legal systems. Civil law is sometimes also used as a synonym for **private law**.

Claim-right: a term from Wesley Hohfeld's theory of rights describing the correlative of a duty. For example, to say that A has a claim-right to B's book means that B has a duty to give A the book.

Code: a systematic written formulation of a certain area of law (eg **criminal law**) enacted through legislation, typical for **civil law** systems.

Common law: a category of legal systems (including eg UK, Ghana, and Pakistan) that focus on law developed by courts following the doctrine of **precedent**. This category is distinguished from **civil law** systems.

Competence norms: legal rules, usually found in constitutions, allocating the authority to regulate a certain subject matter (eg animal protection law) to specific bodies.

Consciousness: a concept without settled meaning that can be taken to refer to the capacity to be aware of and respond to (rather than simply register) sensory stimuli. Consciousness is sometimes used as a synonym for **sentience**, although this usage is contested.

Conservationism: a view and movement aimed at conserving and protecting natural resources and biodiversity. Philosophically, many conservationists believe that what ultimately matters is not the individual animal, but the biological community (see also **land ethic**). Compassionate conservationists disagree with this type of conservationism and argue that both individuals and the biological community matter.

Constitutional law: a branch of law that is part of **public law** and that is concerned with regulating the rights of people, the structure of government, and the powers of public authorities.

Constitutional norms: the legal rules and principles contained in constitutions.

Contractualism: a philosophical approach according to which what is morally right and wrong depends on a (hypothetical) contract or agreement between people. The philosopher Tim Scanlon is the most prominent contemporary defender of this approach, and Peter Carruthers has developed a contractualist critique of **animal rights**.

Criminal law: a branch of law that is part of **public law** and that is concerned with determining and punishing criminal activities.

Deontology: a philosophical approach according to which what is morally right and wrong depends on rules rather than the consequences of people's actions. The German philosopher Immanuel Kant was the most prominent advocate of this approach. Tom Regan has defended a deontological approach to animal ethics (see **subject-of-a-life**).

Dereification: the process of undoing the **property** status of animals.

Dignity: a contested concept that, in the context of **animal rights law**, can be taken to refer to the **inherent value** of animals that requires protecting them as beings who matter for their own sake. Switzerland was the first and remains the only country to enshrine animal dignity in its Constitution.

Dissenting opinion: an opinion in a legal case whereby at least one judge disagrees with the majority judgment of the court. Dissenting opinions are not binding **precedent**, but can indicate directions in which the law may be developed in the future.

Domesticated animals: animals who have been selectively bred to live with or near humans, including in homes (eg cats, dogs, rabbits, fish, and birds), in which case they are called companion animals or 'pets', and on farms (eg chickens, cows, pigs, turkeys, sheep, and fish). Domesticated animals are distinguished from **wild animals** and **liminal animals**.

Dualism: a concept used, particularly by **ecofeminists** and other critical thinkers, to describe the construction of hierarchies, usually expressed in binary form (eg man/woman, white/black, human/animal), in which the binary's left side represents the dominant element and the right side the oppressed element.

Ecofeminism: a branch of feminism and ecology focused on the connections between women and the natural world. Developed in the human context by the psychologist Carol Gilligan and the philosopher Nel Noddings, it was later applied to animals by the literature scholar Josephine Donovan and the activist and writer Carol Adams.

Ecofeminists emphasise the interlocking nature (see **intersectionality**) of different forms of oppression such as sexism, racism, and **speciesism**.

Elite species approach: a strategy for achieving legal **animal rights** by focussing on only a few species which are popular with the public and whose rights protection would have limited adverse economic and social consequences. For example, the cases brought by the Nonhuman Rights Project (NhRP) have been on behalf of elite species such as chimpanzees and elephants.

Five Freedoms: a set of non-binding principles for **animal welfare**, developed by the Brambell Committee in 1965 in the UK and later codified by the UK Farm Animal Welfare Council. The Five Freedoms are: freedom from hunger and thirst; freedom from discomfort; freedom from pain, injury or disease; freedom to express normal behaviour; freedom from fear and distress.

Foundationalism: a philosophical approach to rights that explains rights by reference to their holders' empirical properties (eg the ability to reason). Foundationalism is contrasted with **anti-foundationalism**.

Guardian: a formally appointed person or authority looking after the interests of someone else, called ward.

Habeas corpus: a legal instrument available in **common law** as well as some **civil law** systems that allows a challenge to the unlawful detention of a person.

Human abolitionism: refers to the movement that started in the eighteenth century in Europe whose objectives were to abolish human slavery and the slave trade.

Inherent value: a term from ethics denoting value that its holders have in and of themselves, regardless of whether they are useful or valued by someone else. Inherent value is often employed synonymously with 'intrinsic value', and is contrasted with **instrumental value**.

Instrumental value: a term from ethics describing the value that someone or something has because it is useful to or valued by someone else. Instrumental value is contrasted with **inherent value**.

Interest-based approach to rights: an approach to the function of rights according to which rights serve to protect the interests (ie wellbeing) of their holders. This approach is usually contrasted with the **choice-based approach to rights**.

International declaration: a written international statement that, in contrast to **international treaties**, is not legally binding. Some declarations, such as for example the Universal Declaration of Human Rights (UDHR), reflect (binding) customary **international law**.

International law: the branch of law governing the relationship between states and international organisations (such as the United Nations) which is primarily applicable to states, but in some cases also to individuals (eg in the case of international human rights protection). The sources of international law are **treaties**, customary international law, and general principles of law. Some international law has a regional focus (eg the Conventions of the Council of Europe are focused on European states).

Intersectionality: a term coined by critical race theorist Kimberlé Crenshaw to describe the ways in which race, class, gender, disability, and other ideas intersect and overlap to become more than the sum of their parts. This term is often used by **ecofeminists** to include species as another oppressed part.

Kantianism: a term describing the philosophical views of the German philosopher Immanuel Kant and his followers. Regarding animals, Kant held that we ought not to protect them for their own sakes, but only because doing so helps us better protect humans (see **instrumental value**).

Land ethic: the ethical position of the author and ecologist Aldo Leopold according to whom human morality should evolve to extend to nature more generally. Leopold argued that the good of the biotic community, not of individuals, is what is most valuable (see **conservationism**).

Legal personhood: a **legal status** that distinguishes its holders from legal things. Legal personhood is often seen as a precondition for having legal rights and legal persons generally have **legal standing** to enforce their rights. Legal personhood is sometimes used as a synonym for 'legal subjecthood'.

Legal standing: the right to initiate a lawsuit against someone else, a law, policy, or decision, usually dependent on the condition that one is sufficiently affected and is a **legal person**.

Legal status: a term we use to denote the set of legal positions (eg legal capacities, entitlements, and duties) attached to someone or something. **Legal personhood** and legal thinghood (ie being an ownable thing, see **property**) are two different legal statuses with largely opposed legal positions.

Legal theory: the theoretical study of law, legal systems, legal institutions, legal reasoning, and the role of law in society.

Liminal animals: animals who are neither fully **domesticated** nor fully **wild**, who live among or near humans or their homes. This includes rats, foxes, squirrels, raccoons, sparrows, deer, coyotes, mice, and other species. In the political theory of Sue Donaldson and Will Kymlicka, liminal animals are viewed as denizens similar to human migrants.

Negative rights: entitlements against certain things, particularly interference from others. Negative rights are contrasted with **positive rights**.

New Welfarism: the view ascribed to the political scientist Robert Garner as well as others who believe that animals should have certain rights that can be achieved through **animal welfare** reforms. New Welfarists are generally seen as successors of **Classic Welfarism** and opponents of **Abolitionism**.

Othering: a term describing processes that lead to certain groups being seen as subordinate others, thereby marginalising them (see **dualism**). In **animal rights law**, the term is often used by **ecofeminists** to critique the marginalisation of animals.

Plaintiff: someone who initiates court proceedings, usually to seek a legal remedy.

Political turn: a term that, in animal ethics, describes the shift away from focusing on individuals' moral duties, and toward the duties of society to govern humans and animals justly.

Positive rights: entitlements to certain things, such as to be provided with a suitable habitat, safe neighbourhoods, and care.

Precedent: a judicial decision which is considered binding in future cases. Precedent is of primary relevance in **common law** systems.

Private law: a branch of law that is concerned with regulating relationships between individuals, rather than between individuals and the state (see **public law**). Family law, **tort law**, and contract law are some of the sub-branches of private law.

Procedural rights: entitlements and processes relating to the enforcement of **substantive rights** (eg **legal standing** or the right to an attorney).

Property: the **legal status** of being an ownable thing. Animals are considered property in all legal systems, meaning that they can be owned, bought, used, inherited, rented out, sold, and destroyed in similar ways to other objects (eg books or bikes). That animals can be owned in the first place is often traced back to the fact that they are not **legal persons**. Some states no longer treat animals as simple property (ie like books or bikes) but as more than simple property (see **dereification**).

Proportionality test: a procedure employed by courts in most legal systems in cases of conflict between two rights or between a right and the public interest. The test allows determining whether a right can justifiably be limited (see **relative (or qualified) rights**). Many courts adopt a three-pronged version of the test which requires them to examine the suitability of the rights limitation, its necessity, and whether the interest behind the limitation is weightier than the interest in the right (**balancing**).

Public law: a branch of law that is concerned with regulating relationships between individuals and the state, rather than between individuals (see **private law**). **Constitutional law**, **criminal law**, and **administrative law** are some of the sub-branches of public law.

Relative (or qualified) rights: rights that can be justifiably limited in order to protect the rights of others or the public interest. Most courts determine whether a limitation is justified by applying the **proportionality test**. Relative (or qualified) rights are contrasted with **absolute rights**.

RSPCA: the Royal Society for the Prevention of Cruelty to Animals, a UK animal protection organisation founded in 1824.

Scope: a term we use to describe the breadth of coverage of a law, in particular an **animal rights** law.

Sentience: a term generally taken to denote the capacity to have feelings. Sentience is sometimes also used as a synonym for **consciousness**, although this usage is contested. Sentience is often used as the basis for both **animal welfare laws** and **animal rights** laws.

Single-issue campaigns: **animal rights** campaigns that are focused on abolishing animal exploitation in one area (eg circuses) rather than wholesale.

Social justice: a concept concerned with the distribution of privileges, wealth, and opportunities on the level of society. Social justice movements such as for example the feminist movement seek to address existing imbalances in this distribution and bring about more fairness by changing the system and people's attitudes and behaviours. **Animal rights** is increasingly seen as a social justice issue.

Species Membership Approach (SMA): an approach developed by the legal scholar Raffael Fasel with a view to facilitating decisions on which animals should have what legal rights. According to SMA, in law, fundamental rights (and similar legal protections and **legal status**es such as **legal personhood** and **dignity**) should be extended to deserving animals based on species membership, not individual **sentience** or interests.

Species norm: a term coined by philosopher Martha Nussbaum to describe the fact that every species has abilities and needs that are characteristic of it and that need to be promoted so that individual members of that species can flourish (see **capabilities approach**).

Speciesism: coined by the psychologist and activist Richard Ryder and popularised by the philosopher Peter Singer, this term describes prejudicial attitudes and views against animals based simply on their species. The term is intentionally modelled on analogous terms such as sexism and racism.

State objective: provisions, generally found in constitutions, which set out the goals that the state should achieve. In contrast to other types of **constitutional norms**, state objectives are primarily aspirational and of symbolic importance, and do not create any binding obligations that could be enforced in court. Several states have enshrined animal protection as a state objective in their constitutions.

Statute: an act of legislation passed by parliament.

Subject-of-a-life: a term coined by philosopher Tom Regan to describe the kind of being that has **inherent value** and deserves equal respect of their rights. To be a subject-of-a-life, a being has to possess a complex set of abilities, including the ability to perceive and remember and to have beliefs, desires, and preferences, which they have to be able to pursue intentionally. They must also be able to anticipate the future and have an individual welfare that is not simply of **instrumental value**. According to Regan, most mammals above the age of one are subjects-of-a-life.

Substantive rights: entitlements that protect certain primary interests of their holders such as in life, bodily integrity, or family life. Substantive rights are usually contrasted with **procedural rights**, although the latter are often used to promote the former.

Thick rights: a term we use to describe entitlements that are modelled on fundamental human rights. Thick rights consist of complex legal positions, protect individuals' fundamental interests, have a high threshold for justifying limitations (see **relative (or qualified) rights**), are directly enforceable by the individual or their representatives, and have a dynamic character. Thick rights can be contrasted with **thin rights**.

Thin rights: a term we use to describe entitlements (primarily **claim-rights**) that arise for animals in virtue of there being animal protection laws that impose corresponding duties on humans with regard to those animals. For example, the duty not to impose **unnecessary suffering** on animals is seen as giving rise to a thin right in animals not to be imposed unnecessary suffering. Sometimes also called 'simple rights' or 'animal welfare rights', these rights are often criticised for not providing sufficient protection to animals, and therefore not being proper 'rights'. Thin rights are contrasted to **thick rights**.

Tort law: a branch of law that is part of **private law** and that is concerned with providing compensation for injury or damage caused by another.

Treaties: a legally binding agreement in **international law** between two or more states. Treaties are sometimes also called conventions or pacts and are generally concluded through national ratification.

Unnecessary suffering: a term describing principles contained in numerous **animal protection laws** which state that animals must not be imposed any suffering that is considered unnecessary. While 'suffering' is a largely descriptive category, assessed in veterinary terms, 'unnecessary' is a normative category that gives courts and other law interpreters considerable discretion. **Animal rights** proponents disagree about whether unnecessary suffering principles are useful or harmful.

Utilitarianism: a philosophical approach according to which what is morally right and wrong depends on whether it promotes utility (ie good consequences). The philosophers Jeremy Bentham and JS Mill have formulated classic versions of utilitarianism, and the contemporary philosopher Peter Singer has popularised utilitarianism in animal ethics. According to Singer, animals deserve equal consideration of their interests in virtue of the fact that they are **sentient**. To deny them such consideration is to commit **speciesism**.

Welfarism (or Classic Welfarism): an approach according to which animals should be treated humanely because they can suffer (ie they have welfare), but they may nevertheless be owned, used, and killed because human interests are considered to be morally weightier than non-human interests. Classic Welfarism is the philosophy underlying **animal protection laws** around the world. It is the predecessor of **New Welfarism** and is seen as being opposed to **Abolitionism**.

Wild animals: animals who have not been domesticated and live in their own habitats, with little to no interaction with humans (eg wolfs, bears, meerkats, and tundra swans).

Index